Cooking for Health & Flavor

Health & Wellness Cooking Library™

About the Author

Patsy Jamieson is a food writer and recipe developer who specializes in healthy cooking. She contributes articles to *Today's Health & Wellness, Cooking Pleasures, Vegetarian Times, Cooking Light* and *Tufts University Health & Nutrition Letter*. Her most recent cookbook is *Celebrating Herbs* (for the Cooking Club of America). She serves as Food Editor for *Eating Well* magazine. She has conducted cooking classes and demonstrations across the country and has appeared on numerous television shows, including ABC's "Good Morning America," NBC's "Today Show," CNN's "On the Menu" and the Television Food Network's "Chef du Jour." Patsy is a graduate of La Varenne Ecole de Cuisine in Paris. She lives in Burlington, Vermont.

Cooking for Health & Flavor

1 2 3 4 5 6 7 8 / 05 04 03 02
ISBN 1-58159-177-2

National Health & Wellness Club
12301 Whitewater Drive
Minnetonka, MN 55343
www.healthandwellnessclub.com

Tom Carpenter
Creative Director

Heather Koshiol
Book Development Coordinator

Laura Holle
Book Development Assistant

Greg Schwieters
Book Design and Production

Susan Brosious, Food Stylist
Jerry Dudycha, Food Stylist Assistant
Eric Melzer, Assistant Photographer
Amy Peterson, Food Stylist Assistant
Mark Macemon, Photographer

Special thanks to:
Marcia Brinkley, Felicia Busch, Janice Cauley, Jill Crumm, Liz Gunderson, Hallie Harron, Pegi Lee, Nancy Maurer, Mary Jane Miller, Ruth Petran, Deborah Prelesnik and Sandy Zilka.

On the cover: Roasted Chicken & Vegetables, page 116.
On the title page: Pasta & Garbanzo Bean Soup, page 46.

Contents

Introduction

Can you really blend healthy eating with good taste? After a dozen years of focusing my professional energies on creating nutritious recipes that do not compromise flavor, my answer is a resounding "Yes!" Food that nourishes your body can actually taste great as well.

Fat is not the only thing that creates flavor in a recipe. I have always relished the challenge of transforming a traditional fat-laden recipe into a leaner version that tastes just as good. Over the years, I have had the opportunity to experiment with numerous fat substitutes and low-fat cooking techniques that yield big flavors. This experience is reflected in the recipes and tips in *Cooking for Health & Flavor*.

But there is more to eating well than just trimming fat grams and counting calories. You must get enough key nutrients every day. Fruits, vegetables, legumes and whole grains are packed with vitamins, minerals and phytochemicals that provide protection against chronic diseases. These nutrient-dense foods taste great as well. Colorful fruits and vegetables contribute visual appeal, texture and flavor to dishes. Whole grains have a delicious nutty flavor. Learning to accentuate the positive things in food is a big step toward enjoying a healthier diet.

The recipes in this volume were carefully developed with your busy schedule and your family's well-being in mind. The recipes use ingredients readily available in any supermarket and take advantage of convenient items like frozen vegetables (lots of them) to give you the tools you need to eat healthfully *every day*.

And to help you put it all together, I have compiled the recipes into 52 menus that suit occasions ranging from solo breakfasts to family dinners to casual gatherings with friends. You will also find numerous practical tips for reducing fat, improving taste and increasing whole grains, fruits and vegetables in your diet.

Ultimately, good food is about nourishment. I hope that the recipes and tips in *Cooking for Health & Flavor* will help you meet your goal of living a healthier life in many delicious ways.

Patsy

Patsy Jamieson

A Nutrition Primer

What to grab for breakfast before rushing off to work; what to snack on mid-morning; what to order for lunch; what to make for dinner? Numerous decisions concerning your diet face you every day. If you understand the principles of good nutrition, you will be more likely to make smart choices. Here are the fundamentals of good nutrition, along with practical tips for putting it all into practice.

The Benefits: Why a Healthy Diet Is Important

Throughout one's lifetime, overall health and well-being are inextricably linked to diet. A healthy diet can significantly impact the way you age and can reduce your risk of common serious chronic diseases like heart disease, certain cancers, diabetes and osteoporosis.

Diet is a key component in maintaining an appropriate weight. In recent years, the incidence of obesity has increased at an alarming rate. Current estimates indicate that 55% of American adults are overweight. Carrying too much weight greatly increases your risk for high blood pressure, high cholesterol, heart disease, stroke, diabetes, some cancers, arthritis and respiratory problems.

Remember that as important as diet is in promoting good health, it is only part of the equation. Other lifestyle factors—exercising regularly, not smoking and using alcohol in moderation—also have a significant bearing on health.

Principles of Healthy Eating

The Food Guide Pyramid developed by the United States Department of Agriculture (USDA) breaks down your basic food choices into five categories: bread, cereal, rice and pasta; vegetables; fruits; milk, yogurt and cheese; meat, poultry, fish, dry beans, eggs and nuts.

It is important to eat a variety of foods from each category every day to ensure that you meet your dietary goals.

- Make plant foods from the first 3 categories (grains, vegetables and fruits) the foundation of your diet. They are low in saturated fat, but high in components such as fiber, antioxidant vitamins and phytochemicals that protect against chronic diseases like heart disease, cancer and diabetes.

- Choose whole grains. From the 6 to 11 servings of grain foods recommended each day, make sure that at least 3 of those are whole grains. In addition to fiber, whole grains such as brown rice, rolled oats and whole wheat bread contain vitamins, minerals and phytochemicals.

- Eat at least 2 servings of fruit and 3 servings of vegetables each day. But consider 5 daily servings from both these categories a minimum; aim for 9 servings of fruits and vegetables. Eating a variety of different-colored fruits and vegetables helps ensure that you are getting the nutrients you need. Be sure to include leafy dark green vegetables, deep orange or yellow fruits and vegetables, and citrus fruits in your diet every day.

- Limit saturated fat and trans fatty acids because they raise blood cholesterol and increase risk of heart disease. Fatty meats, butter, cream, cheese, lard and coconut oil are high in saturated fat. Trans fatty acids are formed when liquid vegetable oils are made creamy and thick through a process called hydrogenation. They are found in many margarines and shortenings, and are

Food Guide Pyramid
A Guide to Daily Food Choices

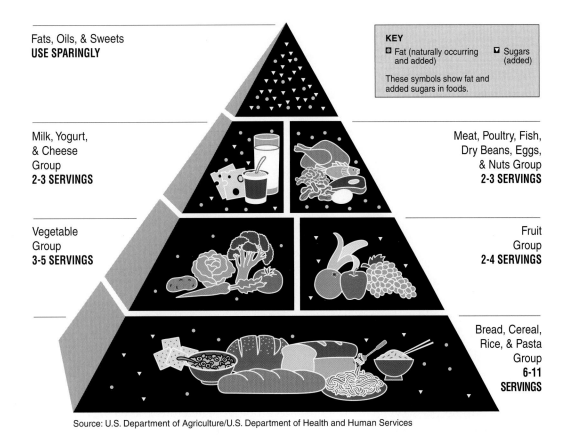

Fats, Oils, & Sweets
USE SPARINGLY

KEY
☐ Fat (naturally occurring and added)   ☑ Sugars (added)

These symbols show fat and added sugars in foods.

Milk, Yogurt, & Cheese Group
2-3 SERVINGS

Meat, Poultry, Fish, Dry Beans, Eggs, & Nuts Group
2-3 SERVINGS

Vegetable Group
3-5 SERVINGS

Fruit Group
2-4 SERVINGS

Bread, Cereal, Rice, & Pasta Group
6-11 SERVINGS

Source: U.S. Department of Agriculture/U.S. Department of Health and Human Services

The USDA Food Guide Pyramid presents a simple, smart and healthy eating plan.

widely used in commercial baked goods and snacks. Replace these fats with unsaturated fats like olive oil and nuts, which do not raise cholesterol. However, all fats are high in calories, so use them in moderation.

- Use a light hand with salt and other high-sodium ingredients, such as soy sauce, and limit processed foods, which are typically high in sodium.

- Minimize empty calories from sugar and other caloric sweeteners like honey. When you eat sweetened, starchy foods, you consume a lot of calories but few, if any, key nutrients.

- Enjoy your food and emphasize nutrient-dense foods like leafy dark greens, winter squash, oranges, wheat germ, beans and lentils.

Your Daily Diet: The Lowdown on Calories, Fat, Sodium & Serving Sizes

Calories

Most of us are used to thinking about food and diet in terms of calorie counts. But have you ever wondered just what a calorie is? Simply put, a calorie is a unit that measures the energy a food contains. The number of calories you need each day ranges from 1,600 to 2,800, depending on various factors including age, sex, height, metabolism, activity level and whether you have a weight problem or are pregnant or breastfeeding. The average adult should consume about 2,000 calories per day. One way to determine your individual caloric needs for weight maintenance is to multiply your ideal weight by 13.2 if you are a woman, or by 13.5 if you are a man.

As you age, the number of calories you need decreases. As part of the aging process, the proportion of lean muscle mass to fatty tissue in your body declines. Because muscle burns more calories than fat, it is easy to gain unwelcome pounds if you are not vigilant about calories and exercise. And as you eat fewer calories, make sure that the foods you choose deliver the nutrients you need.

Fat

The public's awareness of the link between high-fat diets and health problems, specifically heart disease, has increased dramatically in the last decade. Most people are aware of the recommendation that you get no more than 30% of your calories from fat. This guideline is easy to remember, but a little more difficult to interpret. Keep in mind that it does not refer to the percentage of fat in the food; rather, it refers to the relationship between calories contributed by fat to total calories. To determine the percentage of calories from fat, multiply the number of grams of fat by 9 (the number of calories in one gram of fat), then calculate percentage of fat calories to total calories. For example, the recipe for Multi-Grain Pancakes or Waffles (page 35) contains 330 calories and 5 grams fat per serving, with 45 calories from fat. Therefore, the recipe contains 13.6% calories from fat (45 divided by 330).

Percentage of calories from fat is a useful measure for evaluating overall diet, but not for individual dishes. For example, a salad made with low-calorie (but nutrient-rich) vegetables and caloric (but heart-healthy) olive oil would have a high percentage of calories from fat. On the other hand, a low-fat dessert comprised primarily of sugar and flour (these carbohydrates contain 4 calories per gram) would weigh in with a low percentage of calories from fat. Clearly, despite the percentages, the salad is a more healthful food. The low-fat dessert can be included in an overall diet as an occasional treat.

These numbers and calculations might seem intimidating. However, monitoring your fat intake over the course of a day is easier because the numbers are more manageable. Most packaged food lists fat content on the Nutrition Facts label. How many grams of fat are you allowed per day? The upper limit of total fat recommended for a person on a 2,000-calorie per day diet is 65 grams. To estimate your individual fat allowance, simply divide your ideal body weight by 2. For example, if your ideal weight is 150 pounds, you should consume no more than 75 grams of fat per day.

There are several types of fat and, when it comes to health, it is important to note that not all fats are created equal. The 4 main types of dietary fat are saturated fat, monounsaturated fat, polyunsaturated fat and trans fatty acids. Here are some facts on fats:

- **Saturated fat.** Saturated fats are associated with heart disease. No more than 10% of your calories (20 grams for a 2000-calorie-per-day diet) should come from saturated fat. Saturated fats are found in meats, some dairy products, coconut oil and palm oil. You can identify these fats because they are solid at room temperature.

- **Monounsaturated fat.** When used to replace saturated fat in the diet, monounsaturated fat can lower blood cholesterol. Olive oil is usually associated with monounsaturated fat. But canola oil, avocados and almonds also contain a high percentage of monounsaturated fat. At room temperature, monounsaturated fats are liquid.

- **Polyunsaturated fat.** Polyunsaturated fats are divided into 2 categories: omega-3 fatty acids and omega-6 fatty acids. Omega-3 fatty acids, in particular, have significant benefits: They provide protection against heart disease, promote eye and brain health, and aid the immune system. Fatty fish like salmon, flaxseeds and walnuts are sources of omega-3s. Omega-6 fatty acids are found in vegetable oils such as corn oil and safflower oil. These fats are liquid at room temperature.

- **Trans fatty acids.** Not only do trans fatty acids raise LDL ("bad") cholesterol, they lower HDL ("good") cholesterol, thereby increasing risk of heart disease. Trans fats are made through a process called hydrogenation, which transforms liquid vegetable oil into a more stable solid state. Essentially, this is how margarine and vegetable shortenings are made. Because hydrogenation increases shelf life and flavor stability of food products, it is not surprising that trans fats abound in the fast food industry and in commercial baked goods and snack foods. Obviously, you want to avoid trans fatty acids, but identifying them can be tricky. At the time of this writing, the United States Food and Drug Administration (FDA) is considering, but has not yet implemented, regulations requiring that Nutrition Facts labels list the number of grams of trans fatty acids in a product. In the meantime, scrutinize the ingredient list on the label for the words "hydrogenated oil" and "partially hydrogenated oil," indications that a product contains trans fatty acids.

Sodium

Most American diets are too high in sodium, due mostly to the large amounts of processed and prepared foods we consume. In some individuals, too much sodium contributes to high blood pressure. While your body needs some sodium—about 500 mg (the amount in ¼ teaspoon salt)—it is prudent to limit your sodium intake. It is recommended that you consume no more than 2,400 mg sodium (the amount found in 1 teaspoon salt) per day. The recipes in this book are seasoned with a moderate amount of salt for flavor. If you are on a sodium-restricted diet, omit the salt. Note that canned beans offer convenience but tend to be high in sodium. When dishes call for canned beans, you can reduce sodium levels by using dried beans instead. (See page 173 for substitution guidelines.)

What Counts as a Serving?

You know that you should eat 6 to 11 servings of grains and 3 to 5 servings of vegetables each day. But just what constitutes a serving? The USDA's *Dietary Guidelines for Americans* offers some examples:

- **Bread, Cereal, Rice and Pasta:** 1 slice bread; 1 cup ready-to-eat cereal.

- **Vegetables:** 1 cup raw leafy vegetables; ½ cup other vegetables—cooked or raw; ¾ cup vegetable juice.

- **Fruits:** 1 medium apple, banana, orange or pear; ½ cup chopped, cooked or canned fruit; ¾ cup fruit juice.

- **Milk, Yogurt and Cheese:** 1 cup milk or yogurt; 1½ oz. natural cheese; 1 oz. processed cheese.

- **Meat, Poultry and Fish:** 2 to 3 oz. cooked lean meat, poultry or fish.

- **Meat Alternatives (Dry Beans, Eggs and Nuts):** Each of these counts as 1 oz. meat: ½ cup cooked dry beans; ½ cup tofu; 2½-oz. soyburger; 1 egg; 2 tablespoons peanut butter; ⅓ cup nuts.

Some Key Nutrients & Protective Components In Food

Antioxidants

Antioxidants are substances that protect the body's cells and tissues by inhibiting oxidation. When body cells burn oxygen, they form by-products called free radicals. These free radicals cause cell damage associated with degenerative diseases such as cancer, heart disease, arthritis and cataracts. Antioxidants provide protection against disease because they neutralize free radicals before they can cause damage.

The best known antioxidants are vitamin C, vitamin E, beta carotene and the mineral selenium. They work synergistically to reduce oxidization. While studies have shown

Sweet potatoes and kale provide your body with important antioxidants.

that a diet rich in antioxidants provides benefits, the various individual antioxidants have not been shown to reduce risk of heart disease and cancer when taken in supplement form. To maximize your antioxidant defenses, the best strategy is to eat plenty of fruits, vegetables and whole grains, and to include nuts in your diet. Foods such as kale, sweet potatoes, citrus fruits, berries and nuts are all good sources of antioxidants.

Calcium

Calcium is an essential mineral that builds and maintains strong bones and teeth. A diet that is deficient in calcium leads to bone mass depletion and can eventually result in osteoporosis. In addition to bone health, adequate calcium intake has been linked to reduced risk of colon cancer and high blood pressure.

Most people do not get enough calcium. Adults need 1,000 mg per day. As you age, you need more calcium to minimize bone loss. Women over age 50 and men over age 65 should get 1,200 to 1,500 mg calcium per day. Calcium needs help to be absorbed; vitamin D is necessary for calcium absorption.

Milk products are classic calcium providers, but you can also get calcium by eating broccoli or dried beans.

Low-fat or nonfat dairy products are the easiest way to meet your calcium needs through diet. A cup of milk or yogurt provides more than 300 mg of calcium, so just three servings puts you well on your way to meeting your daily goal. Some good nondairy sources of calcium include kale, broccoli, dried beans, figs and tofu processed with calcium sulfate.

Fiber

Found only in plants, fiber is the part that cannot be completely digested. Fiber is a nutrient but it does not supply calories, vitamins and minerals. However, it plays an important role in promoting good health and reducing risk of some chronic diseases.

There are two types of fiber. Soluble fiber offers protection against heart disease. So named because it dissolves in water, soluble fiber is found in fruits, some vegetables, oatmeal, oat bran, barley and dried beans. Insoluble fiber is valued for its positive effects on gastrointestinal health. Insoluble fiber can be found in wheat bran and whole wheat products, seeds, nuts, certain vegetables and fruit skins. Most fiber-rich foods contain a mixture of both kinds of fiber, but one type

A single medium-size apple provides about 4 grams of fiber.

might predominate. While soluble fiber has received a lot of press because of its potential for reducing cholesterol, both types are important components of a healthy diet.

Most nutrition experts recommend that you consume 25 to 35 grams of fiber per day, yet most Americans get only 11 to 13 grams. The best way to be sure you get enough fiber is to eat a variety of whole grains, beans, fruits and vegetables. Note that you should increase fiber intake gradually; drastic increases can result in gas and bloating.

Lentils are a great source of folic acid.

Folic Acid

Folic acid, also known as folate, is a B vitamin that plays an essential role in making new body cells. It is especially important that pregnant women get enough folic acid because a deficiency increases risk of delivering a baby with neural tube defects. And because folic acid helps lower homocysteine, it may protect against heart disease.

The Recommended Dietary Allowance (RDA) for folic acid is 400 mcg per day for adults. Fortified cereals, lentils, dried beans, wheat germ, leafy green vegetables, oranges and peanuts are some common foods that provide folic acid.

Omega-3 Fatty Acids

Omega-3 fatty acids are a type of polyunsaturated fat. They are important because they promote cardiac health by reducing blood clotting and abnormal heart rhythms. In addition, omega-3s may help with autoimmune diseases and may have a positive effect on mood because they are important for proper brain function. The best sources of omega-3s are cold-water fatty fish such as salmon, mackerel and bluefish. Flaxseeds, walnuts, legumes and green leafy vegetables are good plant sources of omega-3s.

Fish provides essential omega-3 fatty acids.

Phytochemicals

Vitamins and minerals are not the only components in food that promote good health. Compounds called phytochemicals, also known as phytonutrients, are naturally occurring plant chemicals found in plant foods like fruits, vegetables, grains, nuts and tea; *phyto* is the Greek word for plant. Phytochemicals are being studied for the potential they offer to fight cancer and reduce risk of heart disease. In contrast to vitamins and minerals (classified as nutrients because they are essential), a lack of phytochemicals in the diet has not led to any documented deficiencies. However, it is believed that phytochemicals may be one of the components responsible for the extraordinary health benefits of a diet rich in fruits, vegetables and whole grains.

Phytochemicals play a protective role in several ways. Many phytochemicals are powerful antioxidants. Some are phytoestrogens, which help regulate hormone levels and may have a positive impact on hormone-related cancers. Others serve as detoxifiers and cell regulators, which may shrink cancerous tumors. Phytochemicals are often responsible for a plant's vivid color and distinctive color and flavor. There are thousands of these compounds—many have yet to be identified—and research on them is still in the early stages. At the risk of sounding like a broken record, the best way to take advantage of the protective powers of phytochemicals is to eat a wide array of fruits, vegetables, whole grains, legumes and nuts.

There are too many phytochemicals to cover in this book, but here are a few that you may have heard of and are sure to hear more about as research on the subject progresses.

Grapes and berries offer anthocyanins.

• **Anthocyanins.** This is the reddish pigment in many fruits. It is found in blueberries, grapes, raspberries and cherries. Anthocyanins, which are antioxidants, are linked to reduced risk of heart disease.

• **Carotenoids.** These are the red, orange and yellow pigments in foods. There are hundreds of carotenoid compounds and they all have significant antioxidant potential. Some of the most familiar are beta carotene, lycopene, lutein and zeaxanthin. Beta carotene, found in sweet potatoes, pumpkins and apricots, is associated with reduced risk of cancer. Lycopene, which has been shown to inhibit prostate tumors, is found in cooked tomato products, pink grapefruit, dried apricots and watermelon. Lutein and zeaxanthin are particularly interesting because they may help preserve eyesight by preventing macular degeneration and cataracts. These carotenoids are abundant in leafy greens, such as kale, broccoli, mustard greens and collards.

Broccoli is just one carotenoid source.

• **Isoflavones.** These phytoestrogens have received a lot of attention because they show potential for decreasing the incidence of breast cancer, lowering cholesterol, protecting bone mass and easing symptoms of menopause. Isoflavones are found mainly in soy foods, such as tofu, soymilk and edamame beans.

• **Lignans.** Another phytoestrogen that may lower cholesterol and reduce risk of cancer, lignans are found in flaxseeds, sesame seeds and whole grains.

Flaxseeds are a great source of lignans.

Soy foods are rich in isoflavones.

Eating More Whole Grains

If you think whole grains are mysterious foods that take forever to cook and can only be found in health food stores, think again. Increasing your consumption of whole grains can be as easy as ordering a sandwich on whole wheat bread or cooking instant brown rice for dinner. What follows are some tips for selecting and cooking whole grain foods.

Whole grains are simple to find if you know where and how to look.

Defining Whole Grains

Whole grains consist of the entire grain kernel, which comprises the endosperm, germ and bran. When grains are refined, as they are to make white flour or white rice, the germ and bran are removed, leaving the starchy endosperm portion. Since the vitamins, minerals, fiber and phytochemicals are concentrated in the germ and bran of the grain, refined grains don't measure up nutritionally to intact grains.

Finding Whole Grains

Breakfast cereals. Entire supermarket aisles are devoted to packaged cereals. How do you separate sugar-coated cereals made with refined grains from healthful whole grain options? Rolled oats are an excellent whole grain option. When purchasing ready-to-eat cereals, look for the whole grain health claim on the label. Check the ingredient list carefully. The first ingredient listed should be *whole* wheat, *whole* oats or *whole* barley.

Bread and Crackers. Look for packaged bread labeled 100% whole wheat flour. Many breads are made with a mixture of whole wheat flour, other whole grains like rye and oats, and refined white flour. Check the ingredient list; the first ingredients listed should be qualified with the word "whole." Note that the term "wheat" flour does not necessarily mean whole wheat flour. If you purchase bread at a bakery, ask what percentage of a loaf is whole wheat. My local supermarket sells a wholesome-sounding multigrain loaf. But when I inquired about the loaf's ingredients, I learned that it contained only 15% whole wheat. Similarly, choose crackers made with whole grains and avoid brands that contain trans fats (hydrogenated vegetable oil). Some healthful brands are Wasa, Ry-Krisp and Kavli crispbreads.

Rice. In addition to standard long-grain brown rice, you can now find basmati, short-grain and medium-grain varieties of brown rice in supermarkets. Basmati is prized for its fragrance and nutty taste. Short- and medium-grain rices have an appealing, almost creamy consistency. Granted, it takes twice as long to cook brown rice (40 to 50 minutes) than it does white rice. However, the cooking process is easy and brown rice reheats well in the microwave. If you make up a large batch when you have time on the weekend, it will be ready for a quick reheat on busy weeknights. Instant brown rice, which is available in supermarkets, is useful when you are pressed for time. Brown rice is more perishable than white rice; store in an airtight container in the refrigerator or freezer.

Barley. This versatile grain with a nutty flavor and chewy texture can be used in soups, pilafs and salads. The most common forms found in supermarkets are pearl barley and quick barley. Pearl barley takes about 45 minutes to cook, but quick barley, which cooks in about 15 minutes, is a convenient alternative. Quick barley is simply pearl barley that has been rolled thinner to speed up cooking.

Bulgur. Essentially a whole grain convenience food, bulgur is made from wheat kernels that are steamed, dried and cracked. Its nutty taste and chewy texture are highlighted in salads, tabbouleh and pilafs. Because bulgur is pre-cooked, cooking time is minimal. To prepare it for use in salads, simply cover with boiling water, let soak 20 minutes, then drain. As a pilaf, bulgur takes only 20 minutes to cook. You can find bulgur in the natural foods section of some supermarkets, and in health food stores.

Couscous. Most couscous is not a whole grain food. However, you can find whole wheat couscous at health food stores. Couscous, which is actually a form of pasta that resembles rice, is made from semolina wheat. You can't beat couscous for convenience. To prepare it, simply stir it into boiling liquid, remove from heat and let plump for 5 minutes. Whole wheat couscous doesn't take any longer than regular couscous to prepare. Stock up on the whole wheat variety when you get a chance; it is a better nutritional bet.

Whole Wheat Pasta. Most pasta is made from refined wheat, but you can find whole wheat pasta in health food stores and some supermarkets. Pasta is such a handy staple, it is worth trying whole wheat varieties once in a while. Whole wheat pasta doesn't have as much "chew" as regular pasta because it contains a lower percentage of gluten. However, it has a pleasant nutty taste. I think it works best with sauces that have an assertive flavor.

Quinoa. This grain from South America has the distinction of being higher in protein than any other grain. Quinoa is also rich in vitamins and minerals. It has a delicate earthy flavor and pleasant crunchy texture. Quinoa takes only 20 minutes to cook and makes delicious, easy pilaf. This grain makes an especially nice side dish for fish. You can find it in health food stores.

Eating More Beans & Legumes

Dried beans and other legumes such as lentils and split peas provide fiber, protein, B vitamins (including folic acid) and minerals. Dried and canned beans make essential staples because they are easy to store in your pantry. Here are some suggestions for including more beans and legumes in your diet.

• Keep a good supply of canned beans—garbanzo beans, black beans, kidney beans, cannellini beans, pinto beans, black-eyed peas—on hand to give a nutritional boost to soups, salads, stews and pasta sauces. Canned beans are quite high in sodium. If your doctor has prescribed a low-sodium diet, consider substituting dried beans for canned.

• Dried beans are more economical than canned, but require pre-soaking and have a lengthy cooking time. For general instructions for cooking dried beans, see page 173.

Beans provide fiber, protein, B vitamins and minerals.

• Puree cooked or canned beans with seasonings to make a healthful spread or dip. You will find several recipes for bean spreads on page 44.

• Lentils and split peas do not require pre-soaking and cook in about 45 minutes. If you have some in your pantry, you will always have the makings of satisfying soup on hand.

• Look for canned soups that feature beans and legumes. Lentil soup, black bean soup and split pea soup are handy, healthful options.

Eating More Fruits & Vegetables

Five to nine servings a day might seem like a lot, but if you eat fruits and vegetables at every meal, and enjoy them for snacks, your intake of produce adds up quickly. Here are some simple strategies to ensure that you get the benefits that a diet rich in fruits and vegetables provides.

- Celebrate the produce of the season. Shop at farmers' markets and local farm stands whenever you can. Better yet, grow your own. Freshly picked fruits and vegetables taste so good, you will want to eat more of them. Furthermore, when produce is at its peak, it needs very little preparation or rich sauce to taste great.

Frozen or fresh, vegetables and fruits are essential.

- Since most produce is best when consumed shortly after purchasing, you will need to stock up regularly. However, certain fruits and vegetables store well, so keep some hardy produce on hand for those days when you can't make it to the supermarket. You can keep carrots, for example, in a plastic bag in the crisper of your refrigerator for up to 2 weeks. As for fruit, apples and oranges are good standbys. You can store apples, wrapped in a plastic bag in the refrigerator, for 2 to 4 weeks. Oranges will keep in a plastic bag in the refrigerator for 10 to 14 days.

- Keep a cache of frozen vegetables on hand for busy days when you don't have time to shop for fresh produce or prepare it. Since frozen vegetables are usually processed shortly after harvesting, they might even contain more nutrients than those that have spent days in transit and on supermarket shelves. There are numerous choices for high-quality frozen vegetables: corn, green peas, snow peas, broccoli, spinach and squash, to name a few. Frozen berries and peaches are great for smoothies and sauces. One caution: Avoid prepared frozen vegetable mixes with sauce; typically, they are high in sodium. Instead, embellish your vegetables with a drizzle of extra-virgin olive oil, a squeeze of lemon juice and perhaps some fresh herbs or grated citrus peel.

- Dried fruits are easy to store and make tasty, convenient snacks. However, keep in mind that dried fruits are concentrated sources of calories.

- Get a head start on your five-a-day quota by having both a serving of whole fruit—sliced banana on your cereal, for example—and a glass of fruit juice for breakfast. Throughout the day, slip vegetables into meals and snacks at every opportunity. Add lettuce, tomato, sliced cucumber and grated carrots to sandwiches. Try vegetable toppings like broccoli, artichokes, spinach and bell peppers on pizzas. Finish your meals with fruit desserts.

Choosing Low-Fat Dairy Products

Dairy foods offer the most efficient way to get the calcium you need. Not only are they high in calcium, dairy products contain vitamin D, which aids in absorption of calcium. The key is to choose low-fat or fat-free versions. Here is what you should look for.

Low-Fat Milk. While all milk is high in calcium, the fat content of the different types of milk varies considerably. One cup homogenized whole milk contains 150 calories and 8.2 grams fat (5 grams saturated fat), whereas 1 cup low-fat 1% milk contains 102 calories and 2.6 grams fat (1.6 grams saturated fat). Choose low-fat or fat-free skim milk. Note that 2% milk is not considered low-fat. Use milk instead of water to boost calcium in recipes and convenience foods. Some examples: Make hot cereal with milk; dilute condensed soups with milk; or plump couscous in milk.

Yogurt. Plain nonfat or low-fat yogurt is extremely versatile. You can use it as a creamy base for salad dressings and dips and as a substitute for sour cream in baking. To make yogurt creamier and richer-tasting, drain it. Spoon yogurt into a cheesecloth-lined sieve over a bowl and refrigerater for 1 to 1½ hours. Discard whey that drains off. Plain yogurt is most versatile for cooking and baking, but you might prefer vanilla or fruit-flavored yogurt for eating alone.

Buttermilk. Despite its name, buttermilk is not high in fat. Modern buttermilk is made from cultured nonfat or low-fat milk. Its slight acidity makes baked goods especially moist and tender. Buttermilk is also useful for making creamy, low-fat salad dressings.

For creamier, richer yogurt: Let it drain over a cheesecloth-lined sieve for an hour.

Reduced-Fat Sour Cream. This is sometimes labeled as light or lite sour cream. While it is not as rich as regular sour cream, reduced-fat sour cream should not be used with abandon. However, a little can be useful for giving a creamy finish to a soup or stew.

Cheese. Most cheeses are high in total fat as well as saturated fat. However, it is worth seeking out full-flavored cheeses like aged cheddar and Parmesan because just a small quantity delivers a lot of satisfying cheese flavor.

Cooking With Good Fats

While saturated fat and trans fatty acids contribute to health problems, monounsaturated fats and omega-3 fatty acids provide benefits. All fats, however, are concentrated sources of calories; use them in moderation. What follows are descriptions of where you will find the good fats and how to cook with them.

Olive Oil. Valued by nutritionists for its high percentage of monounsaturated fats and appreciated by cooks for its distinctive flavor, olive oil is an excellent all-purpose oil that complements any dish with Mediterranean flavors. As a dip for bread, it makes a healthful alternative to butter. Extra-virgin olive oil, which is made from the first pressing of the olives, is the most flavorful and most expensive. However, the flavor tends to break down during heating. Therefore, it is generally recommended that you reserve your expensive extra-virgin oil for salads and dishes that will not be heated. Note that the word "lighter" on an olive oil label does not signify that it is lower in fat and calories, but simply that the oil has a milder flavor or color.

Canola Oil. There is no such thing as a canola plant. Canola oil is pressed from rapeseeds, which belong to the mustard family. Canola is a made-up name that refers to the oil's country of origin—Canada. This oil also has a high percentage of monounsaturated fat. In addition, it contains omega-3 fatty acids. Its neutral flavor makes it suitable for sweet baked goods and in dishes featuring assertive Asian flavors.

Nuts. Nuts add flavor and texture to both sweet and savory dishes. While nuts are high in fat, most of it is monounsaturated. Nuts also provide protein, fiber, vitamins and minerals. Walnuts contain omega-3 fatty acids. Once you open the package, store nuts in the freezer for up to 6 months. Nuts are high in calories, so do not overuse. To extract maximum flavor from nuts, toast them on a baking sheet in the oven at 350°F for 8 to 10 minutes, or in a small dry skillet over medium-low heat for 2 to 3 minutes, stirring constantly. Many of the recipes in this book call for nuts. If you are allergic to them or cook for someone with a nut allergy, simply omit them.

Cooking Spray. This is an efficient, low-fat way to prepare baking pans and skillets; it is usually not needed on nonstick skillets. Olive oil cooking spray is useful for giving pizza toppings, oven-fried chicken and baked tortilla crisps a very light but uniform protective coating that prevents food from drying out during baking and ensures a crisp result. Coating food with cooking spray adds a negligible amount of fat.

It only takes a few nuts to add great flavor to a dish.

Superfoods

Certain foods like soy and flaxseeds show extraordinary promise for protecting against disease. But these are not the foods we grew up on. Incorporating soy and flax into your diet can be daunting. Here's how to get to know soy foods and flaxseeds, and use them in cooking.

Soy Foods

Soybeans are a good source of protein but do not contain the accompanying saturated fat found in meats. Studies have found that, when used to replace animal protein, soy foods lower cholesterol and reduce risk of heart disease. Soy foods also contain isoflavones, a type of phytoestrogen that shows promise for protecting against hormone-related cancers and lessening symptoms of menopause. Here are some of the most common and easy-to-use soy products.

You can reap the benefits of soybeans in a variety of forms.

Soymilk. This is the creamy liquid extracted from cooked soybeans. Since soymilk is technically not "dairy milk," it may be labeled soy drink, soy beverage or soymilk. Most supermarkets and health food stores carry refrigerated soymilk and aseptic-packaged soymilk. Aseptic-packaged soymilk is pasteurized at a higher temperature than the refrigerated variety. Many people prefer the taste of refrigerated soymilk, but you can't beat the convenience of shelf-stable aseptic packaging. You can substitute soymilk for dairy milk in most recipes; use plain soymilk in savory recipes, vanilla for desserts and beverages. Try soymilk over breakfast cereal, in smoothies and in hot chocolate.

Tofu. Also known as bean curd, tofu is made by curdling soymilk. There are basically two types of tofu: regular and silken. Regular tofu is made by combining soymilk with a coagulant to form curds in a process similar to making cottage cheese. Silken tofu is made by a slightly different method. Less coagulant is used, and the tofu is set directly in the container. This process results in a more custard-like texture.

Tofu has a bland, almost neutral flavor. It comes to life when it takes on the flavors of a vibrant marinade. Since it has a soft texture, it pairs well with textured foods such as crisp salads. Use firm regular tofu for stir-frying, grilling, sautéing and in soups. Silken tofu is great in creamy spreads, salad dressings and sauces. It even works well as a substitute for butter in cookie recipes (see Wholesome Chocolate Chip Cookies, page 219, and Rolled Sugar Cookies, page 221.

Place the leftover tofu in a clean container, cover with water and refrigerate for up to 1 week, changing water daily. Once opened, aseptically packaged tofu should be refrigerated and used within 2 days.

Edamame. Sometimes known as sweet beans or green soybeans, edamame are immature soybeans. They are easy to prepare and delicious—certainly one of the most effortless ways to include more soy in your diet. Edamame are similar to baby lima beans. You can sometimes find fresh beans in supermarkets and farmers' markets. You can find frozen edamame both in pods and shelled, in natural foods stores and some supermarkets.

Flaxseeds

Flaxseeds show considerable potential for providing health benefits because they are rich in some key disease-fighting compounds. They contain both soluble fiber, which has been linked to reduced risk of heart disease, and unsoluble fiber, which provides valuable roughage. Flaxseeds are also one of the best sources of lignans. These phytochemicals have hormone-like effects in the body and may offer protection against hormone-related cancers. In addition, flaxseeds are one of the best plant sources of beneficial omega-3 fatty acids, which may have a bearing on heart disease, autoimmune disease and mood. As a source of omega-3 fatty acids, flaxseeds are especially important in vegetarian diets that do not include fish.

Flaxseeds have a delicious nutty flavor and are a tasty addition to numerous dishes. Sprinkle ground flaxseeds over cereal, stir into rice pilaf, and use them to thicken salad dressings and enrich baked goods.

To make sure you take advantage of the good things in flax, grind whole seeds in a blender or spice mill. (A coffee grinder reserved for spices, grains and seeds works well as a spice mill.) Don't grind seeds until you need them.

Toasting flaxseeds enhances their nutty flavor. To toast whole flaxseeds, place in a small skillet over medium-low heat. Stir them constantly for 1 to 1½ minutes or until fragrant and popping. Transfer to a small bowl to cool and prevent further cooking.

The Flax Council of Canada recommends storing whole flaxseeds in an airtight container at room temperature for up to one year. However, if you live in a hot climate, keeping them in the refrigerator is a good idea.

Equipment For Healthy Cooking

All you need for healthy cooking is a kitchen stocked with an assortment of pots and pans, and basic tools like knives, cutting board, measuring cups and spoons, a vegetable peeler and colander. However, there are a few pieces of equipment that make healthful cooking easier.

Nonstick Skillet. This is the most useful and versatile item in any health-conscious cook's kitchen. The nonstick surface allows you to use less fat than you might otherwise need in a dish. There are numerous brands of skillets available, ranging from dirt-cheap varieties to ultra-deluxe models. Nonstick surfaces tend to wear off eventually. One strategy for maintaining surface quality is to use a moderately priced skillet and replace it every few years.

Kitchen Scale. Measuring cups and spoons do the job of measuring most ingredients in a recipe, but certain items like pasta and meats can only be measured by weight. A kitchen scale is useful for ensuring appropriate portion sizes. Digital scales are precise but expensive. An inexpensive spring-loaded scale is fine for most purposes.

Instant-Read Thermometer. An instant-read thermometer allows you to determine the temperature of chicken or meat quickly and accurately for food safety.

Spice Mill. If you would like to incorporate beneficial flaxseeds into your diet, a spice mill is useful for grinding them. An inexpensive coffee grinder reserved for flaxseeds and spices works well as a spice mill.

Mortar and Pestle. A mortar and pestle is an efficient way to deal with garlic and mellow its flavor. To accomplish this, mash garlic with a touch of salt into a paste.

The right equipment makes your healthy cooking venture easier.

Healthy Cooking Techniques

If you opt for good fats, such as olive oil and canola oil, and use the bare minimum needed, you can easily accommodate most cooking techniques to healthful cooking. However, certain methods successfully replicate the results traditionally achieved by much higher-fat techniques, while others maximize the natural flavors in foods without drenching them in fat.

You'll find the recipe for Two-Potato Oven Fries *on page 103.*

Steaming is another good option for cooking vegetables.

• When you sauté or stir-fry, use a nonstick skillet or stir-fry pan and a teaspoon or two of oil. Choose olive oil or canola oil instead of butter or margarine.

• To create a crisp crust on chicken pieces or potato wedges, "fry" them in a hot oven rather than in a bath of hot fat. Spritz the surface of the food with cooking spray or toss the food in a small amount of oil before baking. This prevents drying out and promotes a crisp finish.

• Roasting is not just for large cuts of meat and poultry. It works beautifully with vegetables and fruits. High-heat roasting enhances the natural sweetness of vegetables and fruits, and retains nutrients well.

• Braising involves browning and then simmering food in liquid until tender. During simmering, the flavor of the food mingles with the liquid, creating a sauce that has real depth of flavor.

• Steaming vegetables rather than boiling them minimizes vitamin loss. Steaming is also the easiest way to cook many vegetables.

• Poaching is cooking food at a gentle simmer in liquid. It is well suited to fish and poultry because it ensures a moist result. During cooking, the liquid becomes flavorful and provides a good base for a low-fat sauce.

Tips For Healthy Cooking & Savvy Substitutions

The following tips and easy recipe ideas will help you put all the advice outlined here into practice.

Choose Lean Cuts of Red Meat

Lean cuts of meaty beef, which include top loin, sirloin, tenderloin and round, generally come from the hind quarters of the animal. Chuck and shoulder and rib cuts, from the front of the animal, are fattier. Trim meat of visible fat before cooking, and pay attention to portion sizes. Three ounces of cooked meat is the recommended serving size. Because meat shrinks during cooking, allow 4 ounces raw meat per person. If available, venison is always leaner than beef.

Remove Skin from Poultry

Removing poultry's skin saves you about 4 grams of fat per 3-oz. serving. When marinating and sautéing or grilling poultry, remove skin before cooking. But when roasting an entire bird, leave the skin on during roasting to prevent the meat from drying out. Remove skin before serving. Breast meat is far leaner than leg meat. A 3-oz. portion of skinless chicken breast has 3 grams of fat, while the equivalent portion of skinless chicken leg contains 7 grams of fat.

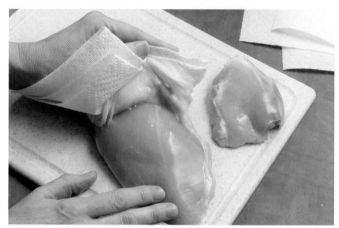

Remove poultry's skin before marinating and sautéing or grilling.

Treat Yourself Smartly

Use "luxury" ingredients such as nuts, cheese and chocolate judiciously, and place them in a prominent place where they will provide maximum impact. For example, instead of burying nuts in muffin batter, sprinkle them over the top. You will get an immediate burst of flavor when you bite into the muffin. That means more flavor impact from a smaller quantity.

Use Whole Wheat Flour

Bake with whole wheat flour. Replace half of the all-purpose flour in yeast breads, quick breads and pancakes with whole wheat flour. This substitution can increase the fiber in your recipe by 10 grams per cup of whole wheat flour used.

Fruit, Not Fat

Substitute fruit puree for much of the fat in simple baked goods. You can find commercial fat replacements for baking, such as Smucker's Baking Healthy and Lighter Bake, in most supermarkets. But applesauce, apple butter and prune pie filling (lekvar) also work well as substitutes for butter, shortening and oil in many cakes, quickbreads, cookie recipes and baking mixes. For best results, replace three-quarters of the fat with fruit puree; leaving in a little bit of fat, preferably in the form of canola oil, improves the texture of low-fat baked goods.

Lighten the Mayo

Moisten sandwich fillings and salads with low-fat mayonnaise instead of regular mayonnaise. Lighten it further by mixing it with an equal part of nonfat plain yogurt. The yogurt brightens the flavor and tempers the sweetness of commercial mayonnaise. One tablespoon regular mayonnaise contains 100 calories and 11 grams fat (1.5 grams saturated fat). One-half tablespoon low-fat mayonnaise mixed with ½ tablespoon nonfat yogurt has 25 calories and 2 grams fat (0 grams saturated fat).

Lose the Sour Cream

- Substitute nonfat plain yogurt for sour cream in baked goods. You will save 48 grams fat and 363 calories per cup.

- Instead of topping your baked potato with sour cream, try Yogurt-Garlic Sauce. Nonfat yogurt becomes exceptionally creamy when it is drained for just 1 hour.

To make Yogurt-Garlic Sauce: Line a sieve with cheesecloth; set over a bowl ½ inch from bottom. (Alternatively, use a large coffee cone lined with filter paper.) Spoon 1⅓ cups nonfat or low-fat plain yogurt into sieve. Cover with plastic wrap; let drain in the refrigerator for 1 hour. Discard whey and transfer drained yogurt to a serving bowl. Use a mortar and pestle or the side of a chef's knife to mash 2 cloves garlic with ¼ teaspoon salt into a paste. Stir into drained yogurt. Stir in 2 teaspoons extra-virgin olive oil. Makes about 1 cup.

Choose an Alternative to Butter

Try spreading bread with Olive Oil-Tofu Dipping Sauce instead of butter. Tofu stretches olive oil and gives it a creamy consistency.

To make Olive Oil-Tofu Dipping Sauce: Mash 2 cloves garlic with ¼ teaspoon salt into a paste in a mortar and pestle or with side of chef's knife. Transfer mixture to a blender. Add ⅓ cup extra-virgin olive oil and ⅓ cup low-fat firm silken tofu; blend until smooth and creamy. Transfer to a serving bowl. Stir in 2 tablespoons chopped fresh parsley. Makes about ½ cup.

Lighten the Cream

Swap whipped cream with Vanilla Cream. Summer berries and many fruit desserts just cry out for a whipped cream topping. Vanilla Cream has the nutrition benefits of yogurt, but uses just enough real whipped cream for a touch of luxury.

To make Vanilla Cream: Line sieve or colander with cheesecloth; set over medium bowl at least ½ inch from bottom. (Alternatively, use a large coffee cone lined with filter paper.) Spoon 1½ cups nonfat or low-fat vanilla yogurt into sieve. Cover with plastic wrap; let drain in refrigerator for 1½ hours. Meanwhile, place small bowl and beaters in freezer to chill. Use the chilled beaters to whip ½ cup whipping cream to soft peaks in the chilled bowl. Push whipped cream to one side of bowl. Discard whey that has drained from yogurt. Add drained yogurt to whipped cream; use rubber spatula to fold gently and mix. Makes 2 cups.

Reduce the Fat

• Rather than munching on deep-fried tortillas chips, enjoy crisp Baked Tortilla Crisps with your snacks. Not only are baked tortilla chips lower in fat than commercial deep-fried chips, they have a richer corn flavor.

You can turn white corn tortillas into crispy low-fat chips.

To make Baked Tortilla Crisps: Stack 1 (9-oz.) pkg. white corn tortillas (12 tortillas); cut into 4 wedges. Spread wedges in a single layer on 2 baking sheets. Spray with cooking spray. Sprinkle with ¼ teaspoon salt. Bake at 400°F 10 to 15 minutes or until light golden and crisp. Makes 6 servings (48 crisps).

• Instead of buying bagel chips or commercial crackers, use Whole Wheat Pita Crisps to scoop your dips and spreads.

To make Whole Wheat Pita Crisps: Cut each of 4 whole wheat pita breads into 4 triangles. Separate each triangle into 2 halves at the fold. Arrange, rough side up, on a baking sheet. Spritz lightly with olive oil cooking spray. Bake at 425°F 8 to 10 minutes or until crisp. Makes 4 servings (32 pita crisps).

Eating Out Healthfully

Cooking at home allows you to see what goes into your food and to control portion sizes. But everyone eats out now and then. Finding healthful fare when you are away from home can be difficult. Restaurants are interested in pleasing the public, not necessarily in making sure that their customers are following a healthy diet. Chefs often rely on generous amounts of butter and cream to achieve full flavors. And during recent years, there has been a trend in food service operations to serve super-sized portions. Here's how to navigate restaurant menus healthfully.

- To combat oversized portions, share the main dish with your dining companion. If you are eating alone, ask about the possibility of getting a half portion.

- Order your salad with dressing on the side. Vinaigrette dressings are generally lower in saturated fat than creamy dressings. Vinegar and olive oil is always a safe choice if you go easy on the oil.

- Avoid items like fried fish and pasta with cream sauce.

- Ask your server what accompaniments are included with the entree. Ask for steamed vegetables or a salad instead of french fries.

You can eat healthfully when you eat out. You just have to investigate your options and make requests.

- If you are going out for a leisurely meal at a fine restaurant, don't arrive ravenous. If you are very hungry, you are more likely to load up on bread and butter while you are waiting for the meal to arrive. To curb your appetite, try eating a small cup of lentil soup before you go out.

- Watch your alcohol consumption. In addition to the extra calories it provides, alcohol stimulates your appetite and puts a damper on your will power, making you more inclined to overeat. Drink lots of water; to make it special, try sparkling water with a twist of lemon or lime.

- Pass on the triple chocolate indulgence cake for dessert, and opt for a fruit sorbet instead.

- When you travel, carry healthy snacks such as dried fruits, sturdy fresh fruit, whole wheat crackers and nuts.

Nutritional Analysis Notes

Each recipe in *Cooking for Health & Flavor* includes a nutritional analysis, which lists values for number of calories, grams of total fat, grams of saturated fat, grams of protein, grams of carbohydrates, milligrams of cholesterol, milligrams of calcium, milligrams of sodium and grams of fiber per serving.

In each recipe, nutrients that provide 25% or more of your daily need are highlighted as "star nutrients." "Noteworthy nutrients" listed provide 15–24% of your daily need. The goal percentages in this book express daily need based on the Recommended Dietary Intake (RDI) published by the USDA. While Recommended Dietary Allowances (RDAs), designed by the National Academy of Sciences, encompass 20 need categories based on age and gender, RDIs are estimated daily needs for individuals 2 years of age and older.

When an alternate ingredient is suggested in a recipe, the first ingredient listed is used for analysis. Optional ingredients are included in the analysis unless otherwise indicated. Where a dressing or other sauce is used, that component is factored into the nutritional analysis for the whole dish. Separate nutritional analyses for dressing and sauce recipes are also included in case you want to use them with other recipes.

Nutritional analysis is done with a computer program. ("Nutritionist Five" was used to analyze the recipes in this book.) Allowances are made for such variables as loss from trimming, and from marinade that is not absorbed by the food. Because nutrient content can vary slightly among brands, cuts of meat and so on, these nutrition figures should be considered general guidelines.

If you are interested in nutrition information for specific foods, the USDA Web site is an excellent resource. Visit www.nal.usda/fnic/foodcomp to access the USDA nutrient database.

Healthy Starts

Whether you are starting your day or looking for an interesting way to begin a meal, this chapter will help you jump-start your healthy diet. The following recipes, ranging from fruit smoothies and cereals to omelets and appetizer spreads, will help get you through every day with style, taste and good health.

Banana-Berry Smoothie

Nothing beats a smoothie for a fast, nutritious breakfast or snack. Packages of frozen mixed berries offer convenient ways to flavor a smoothie and enjoy more of these antioxidant-rich fruits.

1¼ cups orange juice, preferably calcium-fortified
1 ripe medium banana, sliced
1¼ cups mixed frozen berries (blueberries, blackberries, raspberries and/or strawberries)
½ cup (4 oz.) low-fat firm silken tofu
1 tablespoon sugar (optional)

❶ In blender, combine orange juice, banana, berries, tofu and sugar; blend until smooth and creamy.

3 (1-cup) servings.
Preparation time: 5 minutes. Ready to serve: 5 minutes.

Per serving: 145 calories, 0.5 g total fat (0 g saturated fat), 4 g protein, 32 g carbohydrate, 0 mg cholesterol, 33 mg sodium, 3 g fiber. **Star nutrients:** Vitamin C (99%). **Noteworthy nutrients:** Vitamin B6 (15%), Calcium (17%).

NUTRITION NOTE One cup of this smoothie provides 2 servings of fruit and 2 grams of soy protein.

VARIATION Peach or Mango Smoothie
Substitute frozen sliced peaches or diced mango for mixed berries.

Muesli

Muesli is a Swiss breakfast specialty. This is a creamy and refreshing yet substantial summer breakfast; it is practical because it keeps well for several days in the refrigerator.

2½ cups low-fat vanilla yogurt
1 cup old-fashioned rolled oats
1 (8-oz.) can crushed pineapple
1 tablespoon honey

½ cup raisins
1 cup sliced strawberries, blueberries
   or raspberries

❶ In medium bowl, stir together yogurt, oats, pineapple, honey and raisins. Cover; refrigerate at least 8 hours or overnight. Top each serving with strawberries.

8 (½-cup) servings.
Preparation time: 10 minutes. Ready to serve: 8 hours, 10 minutes.

Per serving: 170 calories, 2 g total fat (1 g saturated fat), 6 g protein, 34 g carbohydrate, 4 mg cholesterol, 52 mg sodium, 2 g fiber. **Noteworthy nutrients:** Vitamin C (23%), Calcium (15%), Phosphorus (17%).

MAKE AHEAD Cover and refrigerate for up to 4 days. Top with strawberries just before serving.

Banana-Berry Smoothie

Hot Oatmeal Cereal with
Dried Cranberries & Flaxseeds

In the deep chill of a Vermont winter, I look forward to a bowl of hot oatmeal after my morning walk. This recipe is a delicious and particularly healthful way to start the day. Flaxseeds contribute a deliciously nutty taste and provide unique nutritional benefits. Cooking the oatmeal in low-fat milk, rather than water, makes the porridge creamy and boosts calcium. If you have time, add a grated apple to the oatmeal at the beginning of cooking.

2 cups low-fat (1%) milk or vanilla soymilk
¾ cup old-fashioned rolled oats
⅓ cup dried cranberries, raisins or chopped pitted dates
¼ cup flaxseeds
¼ cup nonfat plain or vanilla yogurt
¼ cup maple syrup, warmed, or 2 tablespoons packed brown sugar

❶ In heavy medium saucepan, combine milk, oats and dried cranberries; bring to a simmer over medium-high heat, stirring constantly. Reduce heat to medium-low; Stirring often, cook 4 to 5 minutes or until creamy and thickened. Remove from heat; cover. Let stand 1 to 2 minutes.

❷ Meanwhile, in spice mill or blender, pulse flaxseeds until coarsely ground.

❸ Stir ground flaxseeds into hot cereal. Spoon into individual bowls; top each with dollop of yogurt and drizzle of maple syrup.

4 (⅔-cup) servings.
Preparation time: 5 minutes.
Ready to serve: 15 minutes.

Per serving: 280 calories, 6.5 g total fat (1.5 g saturated fat), 10 g protein, 47 g carbohydrate, 5 mg cholesterol, 81 mg sodium, 6 g fiber. **Star nutrients:** Phosphorus (29%). **Noteworthy nutrients:** Calcium (23%), Fiber (16%), Magnesium (24%), Riboflavin (17%).

MAKE AHEAD If you have leftover cereal, cover and refrigerate it for up to 2 days. To reheat, spoon a portion into microwave-safe cereal bowl and add 1 tablespoon water. Cover with vented plastic wrap or wax paper; microwave at High 2 to 3 minutes or until steaming.

Poached Eggs on Veggie Burgers

Prepared veggie burgers make an appealing platform for poached eggs and provide a healthful alternative to bacon or sausage for a hearty weekend breakfast.

4 eggs
2 teaspoons olive oil
1 (10-oz.) pkg. frozen veggie patties, such as Garden Burgers (4 patties)
¼ cup prepared salsa

❶ Fill medium or large skillet with 1 inch water; bring to a boil. Crack each egg into custard cup or small bowl. Carefully slip eggs into water, taking care not to break yolks. Reduce heat to low. Cover skillet; poach eggs 3 to 5 minutes or until yolks are just set.

❷ Meanwhile, in large nonstick skillet, heat olive oil over medium heat until hot. Add veggie patties; cook 2 to 3 minutes per side or until browned and heated through.

❸ Place patties on plates. Use slotted spoon to remove eggs from water. Blot eggs dry with paper towel; set on top of veggie burgers. Serve with salsa.

4 servings.
Preparation time: 5 minutes.
Ready to serve: 10 minutes.

Per serving: 225 calories, 10.5 g total fat (3 g saturated fat), 13 g protein, 19 g carbohydrate, 228 mg cholesterol, 388 mg sodium, 4 g fiber. **Noteworthy nutrients:** Fiber (16%), Phosphorus (22%), Riboflavin (24%).

Multi-Grain Pancakes or Waffles

These easy griddle cakes and waffles create a good opportunity for incorporating a variety of whole grains.

2 cups buttermilk
½ cup old-fashioned rolled oats
⅔ cup whole wheat flour
⅔ cup all-purpose flour
¼ cup toasted wheat germ
1½ teaspoons baking powder
½ teaspoon baking soda
¼ teaspoon salt

1 teaspoon ground cinnamon
2 eggs
¼ cup packed brown sugar
1 tablespoon canola oil
2 teaspoons vanilla extract
2 bananas, sliced, or 1½ cups sliced strawberries
1 cup maple syrup, warmed

❶ In small bowl, mix buttermilk and oats; let stand 15 minutes. In large bowl, whisk whole wheat flour, all-purpose flour, wheat germ, baking powder, baking soda, salt and cinnamon.

❷ In medium bowl, whisk eggs, brown sugar, canola oil and vanilla. Add buttermilk mixture. Add this mixture to flour mixture; mix with rubber spatula just until flour mixture is moistened.

To make pancakes

❸ Coat large nonstick skillet with nonstick cooking spray; heat over medium heat. Spoon about ¼ cup batter for each pancake into skillet; cook about 3 minutes or until bottoms are golden and small bubbles start to form on top. Flip; cook an additional 1 to 2 minutes or until pancakes are browned and cooked through. (Adjust heat as necessary for even browning.) Top with bananas and maple syrup.

To make waffles

❸ Coat waffle iron with nonstick cooking spray; heat iron. Spoon in enough batter to cover three-quarters of surface; close iron. Cook 4 to 5 minutes or until waffles are crisp and golden brown. Top with bananas and maple syrup.

8 servings (16 pancakes or waffles).
Preparation time: 20 minutes. Ready to serve: 35 minutes.

Per serving: 330 calories, 5 g total fat (1 g saturated fat), 8 g protein, 65 g carbohydrate, 55 mg cholesterol, 314 mg sodium, 3.5 g fiber. **Noteworthy nutrients:** Vitamin B6 (15%), Calcium (17%), Magnesium (15%), Phosphorus (20%), Riboflavin (18%), Thiamin (17%), Zinc (22%).

TIP To keep cooked batches warm until serving time, place pancakes or waffles in single layer on baking sheet in 200°F oven.

LEFTOVERS Wrap any leftover pancakes or waffles individually in plastic wrap; refrigerate up to 2 days or freeze up to 1 month. Unwrap frozen pancakes or waffles and reheat in toaster or toaster oven.

French-Style Omelet with Goat Cheese Filling

Recent studies indicate that egg consumption is not as closely linked to heart disease as was once believed. The American Heart Association has revised its guidelines to allow seven eggs per week. A basic French-style folded omelet is one of the fastest and most satisfying instant meals you can make. Goat cheese gives this omelet a sophisticated edge, but you can certainly substitute ¼ cup grated cheddar or Swiss cheese and omit green onion and parsley.

¼ cup crumbled goat cheese	¼ teaspoon hot pepper sauce, such as Tabasco
1 tablespoon chopped green onion	Dash salt
1 tablespoon chopped fresh parsley	Dash freshly ground pepper
2 eggs	1 teaspoon olive oil

❶ In small bowl, combine goat cheese, green onion and parsley. In medium bowl, blend eggs, hot pepper sauce, salt and pepper briskly with fork. In 7- to 10-inch nonstick skillet, heat olive oil over medium-high heat until hot. Tilt skillet to swirl oil over surface. Pour in egg mixture. Immediately stir eggs with fork for a few seconds. Then use rubber spatula to push cooked portions at edges toward center, tilting skillet to allow uncooked egg mixture to fill in areas around edges.

❷ Sprinkle goat cheese mixture down center of omelet. Continue to cook until bottom is lightly browned and no visible egg remains on top. Entire cooking process should take about 1 minute. Use rubber spatula to lift one-third of omelet closest to skillet handle and fold it over filling. Tip skillet and, using spatula as a guide, slide omelet onto plate so that it lands, folded in thirds, seam-side down.

1 serving.
Preparation time: 5 minutes.
Ready to serve: 10 minutes.

Per serving: 330 calories, 26 g total fat (11.5 g saturated fat), 21 g protein, 3 g carbohydrate, 455 mg cholesterol, 621 mg sodium, 0.4 g fiber. **Star nutrients:** Vitamin A (30%), Phosphorus (32%), Riboflavin (45%). **Noteworthy nutrients:** Vitamin B12 (18%), Calcium (17%).

VARIATION   **French-Style Potato (or Mushroom) Omelet**

Omit goat cheese. In Step 1, heat 1 teaspoon olive oil in small or medium nonstick skillet. Add ½ cup frozen hash browns or diced cooked potatoes (or sliced mushrooms). Cook 3 to 5 minutes or until browned. Stir in 1 tablespoon parsley, dash salt and dash freshly ground pepper. In Step 2, sprinkle potato (or mushroom) mixture down center of omelet.

Frittata with Potatoes & Canadian Bacon

This Italian omelet is quite substantial and makes a good option for a leisurely weekend breakfast or quick supper. Frozen hash browns are a handy staple; check the label to be sure that the potatoes you purchase have not been previously deep-fried. Nutrition Facts should indicate that the potatoes contain less than one gram of fat per serving.

3 teaspoons olive oil, divided
¾ cup frozen hash browns or diced cooked potatoes
4 slices (2 oz.) Canadian-style bacon, finely diced (½ cup)
½ cup chopped onion (1 small)
4 eggs
1½ teaspoons hot pepper sauce, such as Tabasco
⅛ teaspoon salt
⅛ teaspoon freshly ground pepper
½ cup (1½ oz.) grated mozzarella cheese
2 tablespoons chopped green onions (green parts only)

❶ In 10-inch nonstick skillet, heat 2 teaspoons of the olive oil over medium-high heat. Add potatoes and bacon; cook 5 to 10 minutes or until golden brown, shaking pan and occasionally tossing potatoes and bacon. Add onion; cook, stirring often, 1 to 2 minutes or until onion has softened. Transfer to plate; let cool. Rinse and dry skillet.

❷ In medium bowl, blend eggs, hot pepper sauce, salt and pepper briskly with fork. Stir in cooled potato mixture, cheese and green onions.

❸ Heat broiler.

❹ Brush skillet with remaining 1 teaspoon of the olive oil; heat over medium heat. Pour in egg mixture. Reduce heat to medium-low; cook 3 to 4 minutes or until bottom is light golden, lifting edges and tilting skillet as eggs become firm to allow uncooked egg to flow underneath. Place skillet under broiler; cook 1½ to 2½ minutes or until top is light golden and set. Slide frittata onto platter; cut into wedges.

4 servings.
Preparation time: 15 minutes.
Ready to serve: 30 minutes.

Per serving: 195 calories, 11.5 g total fat (3.5 g saturated fat), 13 g protein, 10 g carbohydrate, 226 mg cholesterol, 406 mg sodium, 1 g fiber. **Noteworthy nutrients:** Phosphorus (20%), Riboflavin (19%).

Roasted Red Pepper-Walnut Spread

This easy Middle Eastern spread is delicious. Serve with toasted Whole Wheat Pita Crisps (page 26) or sesame crackers.

⅔ cup (2½ oz.) chopped walnuts, toasted*
4 (½-inch-thick) slices baguette, lightly toasted
2 garlic cloves, crushed, peeled
1 tablespoon ground cumin
¼ teaspoon crushed red pepper
¼ teaspoon salt
1 (12-oz.) or 2 (7-oz.) jars roasted red bell peppers, drained, rinsed
4 teaspoons lemon juice
1 tablespoon extra-virgin olive oil

❶ In food processor, combine walnuts, baguette slices, garlic, cumin, crushed red pepper and salt; process until walnuts are ground. Add roasted bell peppers, lemon juice and olive oil; process until smooth.

6 (¼-cup) servings.
Preparation time: 10 minutes.
Ready to serve: 10 minutes.

Per serving: 175 calories, 11 g total fat (1 g saturated fat), 6 g protein, 15 g carbohydrate, 0 mg cholesterol, 202 mg sodium, 2.8 g fiber. **Star nutrients:** Vitamin A (66%), Vitamin C (183%).

MAKE AHEAD Cover and refrigerate for up to 4 days.

TIP *To toast walnuts, spread on baking sheet; bake at 375°F 7 to 10 minutes or until lightly browned. Cool.

Quick Bites

Appetizers are a lovely way to welcome your guests and relax before enjoying a meal. But who wants to spend too much time preparing them? Here are some quick, easy ideas for tasty tidbits to stimulate your appetite and create an inviting setting.

Marinated Olives. Heat 2 teaspoons olive oil in medium skillet over low heat until warm. Add 2 cloves peeled garlic, 4 (2x½-inch) strips orange peel and 1½ teaspoons fennel seeds; cook 30 to 60 seconds or until fragrant, stirring. Add 2 cups rinsed Kalamata olives; cook, stirring, 1 minute or until warmed through but not hot. Remove from heat; stir in 2 tablespoons orange juice. Cover; let stand at room temperature 1 hour. Olives will keep, covered, in refrigerator up to 2 weeks. Serve at room temperature. Makes 1 cup (8 servings).

Spiced Almonds. Toss 1 cup unpeeled whole almonds with 1 teaspoon olive oil, ¾ teaspoon ground cumin, ¼ teaspoon salt and ⅛ teaspoon cayenne pepper in pie plate or shallow baking dish. Bake at 350°F 25 to 30 minutes or until fragrant, stirring occasionally. Let cool. Almonds will keep in airtight container up to 1 week. Makes 1 cup (8 servings).

Tomato Bread. This is a popular snack in the tapas bars in and around Barcelona. To make it, halve 2 tomatoes crosswise. Toast 4 (½-inch-thick) slices whole wheat country bread; rub with cut sides of garlic clove. Rub tomato half over each piece of bread, squeezing and pressing pulp into bread. Drizzle each bread slice with ½ teaspoon extra-virgin olive oil; sprinkle with salt and freshly ground pepper. Makes 4 servings.

Edamame Beans. Cook 1 (10- or 12-oz.) pkg. frozen edamame beans in pods according to package directions. Drain and rinse under cold running water. Serve edamame beans in shells; let your guests shell them as they snack. Makes 4 servings.

Creative Crudités. In addition to the standard carrot sticks, celery sticks, cherry tomatoes, bell pepper strips and broccoli florets, expand your crudités selection to include some of the following fun vegetables:
- *Fresh fennel.* Cut into thin slices. Serve with extra-virgin olive oil and kosher (coarse) salt for dipping.
- *Jicama.* Peel and slice. Sprinkle with chili powder and lime juice.
- *Endive lettuce leaves.* Serve with extra-virgin olive oil and kosher (coarse) salt for dipping.

Asian Peanut Dip

Tofu stretches calorie-laden peanut butter and gives this spicy peanut dip a velvety consistency. Serve with crudités or as a spread for grown-up peanut butter sandwiches made with thick slices of whole wheat country bread, grated carrots, sliced cucumber and lettuce. This dip can also be used as a dressing for an Asian noodle salad.

2 garlic cloves, crushed, peeled
3 tablespoons packed light brown sugar
¾ teaspoon crushed red pepper
½ cup natural peanut butter
⅓ cup low-fat firm silken tofu
2 tablespoons reduced-sodium soy sauce
2 tablespoons lime juice

❶ Place garlic in mortar or on cutting board. Sprinkle with brown sugar and crushed red pepper; mash into a paste with pestle or side of chef's knife. Transfer to food processor. Add peanut butter, tofu, soy sauce and lime juice; process until smooth and creamy, stopping once or twice to scrape down sides of bowl.

8 (2-tablespoon) servings.
Preparation time: 10 minutes.
Ready to serve: 10 minutes.

Per serving: 120 calories, 7 g total fat (1.5 g saturated fat), 5 g protein, 10 g carbohydrate, 0 mg cholesterol, 216 mg sodium, 1 g fiber.

MAKE AHEAD Cover and refrigerate for up to 2 days.

Herbed Edamame Spread

This spread will get you hooked on soy foods. Whole Wheat Pita Crisps (page 26) or sesame crackers are appealing accompaniments.

1 (12-oz.) pkg. frozen shelled edamame beans*
4 garlic cloves, crushed, peeled
2 tablespoons extra-virgin olive oil
4 teaspoons lemon juice
1 teaspoon ground cumin
½ teaspoon salt
¼ teaspoon crushed red pepper
⅛ teaspoon freshly ground pepper
1 tablespoon chopped fresh mint
1 tablespoon chopped fresh cilantro
1 tablespoon chopped fresh dill

❶ In large saucepan of lightly salted boiling water, cook edamame beans and garlic about 10 minutes or until tender. Alternatively, cook edamame beans with garlic according to package directions. Remove from heat; let beans and garlic cool in the water.

❷ Reserve about ¼ cup of the cooking liquid; drain beans and garlic. Transfer to food processor. Add olive oil, lemon juice, cumin, salt, crushed red pepper and ground pepper; puree until smooth. Transfer to medium bowl. Stir in mint, cilantro and dill. If spread seems thick, thin with a bit of reserved cooking liquid.

8 (3-tablespoon) servings.
Preparation time: 10 minutes.
Ready to serve: 1 hour.

Per serving: 98 calories, 6.5 g total fat (1 g saturated fat), 6 g protein, 6 g carbohydrate, 0 mg cholesterol, 153 mg sodium, 2 g fiber. **Star nutrients:** Vitamin C (25%). **Noteworthy nutrients:** Folate (18%).

MAKE AHEAD   Cover and refrigerate for up to 4 days.

INGREDIENT NOTE   *For more information on edamame beans, see page 21. If edamame are unavailable, substitute 1 (10-oz.) pkg. frozen lima beans.

Black Bean Spread with Cumin & Lime

Whether served as an appetizer or sandwich spread, a bean "butter" made with canned beans is convenient and healthful. Here are some ideas for super simple homemade spreads. Serve with Baked Tortilla Crisps (page 26) or Whole Wheat Pita Crisps (page 26).

1 garlic clove, crushed, peeled
1 teaspoon ground cumin
⅛ teaspoon salt
1 (15½- or 19-oz.) can black beans,
  drained, rinsed

2 tablespoons fresh lime juice
1 tablespoon olive oil
¼ teaspoon hot pepper sauce, such as Tabasco
⅛ teaspoon freshly ground pepper
2 tablespoons chopped fresh cilantro

❶ In food processor, combine garlic, cumin and salt; process until garlic is minced. Add beans, lime juice, olive oil, hot pepper sauce and pepper; process until smooth, stopping once or twice to scrape down sides of bowl. Transfer puree to medium bowl. Stir in cilantro.

8 (3-tablespoon) servings.
Preparation time: 10 minutes.
Ready to serve: 10 minutes.

Per serving: 65 calories, 2 g total fat (0.2 g saturated fat), 3 g protein, 8 g carbohydrate, 0 mg cholesterol, 208 mg sodium, 3 g fiber.

MAKE AHEAD Cover and refrigerate for up to 4 days.

VARIATION White Bean Spread with Rosemary

In food processor, combine 1 clove crushed garlic and ⅛ teaspoon salt; process until garlic is minced. Add 1 (19-oz.) can rinsed, drained cannellini beans, 2 tablespoons lemon juice, 1 tablespoon extra-virgin olive oil, ⅛ teaspoon freshly ground pepper and dash cayenne pepper; pulse into chunky puree. Transfer puree to medium bowl. Stir in 1½ teaspoons chopped fresh rosemary. Makes 8 (3-tablespoon) servings.

VARIATION Black-Eyed Pea Spread with Caraway Seeds

In food processor, combine 1 clove crushed garlic, 1½ teaspoons caraway seeds and ⅛ teaspoon salt; process until garlic is minced. Add 1 (15½-oz.) can rinsed, drained black-eyed peas, 4 teaspoons cider vinegar, 1 tablespoon olive oil, ½ teaspoon hot pepper sauce and ⅛ teaspoon freshly ground pepper; process until smooth, stopping once or twice to scrape down sides of bowl. Transfer puree to medium bowl. Stir in 2 tablespoons chopped fresh parsley. Makes 6 (3-tablespoon) servings.

Soups

There is nothing like soup for warming hearts and souls. These recipes showcase healthful vegetables, beans and whole grains.

Pasta & Garbanzo Bean Soup

Here you'll find three easy variations for rich, full-bodied Italian soups.

4 (14½-oz.) cans reduced-sodium chicken broth
6 garlic cloves, peeled, crushed
2 (4-inch) sprigs fresh rosemary
¼ teaspoon crushed red pepper
1 (15½- or 19-oz.) can garbanzo beans,
  drained, rinsed, divided
2 teaspoons olive oil
1 medium onion, chopped (1 cup)

2 medium carrots, diced (1 cup)
1 rib celery, diced (⅓ cup)
1 (14½-oz.) can diced tomatoes, undrained
1 cup ditalini pasta
2 cups (6 oz.) individually quick frozen spinach*
¼ teaspoon freshly ground pepper
½ cup (1 oz.) freshly grated Parmesan cheese

❶ In large saucepan, bring broth to a boil. If you have a tea infuser, use it to enclose garlic, rosemary and crushed red pepper; place infuser in broth. Alternatively, add seasonings directly to broth. Partially cover pot; simmer over medium-low heat 15 minutes to intensify flavor. Remove tea infuser or pass broth through strainer.

❷ In small bowl, mash 1 cup of the garbanzo beans with fork. Set whole and mashed garbanzo beans aside. In 4- to 6-quart soup pot, heat olive oil over medium heat. Add onion, carrots and celery; cook 3 to 4 minutes or until softened, stirring often. Pour in infused broth. Add tomatoes, pasta and mashed and remaining whole garbanzo beans. Bring to a simmer, stirring occasionally. Reduce heat to medium-low; cover. Cook 15 to 18 minutes or until pasta is tender.

❸ Stir in spinach; cover. Cook 2 to 3 minutes or until spinach has thawed. Stir in ground pepper. Garnish each serving with 1 tablespoon Parmesan cheese.

8 (1⅓-cup) servings. Preparation time: 30 minutes. Ready to serve: 1 hour.

Per serving: 210 calories, 4.5 g total fat (1.5 g saturated fat), 12 g protein, 32 g carbohydrate, 5 mg cholesterol, 823 mg sodium, 6 g fiber. **Star nutrients:** Vitamin A (162%), Vitamin C (56%), Fiber (25%), Folate (33%). **Noteworthy nutrients:** Vitamin B6 (22%), Calcium (23%), Iron (16%), Magnesium (17%), Phosphorus (19%), Thiamin (15%).

INGREDIENT NOTE *Individually quick frozen spinach is packaged in a plastic bag rather than a box.

MAKE AHEAD Cover and refrigerate soup for up to 2 days or freeze for up to 3 months.

VARIATION Hearty Bean & Barley Soup

Substitute 1 (15½- or 19-oz.) can rinsed, drained dark red kidney beans for garbanzo beans and 1 cup quick-cooking barley for pasta. Quick-cooking barley cooks in about the same amount of time as ditalini.

VARIATION Tuscan Bean Soup with Greens

Substitute 1 (15½- or 19-oz.) can cannellini beans for garbanzo beans and 2 cups (6 oz.) individually quick frozen mustard greens or turnip greens for spinach. Add greens to soup when you add broth in Step 2.

Enhancing Canned Broth

Flavorful broths are key to making tasty soups, but few of us have time to make them from scratch. To give canned chicken broth a rich, full flavor, simmer it with garlic, herbs and seasonings 15 minutes or so. A tea infuser provides a convenient container for the flavorings, because it eliminates the need for straining the broth. If you do not have a tea infuser, you can tie seasonings in a cheesecloth bag. Alternatively, simmer seasonings loose in broth, then strain them out. Although you can now find many varieties of flavored chicken broth in supermarkets, I recommend that you start with basic broth and add your own seasonings; the resulting flavor will be much fresher tasting. In addition, be sure to use reduced-sodium broth; regular canned chicken broth becomes too salty when cooked down. Use any of the following infusions to give your fast soups homemade flavor or simply enjoy as a nourishing broth.

All-Purpose Infused Broth. Tuck 6 crushed garlic cloves, 4 (3- to 4-inch) sprigs fresh thyme (or ½ teaspoon dried) and ¼ teaspoon black peppercorns in tea infuser or cheesecloth bag. Place in large saucepan; add 4 (14½-oz.) cans reduced-sodium chicken broth and 1 bay leaf. Bring to a simmer. Partially cover; simmer over medium-low heat 15 minutes. Remove tea infuser and bay leaf. Makes 6½ cups.

Infused Broth with Italian Flavors. Tuck 6 crushed garlic cloves, 2 (4-inch) sprigs fresh rosemary (or ½ teaspoon dried) and ¼ teaspoon crushed red pepper in tea infuser or cheesecloth bag. Place in large saucepan; add 4 (14½-oz.) cans reduced-sodium chicken broth. Bring to a simmer. Partially cover; simmer over medium-low heat 15 minutes. Remove tea infuser. Makes 6½ cups.

Infused Broth with Asian Flavors. Tuck 4 (¼-inch-thick) slices peeled ginger, 3 crushed garlic cloves and ¼ teaspoon crushed red pepper in tea infuser or cheesecloth bag. Place in large saucepan; add 4 (14½-oz.) cans reduced-sodium chicken broth. Bring to a simmer. Partially cover; simmer over medium-low heat 15 minutes. Remove tea infuser. Makes 6½ cups.

Simple Soup Fixes

Nothing beats homemade soup. But adding just a few ingredients to canned low-fat soups can give store-bought soup homemade flavor in just minutes.

Lentil Soup with Couscous. Combine 1 (19-oz.) can lentil soup, 1 (14-oz.) can reduced-sodium chicken broth, 1 (14½-oz.) can diced tomatoes and 2 teaspoons ground cumin in large saucepan; bring to a simmer. Remove from heat; stir in ½ cup couscous. Cover; let stand 5 minutes. Return to a simmer. Add a squeeze of lemon juice; serve. Makes 5 (1-cup) servings.

Mexican Tomato Soup with Hominy. Combine 1 (19-oz.) can tomato soup (such as Progresso Hearty Tomato), 1 (15½-oz.) can drained, rinsed white hominy, 1½ teaspoons ground cumin and ½ teaspoon dried oregano in medium saucepan; bring to a simmer. Add dash hot pepper sauce and a squeeze of lime juice; serve. Makes 3 (1-cup) servings.

Middle-Eastern Lentil Soup

Cumin-scented lentil soup is popular throughout the Middle East, where it is often thickened with whole grain bulgur—a delicious and healthful combination. Lentils provide plant protein, fiber and folic acid. They are also inexpensive and do not require pre-soaking. Make up a batch of this hearty soup on the weekend and you can look forward to a supper of homemade soup on the weeknights that follow.

2 teaspoons olive oil
2 medium onions, chopped (2 cups)
4 garlic cloves, minced
1 tablespoon ground cumin
4 (14½-oz.) cans reduced-sodium chicken broth
  or 7 cups vegetable broth
¼ cup water
1½ cups brown lentils, rinsed, sorted

⅓ cup chopped sun-dried tomatoes
  (not oil-packed)
1 cinnamon stick
1 bay leaf
⅓ cup bulgur or long-grain white rice
2 tablespoons fresh lemon juice
¼ teaspoon freshly ground pepper
¼ cup chopped fresh mint or parsley

❶ In 4- to 6-quart soup pot, heat olive oil over medium heat. Add onions; cook, stirring often, 3 to 5 minutes or until softened. Add garlic and cumin; cook 30 seconds, stirring. Add broth, water, lentils, sun-dried tomatoes, cinnamon stick and bay leaf; bring to a simmer. Reduce heat to low. Cover; simmer 20 minutes.

❷ Add bulgur; simmer, covered, an additional 20 to 25 minutes or until lentils and bulgur are tender. Discard cinnamon stick and bay leaf.

❸ Transfer 4 cups of the soup, in batches if necessary, to food processor or blender; puree. (Use caution when blending hot liquids.) Return puree to soup; heat through. Stir in lemon juice and pepper. Garnish each serving with mint.

8 (1-cup) servings.
Preparation time: 15 minutes.
Ready to serve: 1 hour.

Per serving: 195 calories, 2 g total fat (0.5 g saturated fat), 14 g protein, 32 g carbohydrate, 0 mg cholesterol, 381 mg sodium, 14 g fiber. **Star nutrients:** Vitamin C (41%), Fiber (57%), Folate (43%). **Noteworthy nutrients:** Vitamin B6 (15%), Copper (22%), Iron (24%), Magnesium (15%), Phosphorus (23%), Thiamin (15%).

MAKE AHEAD Cover and refrigerate soup up to 2 days or freeze for up to 3 months.

Spinach & Parsnip Soup

Vegetables star in soups. This creamy French-style soup pairs spinach with earthy-tasting parsnips.

2 teaspoons olive oil
3 bunches green onions, trimmed, chopped (about 2 cups)
2 garlic cloves, peeled, crushed
2 (14½-oz) cans reduced-sodium chicken broth
1 lb. parsnips, peeled, sliced
1 (10-oz.) pkg. fresh spinach, stems trimmed (10 cups)*
½ cup reduced-fat sour cream
⅛ teaspoon freshly ground pepper to taste

❶ In 4- to 6-quart soup pot, heat olive oil over medium heat. Add green onions and garlic; cook about 2 minutes or until softened, stirring. Add broth and parsnips; increase heat to medium-high. Bring to a simmer. Reduce heat to medium-low. Cover; simmer 15 minutes.

❷ Add spinach; stir to immerse. Cook, covered, 10 minutes or until parsnips are tender and spinach has wilted.

❸ Puree soup, in batches if necessary, in food processor or blender. (Use caution when blending hot liquids.) Return soup to pot. Add sour cream and pepper; whisk until smooth. Heat, stirring occasionally, over medium heat until heated through, but do not boil.

6 (1-cup) servings.
Preparation time: 25 minutes.
Ready to serve: 50 minutes.

Per serving: 125 calories, 4.5 g total fat (2 g saturated fat), 5 g protein, 18 mg carbohydrate, 8 mg cholesterol, 294 mg sodium, 9 g fiber. **Star nutrients:** Vitamin A (54%), Vitamin C (67%) Fiber (37%). **Noteworthy nutrients:** Iron (24%), Folate (19%), Magnesium (17%).

MAKE AHEAD Cover and refrigerate soup for up to 2 days or freeze for up to 3 months.

TIMESAVING TIP *Substitute 1 (10-oz.) pkg. frozen spinach. In Step 1, simmer soup about 25 minutes or until parsnips are tender. Meanwhile, cook spinach separately according to package directions. In Step 3, puree spinach with parsnip mixture.

Asian Noodle Hot Pot

This unique soup is light and satisfying with a spicy broth.

3 (¼-inch-thick) slices peeled fresh ginger

2 garlic cloves, crushed, peeled

¼ teaspoon crushed red pepper

3 (14½-oz.) cans reduced-sodium chicken broth

2 teaspoons canola oil

3½ to 4 oz. fresh shiitake mushrooms, stems removed, sliced

3 cups sliced napa cabbage* (½ medium)

8 oz. firm regular tofu, drained, patted dry, cut into ¾-inch cubes

1 cup grated carrots (2 to 4 carrots)

2 teaspoons reduced-sodium soy sauce

2 teaspoons rice vinegar

1 teaspoon sesame oil

4 oz. linguine

¼ cup chopped green onions

❶ Tuck ginger, garlic and crushed red pepper in tea infuser or cheesecloth bag. Place in large saucepan; add broth. Bring to a simmer. Partially cover; simmer over medium-low heat 15 minutes. Remove tea infuser. (If you do not have tea infuser or cheesecloth, simmer ginger, garlic and crushed red pepper loose in saucepan, then strain.)

❷ In large nonstick skillet, heat canola oil over medium-high heat. Sauté mushrooms 3 to 5 minutes or until tender. Add cabbage; sauté 2 to 3 minutes or until cabbage is almost tender.

❸ Add sautéed mushrooms and cabbage to infused broth in saucepan. Simmer, partially covered, over medium-low heat about 5 minutes or until cabbage is tender. Add tofu and carrots to soup; heat through. Stir in soy sauce, vinegar and sesame oil.

❹ Meanwhile, cook linguine according to package directions. Drain; divide among 4 large soup bowls. Ladle soup over noodles. Garnish each serving with green onions.

4 (1½-cup) servings.
Preparation time: 30 minutes.
Ready to serve: 40 minutes.

Per serving: 230 calories, 6.5 g total fat (1 g saturated fat), 13 g protein, 31 g carbohydrate, 0 mg cholesterol, 627 mg sodium, 5 g fiber. **Star nutrients:** Vitamin A (169%), Vitamin C (69%), Folate (30%), Thiamin (30%), Niacin (27%). **Noteworthy nutrients:** Copper (21%), Fiber (20%), Iron (16%), Phosphorus (20%), Riboflavin (21%).

MAKE AHEAD Prepare recipe through Step 1. Cover and refrigerate broth for up to 2 days or freeze for up to 3 months.

INGREDIENT NOTE *Napa, also known as Chinese cabbage, is a pale green, long, oval-shaped cabbage. Its flavor is more delicate than regular green cabbage.

TIMESAVING TIP *Substitute 4 cups prepared coleslaw mix for the napa cabbage and carrots.

Curried Squash Bisque

Pureeing the squash lends incredible richness to this low-fat bisque, while adding the pear accents the squash's sweetness. Using frozen squash saves you the hard work of cutting and peeling a hard-skinned squash.

2 teaspoons olive oil
1 medium onion, chopped (1 cup)
1 Bartlett pear, peeled, cored, diced
2 teaspoons minced fresh ginger
1 garlic clove, crushed, peeled
2 teaspoons curry powder
1 (12-oz.) pkg. frozen cooked squash

2 (14½-oz.) cans reduced-sodium chicken broth
1 tablespoon orange juice
⅛ teaspoon freshly ground pepper
¼ cup plain nonfat yogurt
2 tablespoons low-fat (1%) milk
2 tablespoons snipped fresh chives or parsley

❶ In 4- to 6-quart soup pot, heat olive oil over medium heat until hot. Add onion; cook 2 to 3 minutes or until softened, stirring. Add pear, ginger, garlic and curry powder; cook 30 seconds, stirring. Add squash. Pour in broth; bring to a simmer over medium-high heat. Reduce heat to medium-low. Cover; cook 10 to 15 minutes or until squash is heated through and pear and onion are tender. Stir in orange juice and pepper. Let cool slightly.

❷ In batches, transfer soup to blender or food processor;* puree until smooth. (Use caution when blending hot liquids.) Return to soup pot; heat through over medium heat, stirring.

❸ In small bowl, whisk yogurt and milk until smooth. Ladle soup into bowls; drop large dollop (or several small dollops) of thinned yogurt onto each. Draw the tip of a knife or toothpick through yogurt to make decorative swirls. Sprinkle with chives.

6 (1-cup) servings. Preparation time: 20 minutes. Ready to serve: 40 minutes.

Per serving: 95 calories, 2 g total fat (0.5 g saturated fat), 4 g protein, 17 g carbohydrate, 0 mg cholesterol, 230 mg sodium, 3 g fiber. **Star nutrients:** Vitamin A (56%), Vitamin C (32%).

MAKE AHEAD   Prepare recipe through Step 2. Cover and refrigerate soup for up to 2 days or freeze for up to 3 months.

TIP *You have several equipment options for pureeing soup:
• An **immersion blender** allows you to puree soup right in the soup pot. Take care to immerse blades in the mixture to avoid splattering.
• To use a **food processor** to puree soup, pass the liquid through a strainer into a bowl. Then transfer solids to food processor to puree. Return pureed solids and reserved liquid to soup pot; heat through.
• A **blender** produces the most velvety texture in a pureed soup. Blend liquids and solids together. Use precautions when pureeing hot liquids. Be sure to fill blender container slightly less than half full. (Puree soup in batches, if necessary.) Place lid on blender securely and cover with kitchen towel. Hold lid on blender container firmly while blending.
• If you don't have any of these electrical appliances, you can use an old-fashioned hand-cranked **mouli food mill** to force solids through small holes of a disk to puree.

Chicken Noodle Soup

There is nothing more comforting than a bowl of homemade chicken noodle soup. And you don't have to spend hours making it. In the version that follows, boneless chicken breasts are poached in canned broth, enriching the broth in very little time. Accompanied by toasted whole wheat country bread, this heart-warming soup makes a satisfying meal.

2 teaspoons olive oil
1 medium onion, chopped (1 cup)
3 garlic cloves, minced
4 (14½-oz.) cans reduced-sodium chicken broth
2 boneless skinless chicken breast halves
   (8 oz. total), trimmed
1 cup sliced carrots (2 to 3 medium)

1 cup sliced parsnips (2 to 3 medium)
4 oz. (2 cups) medium-wide egg noodles
1 cup frozen green peas, rinsed under cold
   water to thaw
¼ cup chopped fresh dill
2 teaspoons fresh lemon juice
⅛ teaspoon freshly ground pepper

❶ In 4- to 6-quart soup pot, heat olive oil over medium heat until hot. Add onion; cook, stirring often, 2 to 3 minutes or until tender. Add garlic; cook 30 seconds, stirring. Add broth; bring to a simmer. Add chicken; reduce heat to low. Cover; simmer 15 to 25 minutes or until chicken is no longer pink in center.

❷ Using tongs, transfer chicken to cutting board. Add carrots and parsnips to broth; increase heat to medium. Partially cover; simmer 10 to 15 minutes or until vegetables are tender.

❸ Meanwhile, cook noodles according to package directions. Drain; refresh under cold running water. Slice cooked chicken.

❹ When carrots and parsnips are tender, add peas, dill, lemon juice, pepper, noodles and chicken to soup; heat through.

8 (1¼-cup) servings.
Preparation time: 30 minutes. Ready to serve: 50 minutes.

Per serving: 120 calories, 2 g total fat (0.5 g saturated fat), 11 g protein, 14 g carbohydrate, 21 mg cholesterol, 370 mg sodium, 4 g fiber. **Star nutrients:** Vitamin A (89%), Vitamin C (39%), Niacin (25%). **Noteworthy nutrients:** Fiber (15%).

MAKE AHEAD   Cover and refrigerate soup for up to 2 days or freeze for up to 3 months.

Down-Home Corn, Potato & Lima Bean Chowder

Mashing a portion of the vegetables is a good technique for adding body to a chunky soup. A garnish of crisp bacon gives this old-fashioned chowder a luxurious finish.

2 teaspoons olive oil or canola oil
1 medium onion, chopped (1 cup)
1 rib celery, diced ($\frac{1}{3}$ cup)
2 garlic cloves, minced
2 (14$\frac{1}{2}$-oz.) cans reduced-sodium chicken broth
2 medium all-purpose potatoes, peeled, diced (2 cups)
1 (10-oz.) pkg. frozen lima beans or frozen shelled edamame beans (2 cups)

$\frac{1}{2}$ teaspoon dried thyme
1 bay leaf
6 slices (3 oz.) reduced-fat bacon or turkey bacon, diced
1$\frac{1}{2}$ cups frozen corn
$\frac{1}{4}$ cup low-fat sour cream
$\frac{1}{8}$ teaspoon freshly ground pepper
Dash hot pepper sauce, such as Tabasco
2 tablespoons chopped fresh parsley

❶ In 4- to 6-quart soup pot, heat olive oil over medium heat until hot. Add onion and celery; cook, stirring often, 2 to 3 minutes or until tender. Add garlic; cook 30 seconds, stirring. Add broth, potatoes, lima beans, thyme and bay leaf; bring to a simmer. Reduce heat to medium-low; partially cover. Cook about 20 minutes or until potatoes are tender.

❷ Meanwhile, in small nonstick skillet, cook bacon over medium heat, stirring frequently, 4 to 5 minutes or until crisp. Transfer bacon to paper towel-lined plate; drain.

❸ When potatoes are tender, use slotted spoon to transfer about 1 cup solids to medium bowl. Discard bay leaf. Mash solids with potato masher or fork. Return mashed solids to soup. Add corn; increase heat to medium. Cook 2 to 3 minutes or until heated through. Add sour cream, pepper and hot pepper sauce; whisk 2 to 3 minutes or until smooth and heated through. Garnish each serving with parsley and bacon.

6 (1-cup) servings.
Preparation time: 20 minutes.
Ready to serve: 45 minutes.

Per serving: 220 calories, 6 g total fat (1.5 g saturated fat), 10 g protein, 34 g carbohydrate, 14 mg cholesterol, 520 mg sodium, 5 g fiber. **Star nutrients:** Vitamin C (46%). **Noteworthy nutrients:** Fiber (21%).

MAKE AHEAD Cover and refrigerate soup for up to 2 days or freeze for up to 3 months.

Hearty Split Pea Soup

Split pea soup may seem thoroughly old-fashioned, but it is well suited to today's focus on healthy eating. Split peas are a good source of plant protein and fiber. And since this legume does not require pre-soaking, you can have a hearty homemade soup ready in just over an hour.

2 teaspoons olive oil
4 slices (2 oz.) Canadian-style bacon, diced (½ cup)
1 medium onion, chopped (1 cup)
2 medium carrots, diced (1 cup)
3 (14½-oz.) cans reduced-sodium chicken broth
1 cup green split peas, rinsed, sorted

1 medium all-purpose potato,
  peeled, diced (1 cup)
Dash cayenne pepper
1 bay leaf
⅛ teaspoon freshly ground pepper
½ cup low-fat croutons

❶ In 4- to 6-quart soup pot, heat olive oil over medium heat until hot. Add bacon, onion and carrots; cook, stirring often, 4 to 5 minutes or until softened and lightly browned. Add broth, split peas, potato, cayenne pepper and bay leaf; bring to a simmer. Reduce heat to medium-low; partially cover. Cook, stirring occasionally, 55 to 60 minutes or until split peas have broken down and thickened soup. Discard bay leaf. Stir in pepper. Garnish each serving with croutons.

4 (1¼-cup) servings.
Preparation time: 15 minutes.
Ready to serve: 1 hour, 15 minutes.

Per serving: 300 calories, 4.5 g total fat (1 g saturated fat), 20 g protein, 46 g carbohydrate, 7 mg cholesterol, 734 mg sodium, 16 g fiber. **Star nutrients:** Vitamin A (173%), Vitamin C (58%), Fiber (63%), Copper (32%), Folate (39%), Niacin (25%), Phosphorus (30%), Thiamin (37%). **Noteworthy nutrients:** Vitamin B6 (17%), Iron (20%), Magnesium (19%).

MAKE AHEAD Cover and refrigerate soup for up to 2 days or freeze for up to 3 months.

BREADS, QUICK BREADS & PIZZAS

Home baking offers great satisfaction, particularly when the recipes are quick and easy and the results are good for you. The following selection offers wholesome loaves, veggie pizzas and breakfast muffins. All the recipes are low in fat and contain whole wheat flour.

Grilled Whole Wheat Flatbreads

This quick food processor yeast dough can be used for grilled flatbreads (this page) as well as pizza and pita breads (page 60) that are stunningly easy to make. The flavor of freshly baked crusty bread just can't be beat. Whole wheat flour gives this basic crust a delightful nutty taste. To make more than four breads, just make two batches.

1 cup whole wheat flour
1 cup all-purpose flour
1 (¼-oz.) pkg. fast-acting dry yeast* (2¼ teaspoons)
1 teaspoon salt

½ teaspoon sugar
¾ cup hot water (120°F to 130°F)
2 teaspoons olive oil

❶ In food processor, combine whole wheat flour, all-purpose flour, yeast, salt and sugar; pulse to mix. In measuring cup, combine hot water and olive oil. With food processor running, gradually pour hot liquid through feed tube. Process until dough forms a ball, then process 1 minute to knead. The dough should be quite soft. If it seems dry, add 1 to 2 tablespoons warm water; if too sticky, add 1 to 2 tablespoons flour. Transfer dough to lightly floured surface. Spray sheet of plastic wrap with nonstick cooking spray; place, sprayed-side down, over dough. Let dough rest 10 to 20 minutes before continuing with recipe.

❷ Heat grill. Divide dough into four pieces. On lightly floured surface, use rolling pin to roll each piece of dough into 7-inch round, about ¼ inch thick. (Keep remaining dough pieces covered while you work.) Place dough rounds on flour-dusted baking sheet.

❸ Lift one dough crust with your hands; place on grill. Repeat with second dough round. Cover grill; cook 1 to 1½ minutes or until dough is puffed and grill marks appear on underside. Using tongs, flip flatbreads over. Working quickly, brush each flatbread with about 1 teaspoon extra-virgin olive oil. Cover grill; cook 1½ to 2 minutes or until bottoms of flatbreads are light golden. Repeat with remaining two dough rounds. Cut into triangles; serve warm.

4 flatbreads. Preparation time: 15 minutes. Ready to serve: 45 minutes.

Per flatbread: 245 calories, 3 g total fat (0.5 g saturated fat), 8 g protein, 47 g carbohydrate, 0 mg cholesterol, 586 mg sodium, 5 g fiber. **Star nutrients:** Thiamin (29%). **Noteworthy nutrients:** Fiber (21%), Folate (18%), Iron (17%), Niacin (23%), Phosphorus (17%), Riboflavin (20%).

MAKE AHEAD Prepare dough; enclose in plastic food storage bag. Refrigerate for up to 2 days. Bring to room temperature before using.

INGREDIENT NOTE *Fast-acting dry yeast is a special variety of yeast that can be mixed directly with dry ingredients; it works with hotter liquids than regular yeast does and requires only a 10-minute rest, rather than the standard 1½-hour rise time. Fleischmann's RapidRise yeast is the most common brand. You can find it in the refrigerated dairy case of your supermarket.

Whole Wheat Pita Breads

Supermarket pita breads just can't compare to the freshly baked homemade version. The trick to making sure that the pitas puff magically is to have a very hot oven; be sure to preheat it properly and close the oven door quickly after putting pitas in.

❶ Follow Step 1 for Grilled Whole Wheat Flatbread (page 58).

❷ Place baking sheet on bottom rack of oven. Heat oven to 500°F.

❸ Divide dough into four pieces. On lightly floured surface, use rolling pin to roll each piece of dough into 7-inch round, about ¼ inch thick. (Keep remaining dough pieces covered while you work.) Place dough rounds on flour-dusted baking sheet.

❹ Using wide metal spatula, transfer two dough rounds to heated baking sheet. Bake pitas 5 to 6 minutes or until puffed and lightly browned around edges. Immediately wrap baked pitas in kitchen towel to keep them warm and soft. Repeat with remaining dough.

4 pitas. Preparation time: 15 minutes. Ready to serve: 45 minutes.

MAKE AHEAD Prepare dough; enclose in plastic food storage bag. Refrigerate for up to 2 days. Bring to room temperature before using.

Whole Wheat Pizza Dough

This is the amount of dough you will need to cover a 12-inch pizza pan. If you would like to make four individual pizzas or a larger pizza on a rectangular baking sheet, use the batch size in the Grilled Whole Wheat Flatbread recipe (page 58).

¾ cup whole wheat flour
¾ cup all-purpose flour
2 teaspoons fast-acting dry yeast*
¾ teaspoon salt
¼ teaspoon sugar
⅔ cup hot water (120°F to 130°F)
1½ teaspoons olive oil

❶ Follow Step 1 for Grilled Whole Wheat Flatbread (page 58).

❷ Use dough in recipes on page 61 or in your favorite pizza recipe.

MAKE AHEAD Prepare dough; enclose in plastic food storage bag. Refrigerate for up to 2 days. Bring to room temperature before using.

Pizza with Broccoli & Black Olives

Baking your own pizza allows you to highlight healthful vegetables and use just enough cheese to meld the pizza without overloading it.

1 recipe *Whole Wheat Pizza Dough*
  (page 60) or purchased pizza dough
Olive oil cooking spray
Cornmeal for sprinkling
2 cups (2 stalks) broccoli florets (¾-inch pieces)*
⅔ cup prepared marinara sauce

1 teaspoon dried oregano
⅛ teaspoon crushed red pepper
1 cup (3 oz.) grated part-skim mozzarella cheese
½ cup diced red onion
¼ cup Kalamata olives, pitted, coarsely chopped

❶ Prepare Whole Wheat Flatbread Dough, if using.

❷ Place inverted baking sheet on lowest shelf of oven; heat oven to 500°F or highest setting. Coat 12-inch pizza pan with olive oil cooking spray; sprinkle with cornmeal.

❸ Place broccoli in steamer over large saucepan of boiling water; cover and steam 2 to 3 minutes or just until tender. Refresh broccoli with cold running water to stop further cooking; drain well.

❹ In small bowl, mix marinara sauce, oregano and crushed red pepper.

❺ On lightly floured surface, roll pizza dough into 12½-inch circle. Transfer to pizza pan. Turn edges under to make a slight rim around perimeter. Spread marinara sauce mixture over crust, leaving ½-inch border. Sprinkle mozzarella cheese over sauce. Scatter broccoli, onion and olives over top. Spritz pizza lightly with olive oil cooking spray. Place pizza pan on heated baking sheet; bake 10 to 14 minutes or until bottom of crust is crisp and golden.

4 servings. Preparation time: 35 minutes. Ready to serve: 45 minutes.

Per serving: 295 calories, 7.5 g total fat (2.5 g saturated fat), 14 g protein, 45 g carbohydrate, 12 mg cholesterol, 792 mg sodium, 7 g fiber. **Star nutrients:** Vitamin C (76%), Fiber (28%), Folate (27%), Phosphorus (28%), Riboflavin (25%), Thiamin (27%). **Noteworthy nutrients:** Vitamin A (21%), Calcium (20%), Iron (20%), Magnesium (16%) Niacin (22%).

TIMESAVING TIP *Use frozen chopped broccoli instead of fresh. Cook according to package directions.

VARIATION **Roasted Red Pepper & Spinach Pizza**
Follow recipe through Step 2. In Step 3, cook 1½ cups individually quick frozen spinach (the kind you purchase in a plastic bag, rather than a box) according to package directions; drain well. In Step 4, mix ⅔ cup marinara sauce, 2 cloves minced garlic and ⅛ teaspoon crushed red pepper. In Step 5, roll out dough according to recipe. Spread marinara sauce mixture over crust. Sprinkle with 1 cup grated part-skim mozzarella cheese. Scatter cooked spinach, 1 cup diced, rinsed, bottled roasted bell peppers and ½ cup diced red onion over top. Spray olive oil cooking spray over pizza. Bake as directed.

Baking with Whole Wheat Flour

Whole wheat flour is simply flour milled from the entire wheat kernel. The process of producing refined white flours removes the nutrient- and fiber-rich germ and bran. Even though refined flour is enriched with some of the vitamins and minerals lost during processing, fiber, phytochemicals and antioxidants are not replaced. Clearly, whole wheat flour is nutritionally superior to white flour; use it as often as you can. Here are some whole wheat flour baking tips.

• Use whole wheat flour in yeast breads. In a basic pizza crust, for example, use half whole wheat flour and half all-purpose white flour. Wholesome baked goods like muffins, quick breads, crumbles, pancakes and oatmeal cookies are good candidates for incorporating whole wheat flour. You can generally replace 50% of the white flour with whole wheat flour. Because whole wheat flour has slightly different baking properties than white flour, a 100% substitution is not recommended. White flour performs better in delicate recipes like angel food cake.

• When making pancakes, crumbles, muffins, quick breads and wholesome cookies, such as oatmeal, replace half of the white flour with whole wheat flour.

• Since whole wheat flour contains more fat (these are beneficial fats) than white flour, it is more perishable. If you bake frequently and do not live in a hot, humid climate, you can store whole wheat flour in an airtight container at room temperature (less than 75°F) for up to six months. Otherwise, refrigerate or freeze it for up to one year; bring to room temperature before using.

• One more reason to bake with whole wheat flour: Taste. Whole wheat flour has a delicious nutty flavor, which enhances numerous recipes.

Whole Wheat-Flaxseed Bread

To save time, use a stand-up mixer equipped with a dough hook to mix and knead the dough.

1 cup lukewarm (about 100°F) low-fat (1%) milk
1 cup lukewarm (about 100°F) water
3 tablespoons packed light brown sugar
1 (¼-oz.) pkg. active dry yeast (2¼ teaspoons)
⅓ cup plus 2 tablespoons flaxseeds, divided
2½ cups whole wheat flour

2 teaspoons salt
1 tablespoon canola oil
2 to 2¼ cups all-purpose flour
1 egg white
1 tablespoon water

❶ In large bowl, whisk milk, lukewarm water and brown sugar until sugar has dissolved. Sprinkle in yeast; let stand 3 to 5 minutes or until creamy. Meanwhile, in clean dry coffee grinder or blender, grind ⅓ cup of the flaxseeds into coarse meal.

❷ Gradually add whole wheat flour to yeast mixture, beating with wooden spoon. Add ground flaxseeds, salt and canola oil; beat well. Gradually beat in enough of the all-purpose flour until dough is too difficult to stir. Turn dough out onto lightly floured surface; knead 10 minutes or until dough is smooth and elastic, adding just enough flour to prevent dough from sticking.

❸ Place dough in large bowl coated with nonstick cooking spray; turn to coat top. Cover; let rise at room temperature 1½ hours or until doubled in size. Punch dough down; let rest 5 minutes.

❹ Coat baking sheet with nonstick cooking spray. Divide dough in half; shape each piece into 8x3¾-inch oval. Place loaves, about 4 inches apart, on baking sheet. Cover with plastic wrap; let rise 1 hour or until doubled in size.

❺ Meanwhile, place small metal baking pan on bottom rack of oven; heat oven to 425°F. When loaves have risen, stir egg white and water briskly with fork until frothy; brush over loaves. Sprinkle loaves with the remaining 2 tablespoons of the flaxseeds. Use serrated knife to score 4 (¼-inch-deep) slashes diagonally on each loaf. Pour 1 cup water into baking pan in oven to create steam. Place baking sheet in oven; bake loaves 20 to 25 minutes or until loaves are golden and sound hollow when tapped. Transfer loaves to wire rack to cool.

2 loaves, about 20 (½-inch) slices. Preparation time: 45 minutes. Ready to serve: 2 hours, 45 minutes.

Per serving: 140 calories, 2.5 g total fat (0.5 g saturated fat), 5 g protein, 25 g carbohydrate, 0 mg cholesterol, 247 mg sodium, 3 g fiber.

> VARIATION **Whole Wheat-Flaxseed Rolls**
>
> In Step 4, divide dough into 16 pieces. Shape each piece into a ball; place 2 inches apart on prepared baking sheet. Cover with plastic wrap; let rise about 1 hour. In Step 5, brush rolls with egg white mixture; sprinkle with flaxseeds. Make ¼-inch-deep slash on each roll. Pour 1 cup water into baking pan in oven to create steam. Bake rolls 18 to 22 minutes. Makes 16 rolls.

Irish Soda Bread

This traditional loaf is actually a quick bread. Since it requires no yeast or lengthy kneading, it is one of the easiest breads you can make. Flaxseeds contribute a pleasant nutty flavor. Serve for breakfast, at tea time or with dinner.

⅓ cup flaxseeds
¾ cup whole wheat flour
¾ cup all-purpose flour
1 teaspoon baking soda
½ teaspoon salt
½ cup baking raisins*

2 teaspoons caraway seeds
¾ cup buttermilk
2 tablespoons packed brown sugar
1 tablespoon canola oil
1½ teaspoons grated orange peel

❶ Heat oven to 400°F. Spray 9-inch pie plate with nonstick cooking spray.

❷ In clean dry coffee grinder or blender, grind flaxseeds into coarse powder. Transfer to mixing bowl. Add whole wheat flour, all-purpose flour, baking soda and salt; whisk to blend. Stir in raisins and caraway seeds.

❸ In glass measuring cup, mix buttermilk, brown sugar, canola oil and orange peel. Make a well in center of dry ingredients. Gradually pour in buttermilk mixture, stirring with fork until dry ingredients are moistened.

❹ Turn dough out onto lightly floured surface; knead several times. Form into a ball; place in pie plate. Flatten dough slightly; dust lightly with flour. With serrated knife, make crisscross slash, ¼ inch deep, on top of loaf.

❺ Bake 25 to 30 minutes or until loaf is golden and sounds hollow when bottom is tapped. Transfer loaf to wire rack to cool slightly before slicing.

1 loaf (8 slices).
Preparation time: 15 minutes.
Ready to serve: 1 hour.

Per serving: 190 calories, 5 g total fat (0.5 g saturated fat), 5 g protein, 32 g carbohydrate, 1 mg cholesterol, 333 mg sodium, 5 g fiber.
Noteworthy nutrients: Fiber (18%).

TIP *Baking raisins are an excellent choice when making lower-fat baked goods. Since they contain more moisture than regular raisins, they draw less moisture from the batter. Look for baking raisins in the dried fruit section of your supermarket. If you do not have baking raisins on hand, substitute regular raisins. Plump regular raisins by soaking them in boiling water 10 minutes; drain well before using.

Whole Wheat Banana-Bran Muffins

When the bananas in your fruit bowl start to turn black, take advantage of that extra sweetness and use them in baking. Mashed banana adds moisture to low-fat muffins.

1 egg	1 teaspoon vanilla extract
1 egg white	1 cup whole wheat flour
¾ cup packed light brown sugar	¾ cup all-purpose flour
1 cup mashed bananas (2 medium, preferably over-ripe)*	1½ teaspoons baking powder
1 cup buttermilk**	½ teaspoon baking soda
1 cup unprocessed wheat bran***	½ teaspoon ground cinnamon
3 tablespoons canola oil	¼ teaspoon salt
	3 tablespoons (¾ oz.) chopped walnuts

❶ Heat oven to 400°F. Coat 12 muffin cups with nonstick cooking spray or line with paper liners. In medium bowl, whisk egg, egg white and brown sugar until smooth. Add bananas, buttermilk, wheat bran, canola oil and vanilla; whisk until blended.

❷ In large bowl, whisk whole wheat flour, all-purpose flour, baking powder, baking soda, cinnamon and salt. Add egg mixture; stir with rubber spatula just until dry ingredients are moistened. Scoop batter into muffin cups. Sprinkle with walnuts.

❸ Bake muffins 18 to 22 minutes or until tops spring back when touched lightly. Loosen edges; turn muffins out onto wire rack. Let cool slightly.

12 muffins. Preparation time: 15 minutes. Ready to serve: 45 minutes.

Per serving: 195 calories, 5.5 g total fat (0.5 g saturated fat), 5 g protein, 34 g carbohydrate, 18 mg cholesterol, 188 mg sodium, 4 g fiber. **Noteworthy nutrients:** Fiber (16%), Magnesium (15%).

MAKE AHEAD To freeze muffins, wrap individually in plastic wrap, enclose in plastic food storage bag and freeze for up to 1 month. To thaw, remove plastic wrap, wrap in paper towel and microwave at Defrost about 2 minutes.

INGREDIENT NOTES *If your bananas are over-ripe, but you are not ready to bake, freeze the bananas. Just peel, wrap individually in plastic wrap and freeze for up to 1 month.

**If you don't bake frequently, you may hesitate to buy a 1-quart carton of buttermilk just to make one recipe. Shelf-stable buttermilk powder is a convenient alternative; substitute according to package directions, but for added calcium and body, replace liquid with low-fat milk instead of water. Another option is to make "sour milk" or "soymilk buttermilk"; mix 1 tablespoon lemon juice into each cup of fresh milk or soymilk. Let stand a few minutes before using.

***Valued as a source of insoluble fiber, unprocessed wheat bran is the outer layer of the wheat kernel that is removed during milling. It is sometimes known as miller's bran. You can find it in the baking section of most supermarkets (Hodgson Mill is a common brand) and in the bulk section of natural food stores. Do not substitute bran cereal in this recipe.

Blueberry-Flaxseed Muffins

In late summer when blueberries are plentiful, I add them to almost everything. One of my favorite ways to enjoy blueberries is in muffins. Here is a healthful spin on a classic blueberry muffin. This recipe includes nutty flaxseeds, whole wheat flour and—of course—blueberries, which are rich in antioxidants.

⅓ cup flaxseeds
1 cup whole wheat flour
¾ cup plus 2 tablespoons all-purpose flour
1½ teaspoons baking powder
½ teaspoon baking soda
¼ teaspoon salt
1 teaspoon ground cinnamon
1 egg
1 egg white

⅔ cup packed light brown sugar
1 cup buttermilk*
3 tablespoons canola oil
2 teaspoons grated orange peel
1 tablespoon orange juice
1 teaspoon vanilla extract
1½ cups fresh blueberries, rinsed, patted dry
1 tablespoon sugar

❶ Heat oven to 400°F. Coat 12 muffin cups with nonstick cooking spray or line with paper liners.

❷ In clean dry coffee grinder or blender, grind flaxseeds into coarse meal. Transfer to large bowl. Add whole wheat flour, all-purpose flour, baking powder, baking soda, salt and cinnamon; whisk to blend.

❸ In medium bowl, whisk egg, egg white and brown sugar until smooth. Add buttermilk, canola oil, orange peel, orange juice and vanilla; whisk until blended. Add egg mixture to flour mixture; mix with rubber spatula just until dry ingredients are moistened. Fold in blueberries. Scoop batter into muffin cups. Sprinkle tops with sugar.

❹ Bake 18 to 22 minutes or until lightly browned and tops spring back when touched lightly. Loosen edges; turn muffins out onto wire rack to cool slightly.

12 muffins.
Preparation time: 20 minutes.
Ready to serve: 50 minutes.

Per serving: 200 calories, 6 g total fat (0.5 g saturated fat), 5 g protein, 33 g carbohydrate, 18 mg cholesterol, 191 mg sodium, 4 g fiber.

TIP *For information on creating a buttermilk substitute, see ingredient note** on page 65.

Carrot-Pineapple Muffins

These fragrant muffins are chock-full of good things. Fruits, vegetables and whole wheat flour all contribute nutrients and good taste.

1 cup whole wheat flour
1 cup all-purpose flour
1½ teaspoons baking powder
½ teaspoon baking soda
¼ teaspoon salt
2 teaspoons ground cinnamon
1 egg
1 egg white

¾ cup packed light brown sugar
3 tablespoons canola oil
1 teaspoon vanilla extract
1 (8-oz.) can crushed pineapple
1 cup finely grated carrots (2 to 4 carrots)
¾ cup baking raisins*
3 tablespoons (¾ oz.) chopped walnuts

❶ Heat oven to 400°F. Coat 12 muffin cups with nonstick cooking spray or line with paper liners.

❷ In large bowl, whisk whole wheat flour, all-purpose flour, baking powder, baking soda, salt and cinnamon.

❸ In medium bowl, whisk egg, egg white, brown sugar, oil and vanilla. Stir in pineapple. Add egg mixture to flour mixture; stir with rubber spatula just until dry ingredients are moistened. Stir in carrots and raisins. Scoop batter into muffin cups; sprinkle with walnuts.

❹ Bake 18 to 22 minutes or until tops spring back when touched lightly. Loosen edges; turn muffins out onto wire rack. Let cool slightly.

12 muffins.
Preparation time: 20 minutes.
Ready to serve: 50 minutes.

Per serving: 220 calories, 5.5 g total fat (0.5 g saturated fat), 4 g protein, 41 g carbohydrate, 18 mg cholesterol, 172 mg sodium, 3 g fiber. **Star nutrients:** Vitamin A (52%).

TIP *For information on baking raisins, see tip on page 64.

Salads

A healthy diet includes lots of salads. A crisp side salad enhances any meal, but a hearty salad can also be the main event. Here are ideas for both side salads and main-dish salads, plus a variety of low-fat dressings to complement your everyday salads.

Caesar Salad Revisited

Caesar salad may well be America's favorite salad choice. But not only are traditional recipes for Caesar dressing high in fat, they typically contain raw eggs, which pose a health risk. In this lightened version, tofu replaces the eggs and much of the oil, significantly reducing fat and eliminating food safety concerns. In addition, using tofu is a delicious and easy way to incorporate beneficial soy into your diet.

1 recipe *Caesar Salad Dressing* (page 72)
1 medium head romaine lettuce, torn into bite-size pieces (10 cups)
1½ cups fat-free croutons
1 cup (2 oz.) Parmesan cheese shavings*

❶ Prepare Caesar Salad Dressing.

❷ In large salad bowl, combine lettuce and croutons. Add dressing; toss to coat well. Divide salad among four plates. Top each serving with Parmesan cheese shavings.

4 servings.
Preparation time: 25 minutes.
Ready to serve: 25 minutes.

Per serving: 170 calories, 8.5 g total fat (3 g saturated fat), 11 g protein, 13 g carbohydrate, 11 mg cholesterol, 556 mg sodium, 3 g fiber.
Star nutrients: Vitamin A (75%), Vitamin C (56%), Calcium (25%), Folate (51%). **Noteworthy nutrients:** Phosphorus (18%).

TIP *Parmesan cheese shavings look attractive and give any salad a delicious Parmesan cheese finish. To make Parmesan cheese shavings, use vegetable peeler to shave curls from a chunk of Parmesan cheese. If you have pre-grated Parmesan cheese, substitute ½ cup grated Parmesan cheese.

VARIATION Chicken Caesar Salad

Grill or broil 1 lb. boneless skinless chicken breasts (see page 123). Slice thinly and arrange over dressed salad before adding Parmesan cheese shavings.

VARIATION Shrimp Caesar Salad

Sauté 1 lb. shelled, deveined uncooked medium shrimp in 2 teaspoons olive oil in large nonstick skillet over medium-high heat 2 to 3 minutes or until shrimp turn pink and are opaque in center. Immediately spoon over dressed salad before adding Parmesan cheese shavings.

Caesar Salad Dressing

You can also try this creamy, full-flavored dressing with pasta salad.

⅓ cup low-fat firm silken tofu
4 teaspoons wine vinegar
1 tablespoon extra-virgin olive oil
1 tablespoon water
1 medium garlic clove, minced
¾ teaspoon Worcestershire sauce
½ teaspoon Dijon mustard
½ teaspoon anchovy paste
¼ teaspoon salt
⅛ teaspoon freshly ground pepper

❶ In blender, combine tofu, vinegar, olive oil, water, garlic, Worcestershire sauce, mustard, anchovy paste, salt and pepper; blend until smooth and creamy, stopping several times to scrape down sides of blender. (If dressing seems thick, thin with a few drops of water.)

½ cup (4 servings).
Preparation time: 10 minutes.
Ready to serve: 10 minutes.

Per serving: 45 calories, 4 g total fat (0.5 g saturated fat), 2 g protein, 1 g carbohydrate, 1 mg cholesterol, 234 mg sodium, 0 g fiber.

MAKE AHEAD Dressing will keep, covered, in refrigerator for up to 2 days.

Best-Dressed Salads

Making good salad dressing is easy. For a basic vinaigrette, simply combine three parts good-tasting oil, one part vinegar or lemon juice, a small dollop of Dijon mustard and salt and pepper to taste in a screw-top jar; shake to blend. To reduce fat and calories, replace half of the oil with brewed black tea or fruit juice. For a creamy dressing, buttermilk and yogurt provide a dairy-rich flavor with a minimum of fat and calories. There is no need to drown your otherwise healthy salads with high-fat dressing.* The following selection of dressings will add variety to your daily salads.

French Dressing. Whisk or shake ¼ cup extra-virgin olive oil, 2 tablespoons wine vinegar, 2 tablespoons water, 1 tablespoon ketchup, 1 teaspoon Dijon mustard, ½ teaspoon dried tarragon, ¼ teaspoon sugar, ⅛ teaspoon salt and ⅛ teaspoon freshly ground pepper in small bowl or jar with tight-fitting lid until blended. Makes ½ cup (4 servings).

Creamy Buttermilk Dressing. Place 2 tablespoons low-fat mayonnaise in small bowl. Gradually whisk in ⅓ cup buttermilk and 1½ teaspoons lemon juice until smooth. Stir in 2 tablespoons chopped green onions, ¼ teaspoon minced garlic, ⅛ teaspoon salt and ⅛ teaspoon freshly ground pepper. Makes ½ cup (4 servings).

Herbed Yogurt Dressing. Whisk ⅓ cup nonfat plain yogurt, 2 tablespoons canola oil, 1 tablespoon lemon juice and ½ teaspoon honey in small bowl until smooth. Stir in 2 tablespoons chopped fresh dill (or parsley or basil), ¼ teaspoon minced garlic, ¼ teaspoon salt and ⅛ teaspoon freshly ground pepper. Makes ½ cup (4 servings).

Asian Dressing. Whisk or shake 2 tablespoons reduced-sodium soy sauce, 2 tablespoons rice vinegar, 2 tablespoons cool brewed green or black tea, 1 tablespoon sugar, 1 tablespoon toasted sesame oil and 2 teaspoons minced fresh ginger in small bowl or jar with tight-fitting lid until blended. Makes ½ cup (4 servings).

Greek Lemon Dressing. Whisk or shake ¼ cup lemon juice, 3 tablespoons extra-virgin olive oil, ½ teaspoon dried oregano, ½ teaspoon honey, ¼ teaspoon salt and ⅛ teaspoon freshly ground pepper in small bowl or jar with tight-fitting lid until blended. Makes ½ cup (4 servings).

MAKE AHEAD Cover and refrigerate dressings for up to 2 days.

TIP *For 1 serving, coat 2 cups salad greens with 2 tablespoons dressing. By tossing salad thoroughly, you use less dressing.

Asparagus Salad with Orange-Sesame Dressing

Celebrate the first stalks of local asparagus in spring by showcasing them in a special salad. Both asparagus and oranges are good sources of folic acid; this salad is a good source of that important nutrient.

1 recipe *Orange-Sesame Dressing* (page 76)
1 lb. asparagus, tough ends snapped off, cut into 1½-inch lengths
1 navel orange
4 cups mesclun salad mix*
½ cup slivered sweet onion, such as Vidalia
2 tablespoons (½ oz.) slivered almonds, toasted**

❶ Prepare Orange-Sesame Dressing.

❷ Place asparagus in steamer basket over boiling water; cover. Steam 2 to 5 minutes or until crisp-tender. Rinse with cold water to stop further cooking.

❸ Using sharp paring knife, peel orange, removing white pith. Quarter and slice orange.

❹ In large bowl, toss mesclun with 1 tablespoon of the dressing. Top with asparagus, onion and orange slices. Drizzle remaining dressing over salads. Sprinkle with almonds.

4 (1½-cup) servings.
Preparation time: 20 minutes. Ready to serve: 25 minutes.

Per serving: 130 calories, 6.5 g total fat (0.5 g saturated fat), 5 g protein, 14 g carbohydrate, 0 g cholesterol, 123 mg sodium, 4 g fiber. **Star nutrients:** Vitamin C (102%), Folate (49%). **Noteworthy nutrients:** Vitamin A (16%), Vitamin E (21%), Copper (16%), Fiber (15%), Thiamin (19%).

INGREDIENT NOTE *Most supermarkets and greengrocers now carry a mixture of baby lettuces called mesclun. Sometimes it is labeled gourmet salad mix. The mixture is prized because it offers a symphony of flavors, ranging from sweet baby leaf lettuce and spinach to bitter greens, such as radicchio, arugula and mizuna. Another reason for mesclun's popularity is that it is quite free of grit. Nevertheless, wash and dry it as you would any salad green.

TIP **To toast almonds, place in a dry skillet. Cook, stirring constantly, over medium-low heat 2 minutes or until light golden and fragrant. Transfer to a small bowl to cool.

Orange-Sesame Dressing

For a light summer entree, toss cooked chicken and salad greens with this vibrant dressing.

⅓ cup orange juice
1 tablespoon rice vinegar or cider vinegar
2 teaspoons reduced-sodium soy sauce
2 teaspoons canola oil
1 teaspoon toasted sesame oil

1 teaspoon honey
1 (¼-inch-thick) slice fresh ginger, peeled,
　coarsely chopped
1 garlic clove, crushed, peeled

❶ In blender, combine orange juice, rice vinegar, soy sauce, canola oil, sesame oil, honey, ginger and garlic; blend until smooth.

⅓ cup (4 servings).
Preparation time: 10 minutes. Ready to serve: 10 minutes.

Per serving: 50 calories, 3.5 g total fat (0.5 g saturated fat), 0 g protein, 4 g carbohydrate, 0 mg cholesterol, 100 mg sodium, 0 g fiber.

MAKE AHEAD　Cover and refrigerate dressing for up to 2 days.

Apricot-Ginger Dressing

This fruity dressing is great with all kinds of greens and grain salads. It also makes a nice marinade for chicken or pork.

¼ cup apricot nectar
2 tablespoons extra-virgin olive oil
4 teaspoons white wine vinegar
½ teaspoon honey
2 (¼-inch-thick) slices fresh ginger, peeled,
　coarsely chopped

1 medium garlic clove, crushed, peeled
¼ teaspoon salt
⅛ teaspoon freshly ground pepper

❶ In blender, combine apricot nectar, olive oil, vinegar, honey, ginger, garlic, salt and pepper; process until blended.

½ cup (6 servings).
Preparation time: 10 minutes. Ready to serve: 10 minutes.

Per serving: 75 calories, 7 g total fat (1 g saturated fat), 0 g protein, 3 g carbohydrate, 0 g cholesterol, 146 mg sodium, 0 g fiber.

MAKE AHEAD　Cover and refrigerate dressing for up to 2 days.

Fruity Tabbouleh

Tabbouleh, the traditional Middle Eastern salad made with whole grain bulgur wheat, tomatoes and herbs, has become popular at salad bars and deli counters across America. Here is a distinctive version of the salad that features a fruity apricot dressing, dried fruit and toasted pine nuts.

¾ cup bulgur
¼ cup chopped dried apricots
⅛ teaspoon salt
1 recipe *Apricot-Ginger Dressing* (page 76)

½ cup chopped green onions
⅓ cup chopped fresh mint
6 leaves Boston lettuce (optional)
¼ cup (1½ oz.) pine nuts, toasted*

❶ In medium bowl, combine bulgur, dried apricots and salt. Cover generously with boiling water. Cover; let stand 30 minutes or until bulgur is tender.

❷ Meanwhile, prepare Apricot-Ginger Dressing.

❸ When bulgur is tender, drain in sieve; press out excess water. Transfer to large bowl. Add green onions and mint. Drizzle with dressing; toss gently to mix. Mound on bed of lettuce leaves, if desired. Sprinkle with pine nuts.

6 (¾-cup) servings.
Preparation time: 15 minutes. Ready to serve: 35 minutes.

Per serving (without lettuce): 160 calories, 8 g total fat (1 g saturated fat), 4 g protein, 21 g carbohydrate, 0 mg cholesterol, 151 mg sodium, 4 g fiber. **Noteworthy nutrients:** Vitamin A (15%), Fiber (17%).

MAKE AHEAD Cover and refrigerate salad for up to 8 hours.

TIP *To toast pine nuts, place in a dry skillet. Cook, stirring constantly, over medium-low heat 2 minutes or until golden brown. Transfer to a small bowl to cool.

Beet & Arugula Salad with Walnuts

When selecting greens for salad, remember that the dark green varieties, such as arugula, are richer in nutrients than pale lettuces like iceberg. In this colorful salad, arugula's distinctive peppery flavor is balanced by the sweetness of beets and a delicate vinaigrette flavored with apple juice concentrate.

1 recipe *Apple-Mustard Vinaigrette* (page 79)
1 (14½-oz.) can sliced beets, drained, or 12 oz. fresh beets, cooked,* peeled, sliced
6 cups arugula or watercress, stems trimmed, torn into bite-size pieces (1 bunch or one 4-oz. pkg.)
¼ cup (1 oz.) chopped walnuts, toasted**

❶ Prepare Apple-Mustard Vinaigrette.

❷ In medium bowl, toss beets with 2 tablespoons of the vinaigrette. (If desired, marinate beets, covered, in refrigerator for up to 2 days.)

❸ In large bowl, toss arugula with remaining vinaigrette. Top each serving with beets and a sprinkling of walnuts.

4 servings.
Preparation time: 20 minutes.
Ready to serve: 20 minutes.

Per serving: 165 calories, 12 g total fat (1.5 g saturated fat), 4 g protein, 13 g carbohydrate, 0 mg cholesterol, 377 mg sodium, 3 g fiber. **Noteworthy nutrients:** Vitamin A (16%), Vitamin C (16%), Folate (17%).

TIP   *To cook beets, scrub them but do not peel. Cook beets in lightly salted boiling water 40 to 50 minutes or until tender. Drain; let cool slightly. Slip off skins. To microwave beets, place in microwave-safe dish with ¼ cup water. Cover; microwave at High 15 to 20 minutes.

TIP   **To toast walnuts, spread on baking sheet; bake at 375°F 7 to 10 minutes or until lightly browned. Cool.

VARIATION   Beet & Arugula Salad with Goat Cheese
Substitute ¼ cup crumbled goat cheese for walnuts.

Apple-Mustard Vinaigrette

This dressing works well with delicate greens, such as Boston lettuce, or more assertive ones such as watercress. You can also use it to make a Waldorf salad with chopped crisp apples, diced celery and walnuts.

2 tablespoons olive oil or canola oil
2 tablespoons apple cider vinegar
4 teaspoons frozen apple juice concentrate
1 tablespoon grainy mustard, such as country-style Dijon
2 tablespoons finely chopped shallot (1 medium)
¼ teaspoon salt
⅛ teaspoon freshly ground pepper

❶ In small jar with tight-fitting lid or small bowl, combine olive oil, vinegar, apple juice concentrate, mustard, shallot, salt and pepper; shake or whisk to blend.

⅓ cup (4 servings).
Preparation time: 10 minutes. Ready to serve: 10 minutes.

Per serving: 80 calories, 7 g total fat (1 g saturated fat), 0 g protein, 4 g carbohydrate, 0 mg cholesterol, 169 mg sodium, 0 g fiber.

MAKE AHEAD Dressing can be prepared up to 2 days ahead. Cover and refrigerate.

Balsamic Vinaigrette

This is a good all-purpose dressing. The sweet taste of balsamic vinegar marries best with strongly flavored greens such as mesclun or arugula.

2 tablespoons extra-virgin olive oil
2 tablespoons balsamic vinegar
1 tablespoon water
½ teaspoon Dijon mustard
⅛ teaspoon salt
Dash freshly ground pepper

❶ In small jar with tight-fitting lid or small bowl, combine olive oil, vinegar, water, mustard, salt and pepper; shake or whisk to blend.

⅓ cup (4 servings).
Preparation time: 5 minutes. Ready to serve: 5 minutes.

Per serving: 66 calories, 7 g total fat (1 g saturated fat) 0 g protein, 1 g carbohydrate, 0 mg cholesterol, 76 mg sodium, 0 g fiber.

Warm Salad with Grilled Vegetables & Garlic Croutons

Meaty portobello mushrooms, sweet bell peppers, onions and tomatoes are incredibly delicious when grilled. Tossed with greens, these vegetables make an elegant main-course salad.

1 recipe *Balsamic Vinaigrette* (page 79)
8 cups mesclun salad mix
4 portobello mushrooms (about 1 lb. total), stem ends trimmed, caps wiped clean, sliced ½ inch thick
2 sweet onions, such as Vidalia (about 1½ lbs. total), cut into ½-inch-thick rounds
1 large red bell pepper, cut into ½-inch strips
16 cherry tomatoes
1 tablespoon olive oil
¼ teaspoon salt
⅛ teaspoon freshly ground pepper
8 (¾-inch-thick) slices whole wheat country bread
1 garlic clove, cut in half
1 cup (2 oz.) Parmesan cheese shavings* or ½ cup crumbled feta cheese

❶ Set fine-mesh grill topper on grill rack. Heat grill.

❷ Prepare Balsamic Vinaigrette.

❸ Place mesclun in large bowl. Spread mushrooms, onions, bell pepper and cherry tomatoes on two baking sheets. Brush both sides of vegetables with olive oil; sprinkle with salt and pepper.

❹ Lightly oil grill topper. In batches, place vegetables on grill topper set on gas grill over medium-high heat or on charcoal grill 4 to 6 inches from medium-hot coals. Cover grill; cook vegetables 2 to 4 minutes per side or until browned and tender. Transfer vegetables to baking sheet as they are done. Grill bread alongside vegetables until lightly toasted.

❺ Add grilled vegetables to mesclun. Drizzle Balsamic Vinaigrette over salad; toss to coat well. Divide salad among 4 plates. Rub grilled bread with cut sides of garlic; place bread alongside each salad. Sprinkle salads with Parmesan cheese shavings.

4 servings.
Preparation time: 30 minutes. Ready to serve: 35 minutes.

Per serving: 480 calories, 20.5 g total fat (5.5 g saturated fat), 17 g protein, 63 g carbohydrate, 18 mg cholesterol, 1,057 mg sodium, 14 g fiber. **Star nutrients:** Vitamin A (65%), Vitamin B6 (27%), Vitamin C (134%), Calcium (25%), Fiber (43%), Folate (35%), Magnesium (30%), Phosphorus (32%). **Noteworthy nutrients:** Copper (22%), Iron (23%), Niacin (21%), Riboflavin (24%), Thiamin (24%), Zinc (18%).

TIP *To make Parmesan cheese shavings, see tip on page 70.

Spinach Salad with Orange Segments & Olives

This salad pairs two nutrient-dense foods—spinach and an orange—in a fresh and appealing way.

1 recipe *Orange-Flaxseed Dressing* (recipe follows)
1 navel orange
8 cups fresh spinach, stems trimmed, torn into bite-size pieces*
½ cup slivered red onion (½ medium)
¼ cup Kalamata olives, pitted, coarsely chopped

❶ Prepare Orange-Flaxseed Dressing.

❷ Using sharp paring knife, peel orange, removing white pith. Quarter and slice orange. In large bowl, combine spinach, onion, olives and orange slices. Drizzle with dressing; toss to coat well.

4 servings. Preparation time: 25 minutes. Ready to serve: 35 minutes.

Per serving: 125 calories, 9 g total fat (1 g saturated fat), 3 g protein, 10 g carbohydrate, 0 mg cholesterol, 300 mg sodium, 8 g fiber.
Star nutrients: Vitamin A (70%), Vitamin C (76%), Fiber (31%), Iron (27%). **Noteworthy nutrients:** Magnesium (18%).

TIMESAVING TIP *Purchase a bag of ready-to-serve, washed spinach.

Orange-Flaxseed Dressing

Ground flaxseeds thicken and flavor this all-purpose, fruit juice-based salad dressing.

1 tablespoon flaxseeds
⅓ cup orange juice
1 tablespoon lemon juice
2 tablespoons extra-virgin olive oil
1 garlic clove, minced

½ teaspoon Dijon mustard
¼ teaspoon sugar
¼ teaspoon salt
⅛ teaspoon freshly ground pepper

❶ In clean dry coffee grinder or blender, grind flaxseeds into coarse meal. Transfer to small jar with tight-fitting lid or small bowl. Add orange juice, lemon juice, olive oil, garlic, mustard, sugar, salt and pepper; whisk or shake to blend.

½ cup (4 servings).
Preparation time: 10 minutes. Ready to serve: 10 minutes.

Per serving: 90 calories, 8 g total fat (1 g saturated fat), 1 g protein, 4 g carbohydrate, 0 mg cholesterol, 150 mg sodium, 1 g fiber.

Carrot Salad with Cumin & Lemon

Because carrots keep well in the vegetable crisper, this is a handy salad for those days when you haven't had time to shop for fresh ingredients. You can also use it to boost the vegetable content in sandwiches; the dill variation is a nice way to perk up a tuna salad sandwich.

1 recipe *Cumin-Scented Lemon Dressing* (recipe follows)
3 cups grated carrots (4 to 6 medium or 1 lb.)
¼ cup chopped green onions
3 tablespoons chopped fresh cilantro or parsley

❶ Prepare Cumin-Scented Lemon Dressing.

❷ In medium bowl, combine carrots, green onions and cilantro. Drizzle with dressing; toss to coat well.

4 (¾-cup) servings.
Preparation time: 15 minutes. Ready to serve: 15 minutes.

Per serving: 105 calories, 7.5 g total fat (1 g saturated fat), 1 g protein, 10 g carbohydrate, 0 mg cholesterol, 179 mg sodium, 3 g fiber.
Star nutrients: Vitamin A (468%), Vitamin C (27%).

MAKE AHEAD Cover and refrigerate salad for up to 8 hours. Toss well before serving.

Cumin-Scented Lemon Dressing

In addition to the carrot salad here, try this dressing with a salad of garbanzo beans, diced red onion and ripe olives.

2 tablespoons lemon juice
2 tablespoons extra-virgin olive oil
1½ teaspoons ground cumin
1 garlic clove, minced
¼ teaspoon salt
⅛ teaspoon freshly ground pepper

❶ In jar with tight-fitting lid or small bowl, combine lemon juice, olive oil, cumin, garlic, salt and pepper; shake or whisk to blend.

¼ cup (4 servings).
Preparation time: 10 minutes. Ready to serve: 10 minutes.

Per serving: 70 calories, 7 g total fat (1 g saturated fat), 0 g protein, 1 g carbohydrate, 0 mg cholesterol, 148 mg sodium, 0 g fiber.

MAKE AHEAD Cover and refrigerate dressing for up to 2 days.

VARIATION Carrot Salad with Lemon & Dill
Omit cumin in dressing. Substitute 3 tablespoons chopped fresh dill for cilantro in salad.

Black Bean & Barley Salad

This salad boasts the goodness of whole grain barley, fiber-rich beans and colorful bell peppers, which are good sources of vitamin C and beta carotene. Accompany with warm corn or flour tortillas.

1¼ cups reduced-sodium chicken broth or
   vegetable broth
¾ cup quick-cooking barley
1 recipe *Orange-Cumin Dressing* (recipe follows)
1 (15½- or 19-oz.) can black beans,
   drained, rinsed

1 large red or yellow bell pepper, diced
1 bunch green onions, trimmed, chopped
   (about ⅔ cup)
½ cup coarsely chopped fresh cilantro
Lime wedges

❶ In medium saucepan, combine broth and barley; bring to a simmer. Cover; reduce heat to low. Simmer about 10 minutes or until barley is tender and most of the liquid has been absorbed. Transfer barley to large bowl. Fluff with fork; let cool.

❷ Meanwhile, prepare Orange-Cumin Dressing.

❸ Add beans, bell pepper, green onions and cilantro to barley. Drizzle with dressing; toss to coat well. Garnish with lime wedges.

6 (¾-cup) servings.
Preparation time: 25 minutes. Ready to serve: 30 minutes.

Per serving: 230 calories, 10.5 g total fat (1.5 g saturated fat), 7 g protein, 29 g carbohydrate, 0 mg cholesterol, 410 mg sodium, 7 g fiber. **Star nutrients:** Vitamin C (117%), Fiber (29%). **Noteworthy nutrients:** Iron (15%).

MAKE AHEAD Cover and refrigerate salad for up to 1 day.

Orange-Cumin Dressing

Well suited to bean and grain salads, this dressing would also be good with a slaw of grated jicama and carrots.

¼ cup cider vinegar
¼ cup orange juice
¼ cup extra-virgin olive oil
1½ teaspoons ground cumin

1 teaspoon dried oregano
1 garlic clove, minced
¼ teaspoon salt
⅛ teaspoon freshly ground pepper

❶ In jar with tight-fitting lid or small bowl, combine vinegar, orange juice, olive oil, cumin, oregano, garlic, salt and pepper; shake or whisk to blend.

¾ cup (6 servings). Preparation time: 10 minutes. Ready to serve: 10 minutes.

Per serving: 90 calories, 9.5 g total fat (1.5 g saturated fat), 0 g protein, 2 g carbohydrate, 0 mg cholesterol, 99 mg sodium, 0 g fiber.

MAKE AHEAD Cover and refrigerate dressing for up to 2 days.

Provençal Salad Platter

This salad makes a satisfying meal during the dog days of summer. Consider the recipe a template and opportunity to use up various ingredients you have on hand. Canned tuna, bottled roasted red bell peppers and feta cheese are all good additions. Accompany this salad with toasted whole wheat country bread.

8 oz. small red potatoes
1 recipe *Anchovy Vinaigrette* (page 87)
4 eggs
8 oz. green beans, stem ends trimmed
1 medium head romaine or leaf lettuce, leaves separated
1 (15½-oz.) can garbanzo beans, drained, rinsed
2 medium tomatoes, cut into wedges
¼ cup finely diced red onion
2 tablespoons chopped fresh parsley

❶ In medium saucepan, cover potatoes with lightly salted water; bring to a boil. Reduce heat to medium-low; cover. Cook 10 to 15 minutes or until tender. Drain; let cool slightly.

❷ Meanwhile, prepare Anchovy Vinaigrette.

❸ When potatoes are cool enough to handle, peel and quarter. Place in medium bowl; toss with 1 tablespoon of the vinaigrette.

❹ In small saucepan, cover eggs with water; bring to a simmer. Reduce heat to low; cover. Simmer gently 10 minutes. Drain; rinse with cold water. Peel and quarter eggs.

❺ Place green beans in steamer basket over boiling water; cover. Steam 4 to 5 minutes or until crisp-tender. Rinse beans under cold water to stop further cooking.

❻ Line large platter with lettuce. Arrange garbanzo beans, tomatoes, eggs, green beans and potatoes over lettuce. Drizzle remaining vinaigrette over salad. Garnish with onion and parsley.

4 servings.
Preparation time: 45 minutes.
Ready to serve: 50 minutes.

Per serving: 390 calories, 17.5 g total fat (3.5 g saturated fat), 16 g protein, 45 g carbohydrate, 213 mg cholesterol, 607 mg sodium, 10 g fiber. **Star nutrients:** Vitamin A (56%), Vitamin B6 (44%), Vitamin C (90%), Fiber (38%), Folate (55%), Phosphorus (28%), Riboflavin (27%). **Noteworthy nutrients:** Copper (23%), Iron (24%), Magnesium (19%), Thiamin (17%), Zinc (15%).

Anchovy Vinaigrette

You can also use this boldly flavored vinaigrette to dress cooked cauliflower or broccoli.

1 garlic clove, crushed, peeled
¼ teaspoon salt
3 tablespoons wine vinegar
½ teaspoon anchovy paste
½ teaspoon Dijon mustard
⅛ teaspoon freshly ground pepper
3 tablespoons extra-virgin olive oil

❶ Using mortar and pestle or side of chef's knife, mash garlic and salt into a paste. Transfer to small bowl, if necessary. Add vinegar, anchovy paste, mustard and pepper; whisk to blend. Gradually whisk in olive oil.

⅓ cup (4 servings).
Preparation time: 10 minutes.
Ready to serve: 10 minutes.

Per serving: 95 calories, 10.5 g total fat (1.5 g saturated fat), 0 g protein, 0 g carbohydrate, 1 mg cholesterol, 197 mg sodium, 0 g fiber.

MAKE AHEAD Cover and refrigerate vinaigrette for up to 2 days.

All-American Coleslaw

Salads made with sturdy, inexpensive cabbage have long been American favorites. There is also good reason to choose cabbage for your health. Cabbage is a member of the cruciferous vegetable family, which is associated with reducing the risk of certain cancers.

1 recipe *Yogurt-Mustard Dressing* (recipe follows)
4 cups shredded green cabbage (½ medium)
1 cup grated carrots (2 to 4 carrots)

❶ Prepare Yogurt-Mustard Dressing.

❷ In large bowl, combine cabbage and carrots. Add dressing; toss to coat well.

6 (¾-cup) servings.
Preparation time: 20 minutes. Ready to serve: 20 minutes.

Per serving: 63 calories, 3.5 g total fat (0.5 g saturated fat), 2 g protein, 7 g carbohydrate, 0 mg cholesterol, 141 mg sodium, 2 g fiber.
Star nutrients: Vitamin A (104%), Vitamin C (28%).

MAKE AHEAD Cover and refrigerate coleslaw for up to 8 hours.

Yogurt-Mustard Dressing

Yogurt, rather than mayonnaise, lends creaminess to this assertive dressing, which is well suited to shredded cabbage.

⅓ cup nonfat plain yogurt
4 teaspoons Dijon mustard
4 teaspoons cider vinegar
4 teaspoons olive oil

1½ teaspoons sugar
½ teaspoon caraway seeds
¼ teaspoon salt
¼ teaspoon freshly ground pepper

❶ In small bowl, whisk yogurt, mustard, vinegar, olive oil, sugar, caraway seeds, salt and pepper until smooth.

½ cup (6 servings).
Preparation time: 10 minutes. Ready to serve: 10 minutes.

Per serving: 45 calories, 3.5 g total fat (0.5 g saturated fat), 1 g protein, 3 g carbohydrate, 0 mg cholesterol, 126 mg sodium, 0 g fiber.

MAKE AHEAD Cover and refrigerate dressing for up to 2 days.

VARIATION **Coleslaw with Asian Flavors**

Substitute Orange-Sesame Dressing (page 76) for Yogurt-Mustard Dressing. Sprinkle 1 tablespoon toasted sesame seeds over coleslaw just before serving. To toast sesame seeds, heat small skillet over medium heat. Add sesame seeds; shake skillet continuously until seeds are lightly browned, 3 to 4 minutes.

Sides

As awareness of the importance of eating more whole grains and vegetables has increased, side dishes have gained new prominence. Here is a selection of quick-cooking whole grain pilafs and convenient vegetable sides to give your meals a healthy balance.

Bulgur Pilaf with Raisins & Pine Nuts

Since it cooks in less than 20 minutes, bulgur could be considered a whole grain convenience food. A pilaf embellished with dried fruit, spices and nuts is a stand-out side dish for poultry or lamb.

¼ cup raisins
2 teaspoons olive oil
1 medium onion, chopped (1 cup)
1 cup bulgur, rinsed
¼ teaspoon ground cinnamon
¼ teaspoon ground allspice

1½ cups reduced-sodium chicken broth or
   vegetable broth
1 bay leaf
¼ cup (1½ oz.) pine nuts, toasted*
3 tablespoons chopped fresh parsley
¼ teaspoon freshly ground pepper

❶ In small bowl, cover raisins with boiling water; set aside to plump.

❷ In large heavy saucepan, heat olive oil over medium heat. Add onion; cook, stirring often, 3 to 5 minutes or until softened. Add bulgur, cinnamon and allspice; cook 1 minute, stirring. Add broth and bay leaf; bring to a simmer. Reduce heat to low. Cover; simmer 15 to 20 minutes or until bulgur is tender and liquid has been absorbed.

❸ When bulgur is ready, discard bay leaf. Drain raisins; add to pilaf along with pine nuts, parsley and pepper. Fluff with fork.

4 (1-cup) servings.
Preparation time: 10 minutes.
Ready to serve: 25 minutes.

Per serving: 260 calories, 9.5 g total fat (1.5 g saturated fat), 7 g protein, 40 g carbohydrate, 0 mg cholesterol, 160 mg sodium, 9 g fiber. **Star nutrients:** Fiber (37%). **Noteworthy nutrients:** Vitamin C (22%), Copper (16%), Magnesium (23%), Niacin (15%), Phosphorus (15%), Thiamin (17%).

TIP   *To toast pine nuts, place in a dry skillet. Cook, stirring constantly, over medium-low heat 2 minutes or until golden brown. Transfer to a small bowl to cool.

VARIATION   **Bulgur Pilaf with Dried Cranberries & Hazelnuts**

Substitute ¼ cup dried cranberries for raisins and ¼ cup toasted chopped hazelnuts (see page 218 for toasting instructions) for pine nuts.

VARIATION   **Bulgur Pilaf with Dried Apricots & Almonds**

Substitute ¼ cup chopped dried apricots for raisins, ¼ cup toasted chopped slivered almonds (see page 118 for toasting instructions) for pine nuts and 3 tablespoons chopped fresh mint for parsley.

Rice & Noodle Pilaf with Toasted Flaxseeds

Rice and noodles might sound somewhat redundant, but the combination makes a delicious and easy pilaf. Flecks of toasted flaxseeds give this dish an interesting presentation and texture, while lemon and fresh herbs provide a refreshing finish. This recipe is a nice accompaniment to fish or chicken.

¼ cup flaxseeds
2 teaspoons olive oil
½ cup thin egg noodles
½ cup long-grain white rice
1 (14½-oz.) can reduced-sodium chicken broth or vegetable broth
¼ cup water
3 tablespoons chopped fresh dill
2 teaspoons freshly grated lemon peel
1 tablespoon fresh lemon juice
⅛ teaspoon freshly ground pepper

❶ In small dry skillet, toast flaxseeds over medium-low heat, stirring constantly, 1 to 1½ minutes or until fragrant and starting to pop. Transfer to small bowl to cool.

❷ In medium saucepan, heat olive oil over medium-low heat. Add noodles; cook about 2 minutes or until lightly toasted, stirring. Add rice; stir to coat. Add broth and water; bring to a simmer. Reduce heat to low. Cover; simmer about 20 minutes or until noodles and rice are tender.

❸ Meanwhile, place cooled flaxseeds in blender; pulse several times just until flaxseeds are broken down, but not ground.

❹ When pilaf is ready, stir in flaxseeds, dill, lemon peel, lemon juice and pepper.

4 (¾-cup) servings.
Preparation time: 10 minutes.
Ready to serve: 25 minutes.

Per serving: 190 calories, 7.0 g total fat (1.0 g saturated fat), 6 g protein, 27 g carbohydrate, 5 mg cholesterol, 170 mg sodium, 4 g fiber. **Star nutrients:** Folate (25%). **Noteworthy nutrients:** Vitamin C (18%), Fiber (17%).

Quinoa Pilaf

Quinoa, considered a supergrain because of its high protein content, is just as easy and fast to cook as long-grain white rice. This delicate pilaf makes a delicious accompaniment to fish.

2 teaspoons olive oil
1 medium onion, chopped (1 cup)
1 cup quinoa,* rinsed
1 (14½-oz.) can reduced-sodium chicken broth or vegetable broth
¼ cup water
⅓ cup chopped fresh parsley
2 teaspoons freshly grated lemon peel
⅛ teaspoon freshly ground pepper

❶ In large saucepan, heat olive oil over medium heat. Add onion; cook 2 to 3 minutes or until softened, stirring often. Add quinoa; stir 30 seconds. Add broth and water; bring to a simmer. Reduce heat to low; cover. Simmer about 20 minutes or until quinoa is tender and most of the liquid has been absorbed. Add parsley, lemon peel and pepper; fluff with fork.

4 (1-cup) servings.
Preparation time: 10 minutes.
Ready to serve: 25 minutes.

Per serving: 205 calories, 5.0 g total fat (0.5 g saturated fat), 7 g protein, 34 g carbohydrate, 0 mg cholesterol, 176 mg sodium, 4 g fiber.
Star nutrients: Vitamin C (30%), Iron (25%). **Noteworthy nutrients:** Copper (21%), Fiber (16%), Magnesium (24%), Phosphorus (20%).

TIP *You can find quinoa in health food stores and in the natural food section of some supermarkets.

Mushroom-Barley Pilaf

Quick-cooking barley makes a barley pilaf a possibility for a weeknight dinner. This recipe takes its inspiration from classic mushroom-barley soup.

4 teaspoons olive oil, divided
1 medium onion, chopped (1 cup)
1 cup quick-cooking barley*
1 (14½-oz.) can reduced-sodium chicken broth
8 oz. mushrooms, stem ends trimmed, sliced (3 cups)
1 medium red bell pepper, diced
1 garlic clove, minced
¼ cup chopped fresh dill
1 tablespoon balsamic vinegar or lemon juice
¼ teaspoon freshly ground pepper

❶ In large saucepan, heat 2 teaspoons of the olive oil over medium heat. Sauté onion 2 to 3 minutes or until softened. Add barley; cook 1 minute, stirring constantly. Add broth; bring to a simmer. Reduce heat to low; cover. Simmer 15 to 18 minutes or until barley is tender and liquid has been absorbed.

❷ Meanwhile, in large nonstick skillet, heat the remaining 2 teaspoons of the olive oil over medium-high heat. Sauté mushrooms, bell pepper and garlic 3 to 5 minutes or until tender.

❸ When barley is ready, add sautéed vegetables along with dill, vinegar and pepper; stir gently to mix.

4 (1-cup) servings.
Preparation time: 15 minutes.
Ready to serve: 35 minutes.

Per serving: 215 calories, 6.5 g total fat (1 g saturated fat), 8 g protein, 36 g carbohydrate, 0 mg cholesterol, 170 mg sodium, 6 g fiber. **Star nutrients:** Vitamin A (35%), Vitamin C (112%). **Noteworthy nutrients:** Vitamin B6 (15%), Copper (21%), Fiber (24%), Niacin (24%), Phosphorus (17%), Riboflavin (18%).

TIP *You can substitute pearl barley for quick-cooking barley. In Step 1, use 2½ cups reduced-sodium chicken broth and increase cooking time to 45 to 50 minutes.

Cajun Corn Sauté

Frozen pepper stir-fry vegetables and prepared salsa allow you to make this dish with a minimum of chopping.

2 teaspoons olive oil
1 cup frozen pepper stir-fry vegetables
2 garlic cloves, minced
3 cups frozen corn

¾ cup mild or hot salsa
⅛ teaspoon hot pepper sauce, such as
    Tabasco, or to taste
⅛ teaspoon freshly ground pepper

❶ In large nonstick skillet, heat olive oil over medium heat until hot. Add stir-fry vegetables and garlic; cook 2 to 3 minutes or until softened, stirring. Add corn; cook 5 minutes, stirring often. Add salsa, hot pepper sauce and pepper; cook 2 minutes or until heated through.

4 (½-cup) servings.
Preparation time: 5 minutes. Ready to serve: 15 minutes.

Per serving: 155 calories, 3.5 g total fat (0.5 g saturated fat), 6 g protein, 31 g carbohydrate, 0 mg cholesterol, 110 mg sodium, 3 g fiber. **Star nutrients:** Vitamin C (39%).

Citrus-Scented Squash Puree

Most people love winter squash, and it is rich in the antioxidant beta carotene. However, peeling, cutting and pureeing hard-skinned squash can be intimidating and time-consuming. Frozen squash provides an excellent solution. Orange juice, lemon peel and a touch of honey bring out the inherent rich taste of squash.

1 (12-oz.) pkg. frozen cooked squash
⅓ cup orange juice
½ teaspoon dried thyme
2 teaspoons honey

1 teaspoon butter
1 teaspoon freshly grated lemon peel
¼ teaspoon salt
⅛ teaspoon freshly ground pepper

❶ In medium saucepan, combine squash, orange juice and thyme; bring to a simmer over medium-high heat. Reduce heat to medium-low. Cover; cook 8 to 10 minutes or until squash has thawed, occasionally turning block of squash. Uncover; simmer, stirring constantly, 1 to 2 minutes or until puree has thickened to desired consistency. Stir in honey, butter, lemon peel, salt and pepper.

2 (¾-cup) servings.
Preparation time: 5 minutes. Ready to serve: 15 minutes.

Per serving: 125 calories, 2 g total fat (1.5 g saturated fat), 2 g protein, 26 g carbohydrate, 5 mg cholesterol, 322 mg sodium, 4 g fiber. **Star nutrients:** Vitamin A (325%), Vitamin C (52%). **Noteworthy nutrients:** Fiber (17%).

Beans & Rice

This combination of whole grain brown rice and fiber-rich beans makes a super side dish nutritionally. And because this recipe uses fast-cooking instant brown rice and canned beans, it is ultra quick. This is a fine accompaniment to pork and chicken.

1 cup instant brown rice
2 teaspoons olive oil
1 medium onion,* chopped (1 cup)
1 medium red bell pepper,* diced
2 garlic cloves, minced
1 (15½- or 19-oz.) can black beans or dark red kidney beans, drained, rinsed
¼ cup reduced-sodium chicken broth or vegetable broth
1 tablespoon cider vinegar
¼ teaspoon hot pepper sauce, such as Tabasco
⅛ teaspoon freshly ground pepper
⅓ cup chopped fresh cilantro

❶ Cook rice according to package directions.

❷ Meanwhile, in large nonstick skillet, heat olive oil over medium-high heat. Add onion; cook 2 minutes, stirring often. Add bell pepper and garlic; cook, stirring often, 2 to 3 minutes or until softened. Add beans, broth, vinegar, hot pepper sauce and pepper; cook 1 to 2 minutes or until heated through. Add cooked rice and cilantro; mix well.

4 (1-cup) servings.
Preparation time: 15 minutes.
Ready to serve: 20 minutes.

Per serving: 65 calories, 3 g total fat (0 g saturated fat), 2 g protein, 11 g carbohydrate, 0 mg cholesterol, 105 mg sodium, 2 g fiber. **Star nutrients:** Vitamin C (30%).

TIMESAVING TIP *Substitute 3 cups frozen stir-fry vegetables for fresh onion and bell pepper; sauté frozen vegetables in 2 teaspoons olive oil 4 to 5 minutes; add garlic and cook 30 seconds.

LEFTOVERS You've got lunch. Reheat beans and rice in microwave (add a little water to moisten) and wrap up in warm flour tortilla with grated Monterey Jack or cheddar cheese and a dollop of reduced-fat sour cream.

How to Cook Nutritious Greens

Although specific nutrient values vary depending on the variety, leafy dark greens boast an impressive nutritional profile. Rich in vitamins A and C, they are also good sources of calcium, iron, folate and magnesium. Greens also contain lutein and zeaxanthin, which are believed to help protect against cataracts and macular degeneration. To help incorporate these nutrient-packed vegetables into your diet, here are some tips for preparing them.

- Leafy greens fall into two categories. The most familiar group consists of tender greens including spinach, beet greens and Swiss chard. The family of sturdy winter greens, which have a characteristic bitter flavor, includes kale, collards, mustard greens and turnip greens.

- To prepare tender greens like spinach, wash thoroughly and trim stems. Then simply wilt them, with just the water clinging to leaves after washing, in a wide pan over medium-high heat, stirring, for 3 to 5 minutes. Drain greens; press out excess moisture.

- To prepare sturdy greens such as kale, you should blanch them to tenderize and mellow their assertive flavor. To blanch greens, after washing and trimming the stems, drop leaves into large pot of lightly salted boiling water, stirring to immerse. Cook, uncovered, until tender. Allow 3 to 4 minutes for broccoli rabe, 6 to 8 minutes for mustard greens and turnip greens, 8 to 12 minutes for collards and kale. Drain and refresh greens under cold running water. Squeeze out excess moisture; chop coarsely. You can then sauté greens in a little olive oil with garlic and dash of crushed red pepper.

- Frozen greens are convenient because you can skip the tedious step of washing and trimming. Frozen spinach is available in any supermarket. Consider it a staple ingredient in your freezer. Some supermarkets and natural food stores carry frozen mustard greens, turnip greens and collards. Cook frozen greens according to package directions. Note that the recommended cooking time for frozen sturdy greens is longer than for fresh.

Braised Kale with Italian Flavors

A touch of prosciutto gives braised kale an incredible depth of flavor. This is a tasty side dish with chicken or pork tenderloin.

1 lb. kale, stems trimmed (12 cups)
2 teaspoons olive oil
1 medium onion, chopped (1 cup)
1 oz. thinly sliced prosciutto, finely chopped (¼ cup)
4 garlic cloves, minced
⅛ teaspoon crushed red pepper
¾ cup reduced-sodium chicken broth
2 tablespoons balsamic vinegar
⅛ teaspoon salt
⅛ teaspoon freshly ground pepper

❶ Drop kale into large pot of lightly salted boiling water; stir to immerse. Cook, uncovered, 8 to 12 minutes or until tender. Drain in colander; refresh under cold running water. Squeeze out excess moisture. Transfer to cutting board; chop coarsely.

❷ In large nonstick skillet, heat olive oil over medium heat. Add onion and prosciutto; cook, stirring frequently, 2 to 3 minutes or until softened. Add garlic and crushed red pepper; cook 30 seconds. Add kale; cook, stirring often, 1½ minutes or until heated through. Add broth; bring to a simmer. Reduce heat to low; simmer, uncovered, 5 minutes. Stir in vinegar, salt and pepper.

4 (¾-cup) servings.
Preparation time: 20 minutes.
Ready to serve: 30 minutes.

Per serving: 165 calories, 4.5 g total fat (0.5 g saturated fat), 10 g protein, 26 g carbohydrate, 5 mg cholesterol, 423 mg sodium, 5 g fiber.
Star nutrients: Vitamin A (358%), Vitamin B6 (33%), Vitamin C (413%), Calcium (29%), Copper (32%). **Noteworthy nutrients:** Fiber (20%), Folate (17%), Iron (21%), Magnesium (19%), Phosphorus (16%), Riboflavin (17%), Thiamin (19%).

Braised Mustard Greens
with Black-Eyed Peas & Bacon

This distinctive side dish balances the assertive taste of winter greens with black-eyed peas and bacon.

12 oz. fresh mustard greens or turnip greens,* stems trimmed (16 cups)
3 oz. reduced-fat bacon or turkey bacon (about 6 slices), diced
1 medium onion, chopped (1 cup)
2 garlic cloves, minced
2 teaspoons caraway seeds
1 (15½-oz.) can black-eyed peas, drained, rinsed
⅓ cup reduced-sodium chicken broth or vegetable broth
2 tablespoons apple cider vinegar
½ teaspoon hot pepper sauce, such as Tabasco
¼ teaspoon salt
⅛ teaspoon freshly ground pepper

❶ Drop greens into large pot of lightly salted boiling water; stir to immerse. Cook, uncovered, 6 to 8 minutes or until tender. Drain in colander; refresh under cold running water. Squeeze out excess moisture. Transfer to cutting board; chop coarsely.

❷ Meanwhile, in large nonstick skillet, cook bacon over medium heat, stirring often, 4 to 6 minutes or until crisp. Transfer bacon to paper towel-lined plate to drain. Discard bacon fat.

❸ Add onion to skillet; cook over medium heat, stirring often, 2 to 3 minutes or until softened. Add garlic and caraway seeds; cook 30 seconds, stirring. Add greens; cook 1½ minutes or until heated through, stirring. Add black-eyed peas and broth; bring to a simmer. Reduce heat to low; simmer, uncovered, 5 minutes. Stir in vinegar, hot pepper sauce, salt and pepper. Sprinkle with bacon.

4 (¾-cup) servings.
Preparation time: 20 minutes. Ready to serve: 30 minutes.

Per serving: 210 calories, 5 g total fat (1 g saturated fat), 15 g protein, 31 g carbohydrate, 15 mg cholesterol, 856 mg sodium, 12 g fiber. **Star nutrients:** Vitamin A (238%), Vitamin B6 (26%), Vitamin C (274%), Calcium (27%), Fiber (499%), Folate (121%), Iron (26%), Magnesium (27%), Copper (25%). **Noteworthy nutrients:** Vitamin E (23%), Phosphorus (20%), Riboflavin (23%), Thiamin (22%).

TIMESAVING TIP *Substitute 1 (16-oz.) pkg. frozen mustard greens or turnip greens; cook according to package directions.

NUTRITION NOTE Rich in vitamins and minerals, winter greens such as mustard and turnip greens also contain the phytochemicals lutein and zeaxanthin, which help protect against cataracts and macular degeneration. These greens have an assertive flavor that some people describe as bitter. Blanching these sturdy greens in boiling water ensures a tender result and mellows their flavor.

Sesame Spinach

Standard Asian seasonings of ginger, soy sauce and sesame seeds perk up a simple side of sautéed spinach.

1 (10-oz.) pkg. fresh spinach,* stems trimmed (12 cups), washed
1 tablespoon reduced-sodium soy sauce
2 teaspoons rice vinegar
1 teaspoon toasted sesame oil
¼ teaspoon packed brown sugar
2 teaspoons canola oil
1 garlic clove, minced
1½ teaspoons minced fresh ginger
Dash crushed red pepper
1 tablespoon sesame seeds, toasted**

❶ With just the water clinging to leaves after washing, cook spinach in large, wide pot over medium-high heat 3 to 5 minutes or just until wilted. Drain; rinse with cold water. Press out excess moisture.

❷ In small bowl, mix soy sauce, vinegar, sesame oil and brown sugar.

❸ In large nonstick skillet, heat canola oil over medium-high heat until hot. Add garlic, ginger and crushed red pepper; stir-fry about 10 seconds or until fragrant but not browned. Add spinach; cook 2 to 3 minutes or until heated through, stirring often. Stir in soy sauce mixture, tossing to coat well. Sprinkle with sesame seeds.

3 (½-cup) servings.
Preparation time: 15 minutes.
Ready to serve: 25 minutes.

Per serving: 65 calories, 4.5 g total fat (0.5 g saturated fat), 4 g protein, 2 g carbohydrate, 0 mg cholesterol, 354 mg sodium, 12 g fiber. **Star nutrients:** Vitamin A (135%), Vitamin C (51%), Fiber (47%), Iron (49%), Magnesium (29%).
Noteworthy nutrients: Vitamin B6 (16%), Riboflavin (15%).

TIMESAVING TIP   *In Step 1, substitute 1 (10-oz.) pkg. frozen spinach for fresh; cook according to package directions.

TIP   **To toast sesame seeds, heat small skillet over medium heat. Add sesame seeds; shake skillet continuously until seeds are lightly browned, 3 to 4 minutes.

Two-Potato Oven Fries

Mixing regular potato with sweet potato creates a delightful contrast of color and texture in these crispy oven fries. But if it is more convenient, use just one type of potato.

1 medium (12- to 16-oz.) sweet potato, peeled
1 large (12- to 16-oz.) russet (baking) potato, peeled
2 teaspoons olive oil
½ teaspoon paprika
¼ teaspoon salt
⅛ teaspoon freshly ground pepper

❶ Heat oven to 450°F. Coat rimmed baking sheet or large roasting pan with nonstick cooking spray.

❷ Cut sweet potato and russet potato in half crosswise, then lengthwise into ½-inch-wide wedges. Place on baking sheet; toss with olive oil, paprika, salt and pepper.

❸ Bake potatoes 25 to 30 minutes or until golden brown and tender, turning wedges over several times.

4 (1-cup) servings.
Preparation time: 10 minutes.
Ready to serve: 40 minutes.

Per serving: 175 calories, 2.5 g total fat (0.5 g saturated fat), 3 g protein, 36 g carbohydrate, 0 mg cholesterol, 161 mg sodium, 4 g fiber. **Star nutrients:** Vitamin A (344%), Vitamin C (59%). **Noteworthy nutrients:** Vitamin B6 (22%), Vitamin E (22%), Copper (18%), Fiber (16%).

Swiss Chard with Red Peppers & Olives

Swiss chard—a member of the beet family—tastes much like spinach. It grows abundantly in the Mediterranean, so it is not surprising that it tastes great with red bell peppers, garlic and olives—ingredients typical of Mediterranean cooking.

1 bunch Swiss chard (1 lb.) stems trimmed*
2 teaspoons olive oil
1 medium onion, slivered (1 cup)
½ red bell pepper, slivered (¾ cup)
2 garlic cloves, minced
Dash crushed red pepper
⅓ cup Kalamata olives, pitted, coarsely chopped
1 tablespoon balsamic vinegar
⅛ teaspoon salt
⅛ teaspoon freshly ground pepper

❶ With just the water clinging to leaves after washing, cook Swiss chard in large, wide pot over medium-high heat 3 to 5 minutes or just until wilted, stirring. Drain; rinse with cold water. Press out excess moisture; chop coarsely.

❷ In large nonstick skillet, heat olive oil over medium-high heat until hot. Add onion and bell pepper; cook, stirring often, 3 to 4 minutes or until softened. Add garlic and crushed red pepper; cook 30 seconds, stirring. Add olives and Swiss chard; cook, stirring often, 2 to 3 minutes or until heated through. Stir in vinegar, salt and pepper.

4 (¾-cup) servings.
Preparation time: 20 minutes.
Ready to serve: 30 minutes.

Per serving: 80 calories, 4.0 g total fat (0.5 g saturated fat), 3 g protein, 11 g carbohydrate, 0 mg cholesterol, 413 mg sodium, 3 g fiber. **Star nutrients:** Vitamin A (108%), Vitamin C (150%), Magnesium (25%). **Noteworthy nutrients:** Vitamin E (15%), Iron (15%).

TIP *Swiss chard stems are tender, but require longer cooking than the leaves. If desired, boil or steam chopped stems separately about 5 minutes or until tender; mix into cooked greens.

TIMESAVING TIP In Step 1, substitute 1 (10-oz.) pkg. frozen spinach for Swiss chard; cook according to package directions. In Step 2, substitute 1¾ cups frozen red pepper stir-fry vegetables for the onion and bell pepper.

Steamed Broccoli with Lemon & Garlic

Broccoli, a member of the cruciferous vegetable family, which is believed to reduce the risk of cancer, contains beta carotene and vitamins A and C. It is widely available in supermarkets year-round, with peak season being winter. Delicious when lightly steamed, broccoli couldn't be simpler to prepare. A light lemon vinaigrette makes a healthful alternative to butter.

2 garlic cloves, crushed, peeled
¼ teaspoon salt
1 teaspoon freshly grated lemon peel
2 tablespoons fresh lemon juice
1 tablespoon extra-virgin olive oil
⅛ teaspoon crushed red pepper
⅛ teaspoon freshly ground pepper
1 large bunch broccoli* (1½ lb.)

❶ Using mortar and pestle or side of chef's knife, mash garlic and salt into a paste. Transfer to large bowl. Add lemon peel, lemon juice, olive oil, crushed red pepper and pepper; whisk to blend.

❷ Separate broccoli florets; cut into 1-inch pieces. Trim about 3 inches from stems. Peel remaining portions of stems with paring knife; slice ½ inch thick. Rinse broccoli. Place in steamer basket over boiling water; cover. Steam 5 to 8 minutes or until crisp-tender. Add to bowl with lemon dressing; toss to coat well.

4 (1-cup) servings.
Preparation time: 15 minutes.
Ready to serve: 20 minutes.

Per serving: 85 calories, 4 g total fat (0.5 g saturated fat), 5 g protein, 10 g carbohydrate, 0 mg cholesterol, 192 mg sodium, 5 g fiber. **Star nutrients:** Vitamin B6 (15%), Vitamin C (272%), Folate (30%). **Noteworthy nutrients:** Fiber (21%).

TIMESAVING TIP *Substitute 1 (16-oz.) pkg. frozen broccoli florets for fresh; cook according to package directions.

Cauliflower & Spinach Casserole

This casserole is great for entertaining and potlucks because it can be prepared in advance and baked just before serving. I like to serve it with lean roast beef.

3 tablespoons dry bread crumbs
1 teaspoon olive oil
¼ teaspoon paprika
1 medium cauliflower (about 2½ lb.), cored, cut into 1½-inch florets (about 7 cups)*
1 (10-oz.) pkg. fresh spinach, stems trimmed (12 cups)*
1¾ cups low-fat (1%) milk, divided
3 tablespoons all-purpose flour
1⅓ cups (4 oz.) grated extra-sharp cheddar cheese
1½ teaspoons dry mustard
½ teaspoon salt
¼ teaspoon freshly ground pepper

❶ Heat oven to 425°F. Coat 12x8-inch (2½-quart) shallow baking dish with nonstick cooking spray.

❷ In small bowl, mix bread crumbs, olive oil and paprika.

❸ In large pot of lightly salted boiling water, cook cauliflower about 6 minutes or until tender. Add spinach to pot; stir to immerse. Cook about 1 minute or until spinach has wilted. Drain cauliflower and spinach; rinse with cold water to stop further cooking. Drain vegetables thoroughly; spread in prepared baking dish.

❹ In small bowl, whisk ¼ cup of the cold milk with flour until smooth. In heavy, medium saucepan, heat the remaining 1½ cups of the milk over medium heat until steaming. Add flour mixture; cook 2 to 3 minutes or until sauce bubbles and thickens, whisking constantly. Remove from heat. Stir in cheese, mustard, salt and pepper. Pour sauce over vegetables, spreading evenly. Sprinkle with bread crumb mixture.

❺ Bake, uncovered, 30 to 35 minutes or until golden and bubbly.

6 (1-cup) servings.
Preparation time: 30 minutes. Ready to serve: 1 hour, 5 minutes.

Per serving: 175 calories, 8.5 g total fat (4.5 g saturated fat), 13g protein, 14 g carbohydrate, 23 mg cholesterol, 519 mg sodium, 10 g fiber. **Star nutrients:** Vitamin A (76%), Vitamin B6 (29%), Vitamin C (209%), Calcium (32%), Fiber (40%), Iron (31%), Phosphorus (28%), Riboflavin (27%). **Noteworthy nutrients:** Magnesium (24%).

MAKE AHEAD Prepare casserole through Step 4. Cover and refrigerate up to 2 days.

TIMESAVING TIP *Substitute 1½ lb. frozen cauliflower and 1 (10-oz.) pkg. frozen spinach for fresh; cook each vegetable separately according to package directions before spreading in baking dish.

Grilled Cherry Tomatoes

In late summer, local cherry tomatoes taste better than candy. But the cherry tomatoes available in supermarkets offer a pretty good fresh tomato taste throughout the year. They become even more delectable and sweet when charred lightly on the grill or in a hot oven. This easy recipe is a great way to add a splash of vivid color to your dinner plate.

1 pint (2 cups) cherry tomatoes or grape tomatoes
2 teaspoons olive oil
⅛ teaspoon salt
⅛ teaspoon freshly ground pepper
2 tablespoons chopped fresh basil or parsley
2 teaspoons balsamic vinegar

❶ Set fine-mesh grill topper on grill rack. Heat grill to medium-high heat.

❷ In medium bowl, toss tomatoes, olive oil, salt and pepper.

❸ Place tomatoes on grill topper set on gas grill over medium-high heat or on charcoal grill 4 to 6 inches from medium-hot coals. Cover grill; cook 4 to 7 minutes or until lightly charred in places and somewhat collapsed, turning several times. Transfer tomatoes to bowl. Add basil and vinegar; toss to coat.

4 (⅓-cup) servings.
Preparation time: 5 minutes.
Ready to serve: 15 minutes.

Per serving: 40 calories, 2.5 g total fat (0.5 g saturated fat), 1 g protein, 5 g carbohydrate, 0 mg cholesterol, 82 mg sodium, 1 g fiber. **Star nutrients:** Vitamin C (33%).

> VARIATION   **Roasted Cherry Tomatoes**
>
> In Step 1, heat oven to 450°F. Coat small baking pan with nonstick cooking spray. In Step 3, spread tomatoes in pan. Bake 20 to 25 minutes or until tomatoes start to collapse, turning several times. Toss with basil and vinegar.

Roasted & Grilled Vegetables

Because flavors are intensified when natural sugars caramelize, roasting and grilling are both excellent techniques for cooking a wide array of vegetables. Here are some easy ways to make sensational vegetable dishes.

Roasted Vegetables

Heat oven to 450°F. Coat rimmed baking sheet with nonstick cooking spray. Place vegetables (see below) on baking sheet; toss with a little olive oil or spritz with olive oil cooking spray. Sprinkle with salt and pepper to taste. Bake until tender and lightly charred using times recommended below as a guide, stirring several times.

Roasted Summer Vegetables. Use sliced zucchini, sliced sweet onion and sliced red bell pepper. Bake 25 to 35 minutes.

Roasted Root Vegetables. Use carrot sticks, parsnip wedges and potato wedges. Bake 25 to 35 minutes.

Roasted Asparagus and Green Onions. Use trimmed asparagus spears and green onions (cut into 2-inch lengths). Bake 10 to 15 minutes.

Grilled Vegetables

To prevent vegetables from falling though the grill rack, place a fine-mesh vegetable grill topper on the grill, then heat up the gas or charcoal grill. Brush vegetables lightly with olive oil or spritz with olive oil cooking spray. Sprinkle with salt and pepper to taste. Moisten a thick ball of paper towel with olive oil and use it to oil the grill topper. Place vegetables on grill. Cover grill and cook until vegetables are tender and lightly charred using times recommended below as a guide, turning once or twice.

Grilled Onions. Cook 5 to 6 minutes.

Grilled Zucchini. Cook 5 to 6 minutes.

Grilled Bell Peppers. Cook 5 to 6 minutes.

Grilled Eggplant (½-inch-thick slices). Cook 8 to 10 minutes.

Grilled Portobello Mushrooms (½-inch-thick slices). Cook 8 to 10 minutes.

Garlic Mashed Potatoes with Greens

Simmering garlic cloves with potatoes is a great, fat-free way to enrich a dish of mashed potatoes. Adding spinach boosts nutrition and contributes even more flavor to this recipe.

2 lb. all-purpose potatoes, such as Yukon Gold (6 to 8 medium), peeled, cut into 2-inch chunks
8 garlic cloves, peeled
1 (10-oz.) pkg. frozen spinach or 4 cups individually quick frozen spinach*
1 cup low-fat (1%) milk
1 tablespoon extra-virgin olive oil
¾ teaspoon salt
⅛ teaspoon freshly ground pepper
Dash nutmeg

❶ Place potatoes and garlic in large heavy saucepan. Cover with lightly salted water; bring to a boil over medium-high heat. Cover; reduce heat to medium-low. Cook about 15 minutes or until potatoes are tender.

❷ Meanwhile, cook spinach according to package directions; drain well. In glass measuring cup or small saucepan, heat milk and olive oil in microwave or on stovetop until steaming.

❸ When potatoes are tender, drain; return to saucepan. Shake pan over low heat, uncovered, for a minute or so to evaporate excess moisture. Remove from heat; mash potatoes and garlic with potato masher. Gradually add enough hot milk mixture to make a smooth puree. Stir in spinach, salt, pepper and nutmeg.

6 (¾-cup) servings.
Preparation time: 20 minutes.
Ready to serve: 45 minutes.

Per serving: 175 calories, 3 g total fat (0.5 g saturated fat), 6 g protein, 32 g carbohydrate, 2 mg cholesterol, 356 mg sodium, 4 g fiber. **Star nutrients:** Vitamin A (75%), Vitamin B6 (26%), Vitamin C (69%), Potassium (30%). **Noteworthy nutrients:** Copper (23%), Fiber (15%), Folate (20%), Magnesium (16%).

TIP   To keep mashed potatoes hot until serving time, place piece of wax paper directly on surface of mashed potatoes; set pot in larger pan of barely simmering water. You can keep potatoes hot up to 1 hour. Any leftovers reheat well in microwave.

INGREDIENT NOTE   *Substitute 4 cups (10 oz.) frozen mustard greens, turnip greens or collards for spinach; cook according to package directions.

Poultry

Looking for new, delicious ways to fix lean poultry? Just turn the page to find a variety of techniques for cooking chicken, turkey cutlets and ground turkey.

Turkey Cutlets with Port
& Dried Cranberry Sauce

Lean turkey cutlets (sometimes labeled turkey breast slices) are ideal for a quick sauté. This sauté lends itself to variations made with different fruits and liquids, each offering an exceptionally rich-tasting and elegant finish.

1 lb. (½-inch-thick) turkey cutlets
¼ teaspoon salt
¼ teaspoon freshly ground pepper
2 teaspoons olive oil
1 teaspoon butter
¼ cup finely chopped shallot (1 large)
¾ teaspoon dried thyme

½ cup port wine
¼ cup balsamic vinegar
1½ cups reduced-sodium chicken broth
⅓ cup dried cranberries
2 teaspoons cornstarch
2 teaspoons water

❶ Pat turkey dry; sprinkle with salt and pepper. In large nonstick skillet, heat olive oil over medium heat until hot. Add turkey; cook 3 to 3½ minutes per side or until browned and no longer pink in center. Transfer to platter; cover to keep warm. (Do not wash skillet.)

❷ Add butter to skillet. Sauté shallot and thyme 30 to 60 seconds or until softened. Add port and vinegar; increase heat to high. Bring to a boil, stirring to scrape up any browned bits. Cook 1½ minutes. Add broth and dried cranberries; return to a boil. Cook 3 minutes. In small bowl, mix cornstarch and water. Add to sauce; stir until slightly thickened. Reduce heat to medium-low; return cutlets (and any juices that have accumulated on plate) to skillet. Turn cutlets over; simmer 1 to 2 minutes or just until heated through.

4 servings.
Preparation time: 10 minutes. Ready to serve: 25 minutes.

Per serving: 275 calories, 6.5 g total fat (2 g saturated fat), 26 g protein, 18 g carbohydrate, 76 mg cholesterol, 380 mg sodium, 1 g fiber. **Star nutrients:** Vitamin B6 (29%), Niacin (27%). **Noteworthy nutrients:** Phosphorus (23%), Zinc (18%).

VARIATION   **Turkey Cutlets with Madeira, Orange & Dried Plum Sauce**

In Step 2, substitute ½ cup Madeira wine for port, ¼ cup orange juice for balsamic vinegar and ⅓ cup quartered pitted dried plums (prunes) for dried cranberries. Add 1 teaspoon freshly grated orange peel to sauce when you return cutlets to skillet.

VARIATION   **Turkey Cutlets with Dried Apricot & Mint Sauce**

In Step 2, substitute 1 teaspoon dried mint for thyme, ½ cup dry white wine for port wine, ¼ cup apricot nectar (or orange juice) for balsamic vinegar and ⅓ cup chopped dried apricots for dried cranberries.

Southwestern Chicken Stew with Red Peppers & Hominy

This recipe provides a delicious way to boost calcium in your diet by incorporating low-fat milk as an ingredient used in cooking. The tortillas thicken the stew and contribute an appealing corn flavor.

4 (6-inch) corn tortillas
12 oz. boneless skinless chicken breast halves, trimmed, cut into ¾-inch chunks
¼ teaspoon salt
¼ teaspoon freshly ground pepper
3 teaspoons olive oil, divided
1 large onion, chopped (1½ cups)
2 small red bell peppers, diced (2 cups)
1 (4½-oz.) can chopped green chiles

2 garlic cloves, minced
1 tablespoon chili powder
1 teaspoon ground cumin
1 teaspoon dried oregano
1 (14½-oz.) can reduced-sodium chicken broth
2 cups low-fat (1%) milk
2 (15-oz.) cans white hominy,* drained, rinsed
⅓ cup chopped fresh cilantro
Lime wedges

❶ Heat heavy dry skillet, such as cast iron, over high heat until hot. Add tortillas, one or two at a time, in single layer; toast 1 minute per side or until golden and fragrant. Cut tortillas into 1-inch-wide strips.

❷ Sprinkle chicken with salt and pepper. In Dutch oven, heat 2 teaspoons of the olive oil over medium-high heat. Add chicken; cook 2 to 3 minutes or until lightly browned, turning occasionally. Transfer to plate.

❸ Add the remaining 1 teaspoon of the olive oil to Dutch oven. Sauté onion and bell peppers about 3 minutes or until softened, stirring often. Add green chiles, garlic, chili powder, cumin and oregano; cook 1 minute, stirring. Add broth and milk; bring to a simmer. (Don't worry if sauce appears curdled; it will smooth out and thicken during cooking.) Add hominy, tortilla strips and chicken.

❹ Reduce heat to low; cover. Simmer, stirring occasionally, about 20 minutes or until chicken is cooked through and stew has thickened. Stir in cilantro. Garnish each serving with a lime wedge.

6 (1½-cup) servings. Preparation time: 20 minutes. Ready to serve: 55 minutes.

Per serving: 255 calories, 5.5 g total fat (1.5 g saturated fat), 20 g protein, 32 g carbohydrate, 36 mg cholesterol, 539 mg sodium, 6 g fiber. **Star nutrients:** Vitamin A (76%), Vitamin B6 (30%), Vitamin C (184%), Niacin (38%), Phosphorus (31%). **Noteworthy nutrients:** Calcium (19%), Fiber (24%), Magnesium (16%), Riboflavin (15%).

MAKE AHEAD Cover and refrigerate for up to 2 days. Stir in cilantro just before serving.

INGREDIENT NOTE *Hominy is made from corn kernels that have been dried, degermed and hulled. You can find canned hominy in the Latin section of many supermarkets, Latin markets and specialty stores.

Easy Chicken Stir-Fry

Hate to chop stir-fry vegetables? Try using convenient frozen vegetables. Serve this simple stir-fry over brown rice.

⅔ cup orange juice
2 tablespoons reduced-sodium soy sauce
2 teaspoons sugar
1 teaspoon toasted sesame oil
¼ teaspoon hot pepper sauce, such as Tabasco
8 oz. boneless skinless chicken breast halves, trimmed, sliced ⅜-inch thick
1 teaspoon cornstarch

2 teaspoons canola oil, divided
1 tablespoon minced fresh ginger
2 garlic cloves, minced
2 cups frozen broccoli florets
1 cup frozen pepper stir-fry vegetables
⅓ cup water
1 tablespoon sesame seeds, toasted*

❶ In glass measuring cup, combine orange juice, soy sauce, sugar, sesame oil and hot pepper sauce; stir to dissolve sugar. Place chicken in medium bowl or shallow glass dish. Add 2 tablespoons of the orange juice mixture, tossing to coat. Cover; refrigerate 15 to 20 minutes. Add cornstarch to remaining orange juice mixture; mix with fork or whisk until smooth.

❷ In large nonstick skillet, heat 1 teaspoon of the canola oil over medium-high heat until hot. Add chicken; stir-fry 4 minutes or until browned and cooked through. Transfer to plate.

❸ Add the remaining 1 teaspoon of the canola oil to skillet. Add ginger and garlic; stir-fry about 10 seconds or until fragrant. Add broccoli and stir-fry vegetables; stir-fry 2 minutes. Add water, cover skillet. Cook 2 to 3 minutes or until vegetables are heated through and tender.

❹ Push vegetables to outside of skillet. Stir reserved marinade to redistribute cornstarch; add to skillet. Cook about 1 minute or until thickened, stirring sauce in center. Stir vegetables toward center of skillet; add reserved chicken. Cook, stirring constantly, about 1 minute or until heated through. Sprinkle with sesame seeds.

2 (1½-cup) servings.
Preparation time: 15 minutes. Ready to serve: 30 minutes.

Per serving: 340 calories, 10.5 g total fat (1.5 g saturated fat), 34 g protein, 28 g carbohydrate, 66 mg cholesterol, 705 mg sodium, 4 g fiber. **Star nutrients:** Vitamin A (30%), Vitamin B6 (35%), Vitamin C (164%), Phosphorus (28%). **Noteworthy nutrients:** Fiber (17%).

TIP *To toast sesame seeds, heat small skillet over medium-low heat. Add sesame seeds; stir continuously until seeds are lightly browned, 2 to 3 minutes.

VARIATION **Easy Tofu Stir-Fry with Broccoli & Peppers**
Substitute 8 oz. drained firm tofu (cut into ¾-inch cubes) for the chicken.

VARIATION **Easy Pork Stir-Fry with Broccoli & Peppers**
Substitute 8 oz. trimmed pork tenderloin (cut into ⅜-inch-thick slices) for the chicken.

Roasted Chicken & Vegetables

A one-pot meal usually conjures up images of simmering stews. But here is a distinctive spin on a practical concept. This heart-warming meal, featuring beautifully caramelized winter vegetables and glazed chicken pieces, is made in a roasting pan.

4 medium all-purpose potatoes, such as Yukon Gold, peeled, cut into 1-inch-wide wedges
4 medium carrots, cut into matchstick-size strips (2x¼ x¼-inch), or 1½ cups baby carrots
4 medium parsnips, cut into matchstick-size strips (2x¼ x¼-inch)
1 tablespoon olive oil
½ teaspoon salt, divided
½ teaspoon freshly ground pepper, divided
2½ to 3 lb. bone-in chicken pieces of your choice, skin removed, trimmed
2 tablespoons grainy mustard, such as country-style Dijon
4 teaspoons honey
2 teaspoons chopped fresh rosemary or ¾ teaspoon dried rosemary

❶ Heat oven to 425°F. Coat large roasting pan with nonstick cooking spray.

❷ In pan, toss potatoes, carrots and parsnips with olive oil, ¼ teaspoon of the salt and ¼ teaspoon of the pepper. Push vegetables toward outside of pan. Sprinkle chicken pieces with the remaining ¼ teaspoon of the salt and the remaining ¼ teaspoon of the pepper. Place chicken pieces, skinned-side down, in center of pan. Bake, uncovered, 20 minutes.

❸ Meanwhile, in small bowl, mix mustard, honey and rosemary.

❹ Turn chicken pieces over; stir vegetables. Brush chicken with mustard mixture. Bake an additional 25 to 35 minutes or until vegetables are tender and chicken pieces are glazed and cooked through. An instant-read thermometer should register 170°F in breast pieces and 180°F in leg pieces.

4 servings (1 cup vegetables per serving).
Preparation time: 30 minutes. Ready to serve: 1 hour, 10 minutes.

Per serving: 565 calories, 13 g total fat (3 g saturated fat), 65 g protein, 45 g carbohydrate, 199 mg cholesterol, 587 mg sodium, 7 g fiber. **Star nutrients:** Vitamin A (346%), Vitamin B6 (84%), Vitamin C (75%), Copper (28%), Fiber (28%), Iron (25%), Magnesium (32%), Niacin (131%), Phosphorus (63%), Riboflavin (31%), Thiamin (29%), Zinc (36%). **Noteworthy nutrients:** Vitamin B12 (17%), Folate (22%).

TIP To make a light pan gravy, remove chicken and vegetables from roasting pan, splash ½ cup port or Madeira wine and ½ cup reduced-sodium chicken broth into pan; simmer a few minutes, stirring. Spoon sauce over chicken and vegetables.

Chicken Salad with Dill

Here is an updated version of classic chicken salad. Low-fat mayonnaise is lightened and brightened with yogurt, while lemon and dill contribute an especially fresh flavor.

½ cup low-fat mayonnaise
½ cup nonfat plain yogurt
1 tablespoon extra-virgin olive oil
1 teaspoon grated lemon peel
3 to 4 teaspoons lemon juice
1 teaspoon Dijon mustard
Dash salt
Dash freshly ground pepper
3 tablespoons chopped fresh dill
2½ cups cubed (½ inch) cooked chicken (1 lb. boneless skinless chicken breasts; to cook see page 123)
¾ cup chopped celery (2 to 3 ribs)
⅔ cup chopped green onions
1 small head Boston or bibb lettuce, leaves separated
¼ cup sliced almonds, toasted* (optional)

❶ In small bowl, whisk mayonnaise, yogurt, olive oil, lemon peel, 3 teaspoons of the lemon juice, mustard, salt and pepper until smooth. Stir in dill.

❷ In large bowl, combine chicken, celery and green onions. Add dressing; toss to coat well. Adjust seasoning with more lemon juice, if desired.

❸ Arrange lettuce leaves on platter or individual plates. Mound chicken salad over lettuce; garnish with almonds, if desired.

6 (¾-cup) servings.
Preparation time: 25 minutes. Ready to serve: 25 minutes.

Per serving: 245 calories, 15.5 g total fat (2 g saturated fat), 20 g protein, 7 g carbohydrate, 52 mg cholesterol, 267 mg sodium, 2 g fiber. **Star nutrients:** Niacin (29%). **Noteworthy nutrients:** Vitamin B6 (16%), Phosphorus (20%).

MAKE AHEAD   Prepare recipe through Step 2. Cover and refrigerate for up to 2 days.

TIP   *To toast almonds, place in a dry skillet. Cook, stirring constantly, over medium-low heat 2 minutes or until light golden and fragrant. Transfer to a small bowl to cool.

Turkey & Bean Chili

There is no better antidote to winter's deep chill than a steaming bowl of robust chili. Serve it over rice, offering a selection of garnishes so your family and guests can personalize their own chili bowls.

12 oz. ground turkey breast
¼ cup chili powder
1 tablespoon ground cumin
1½ teaspoons dried oregano
2 teaspoons canola oil
2 medium onions, chopped (2 cups)
4 garlic cloves, minced
2 (4½-oz.) cans chopped green chiles
1 (28-oz.) or 2 (14½-oz.) cans diced tomatoes, undrained
1 (14½-oz.) can reduced-sodium chicken broth
1 (15½- or 19-oz.) can black beans, drained, rinsed
1 (15½- or 19-oz.) can red kidney beans, drained, rinsed
Optional garnishes: chopped fresh cilantro or parsley; chopped green onions; lime wedges; hot pepper sauce; baked low-fat tortilla chips; nonfat plain yogurt; grated Monterey Jack cheese

❶ In large nonstick skillet, cook ground turkey with chili powder, cumin and oregano over medium-high heat 4 to 5 minutes or until browned, breaking up meat and mixing in spices with large wooden spoon. Remove from heat; set aside.

❷ In Dutch oven, heat canola oil over medium heat. Add onions; cook 3 to 5 minutes or until softened, stirring often. Add garlic and green chiles; cook, stirring frequently, 1 to 2 minutes or until fragrant. Add tomatoes, broth and browned ground turkey; bring to a simmer. Cover; reduce heat to low. Simmer chili 45 minutes, stirring occasionally.

❸ Stir in black beans and kidney beans. Return to a simmer. Cover; simmer over low heat 15 to 20 minutes or until flavors have blended. Serve with your choice of garnishes.

8 (1¼-cup) servings.
Preparation time: 25 minutes.
Ready to serve: 1 hour, 30 minutes.

Per serving (without garnishes): 215 calories, 3.5 g total fat (0.5 g saturated fat), 19 g protein, 27 g carbohydrate, 26 mg cholesterol, 911 mg sodium, 10 g fiber. **Star nutrients:** Vitamin C (52%), Fiber (41%). **Noteworthy nutrients:** Vitamin B6 (20%), Iron (21%), Niacin (18%), Phosphorus (17%).

MAKE AHEAD Cover and refrigerate chili for up to 2 days or freeze for up to 3 months.

Grilled Chicken Breasts with Yogurt-Mint Marinade

A highly seasoned yogurt marinade tenderizes lean chicken breasts and creates a wonderful flavor when caramelized on the grill.

½ cup nonfat plain yogurt
1 tablespoon canola oil
1 tablespoon honey
1 tablespoon lime juice
4 garlic cloves, minced
3 tablespoons finely chopped fresh mint or 1 tablespoon dried
2 teaspoons ground coriander (optional)
½ teaspoon salt
¼ teaspoon freshly ground pepper
4 boneless skinless chicken breast halves (1½ lb. total), trimmed
Lime wedges

❶ In shallow glass dish, whisk yogurt, canola oil, honey, lime juice, garlic, mint, coriander, salt and pepper. Add chicken; turn to coat. Cover; refrigerate at least 30 minutes or up to 8 hours.

❷ Meanwhile, heat grill.

❸ Remove chicken from marinade. Discard marinade. Lightly oil grill rack. Place chicken on gas grill over medium heat or on charcoal grill 4 to 6 inches from medium coals. Cover grill; cook 5 to 6 minutes per side or until chicken is no longer pink in center. An instant-read thermometer inserted in center should register 170°F. Garnish with lime wedges.

4 servings.
Preparation time: 10 minutes.
Ready to serve: 55 minutes.

Per serving: 275 calories, 6 g total fat (1 g saturated fat), 43 g protein, 10 g carbohydrate, 99 mg cholesterol, 430 mg sodium, 1 g fiber. **Star nutrients:** Vitamin A (39%), Vitamin B6 (50%), Vitamin C (78%), Niacin (96%), Phosphorus (39%). **Noteworthy nutrients:** Calcium (17%), Riboflavin (16%), Thiamin (15%).

Cider House Chicken

A simple sauce of apple cider and grainy mustard enhances basic chicken breasts for a quick and satisfying autumn (or anytime!) dinner.

4 boneless skinless chicken breast halves, trimmed
¼ teaspoon salt
¼ teaspoon freshly ground pepper
3 teaspoons olive oil, divided
1 medium onion, chopped (1 cup)
1 cup apple cider
¼ cup dried cranberries
¾ teaspoon dried thyme
2 teaspoons water
1 teaspoon cornstarch
4 teaspoons grainy mustard, such as country-style Dijon

❶ Sprinkle chicken with salt and pepper. In large nonstick skillet, heat 2 teaspoons of the olive oil over medium-high heat until hot. Add chicken; cook about 2 minutes per side or just until browned. Transfer to plate. (Chicken will continue to cook as it simmers later.)

❷ Add remaining 1 teaspoon of the olive oil to skillet; reduce heat to medium. Add onion; sauté 2 to 3 minutes or until softened and lightly browned. Add cider, dried cranberries and thyme; bring to a simmer.* Return chicken to skillet; reduce heat to low. Cover; simmer 6 to 8 minutes or until chicken is no longer pink in center.

❸ Transfer chicken to clean platter or plates. In small bowl, mix water and cornstarch. Add cornstarch mixture to sauce in skillet; increase heat to medium. Cook, stirring constantly, about 1 minute or until slightly thickened. Stir in mustard. Spoon sauce over chicken.

4 servings.
Preparation time: 15 minutes.
Ready to serve: 25 minutes.

Per serving: 230 calories, 5 g total fat (1 g saturated fat), 27 g protein, 12 g carbohydrate, 66 mg cholesterol, 249 mg sodium, 1 g fiber.
Star nutrients: Vitamin B6 (35%), Niacin (65%), Phosphorus (25%).

TIP *If you prefer a sweeter dish, try adding 1 tablespoon packed brown sugar when you add the cider, dried cranberries and thyme.

Boneless Chicken Breast Basics

Ever-popular boneless chicken breasts are convenient and lean. Here is a guide to cooking basic boneless breasts.

To sauté boneless skinless chicken breast halves: Sprinkle 1 lb. chicken with ¼ teaspoon salt and ¼ teaspoon freshly ground pepper. Heat 2 teaspoons olive oil in large nonstick skillet over medium heat. Add chicken; cook 4 to 5 minutes per side or until browned. Pour ¼ cup dry white wine (or reduced-sodium chicken broth) into skillet. Reduce heat to low; cover. Cook an additional 3 to 4 minutes or until chicken is no longer pink in center and instant-read thermometer registers 170°F.

To grill boneless skinless chicken breast halves: Heat grill. Rub 1 lb. chicken with 2 teaspoons olive oil. Sprinkle with ¼ teaspoon salt and ¼ teaspoon freshly ground pepper. Lightly oil grill rack. Place chicken on gas grill over medium heat or on charcoal grill 4 to 6 inches from medium coals. Cover grill; cook 5 to 6 minutes per side or until chicken is no longer pink in center and instant-read thermometer registers 170°F.

To broil boneless skinless chicken breast halves: Heat broiler. Coat broiler pan or baking sheet with nonstick cooking spray. Rub 1 lb. chicken with 2 teaspoons olive oil. Sprinkle with ¼ teaspoon salt and ¼ teaspoon freshly ground pepper. Place chicken on broiler pan. Broil 4 to 6 inches from heat source 5 to 6 minutes per side or until chicken is no longer pink in center and instant-read thermometer registers 170°F.

To poach boneless skinless chicken breast halves: Combine 1 (14½-oz.) can reduced-sodium chicken broth, ½ cup water, 6 cloves peeled garlic, ½ teaspoon dried thyme, 1 bay leaf and ¼ teaspoon black peppercorns in 10- to 12-inch skillet or Dutch oven with tight-fitting lid; bring to a simmer. Add 1 lb. chicken; reduce heat to low. Cover; cook, turning several times adjusting heat as necessary to maintain a very gentle simmer, about 20 minutes or until chicken is no longer pink in center and instant-read thermometer registers 170°F. With tongs, transfer chicken to plate. Pass broth through strainer into medium bowl. Poaching chicken ensures moist results, so poached chicken is ideal for salads and sandwiches. Poaching chicken in canned chicken broth enriches the broth. The broth will keep, covered, in refrigerator up to 2 days or in freezer up to 6 months.

TIP Be sure to trim fat and any membrane (it can be tough) from chicken breasts. You can leave the tenderloin portions on the breasts if you like. However, if you would like an evenly shaped breast, remove tenders and freeze them for use later in stir-fries.

Chicken & Pineapple Kabobs with Greens

Light yet satisfying, this colorful salad is well suited to relaxed summer eating. Pineapple juice is the secret ingredient in the low-fat dressing, which doubles as a marinade for the chicken.

½ cup pineapple juice
2 tablespoons reduced-sodium soy sauce
2 tablespoons rice vinegar
1 tablespoon canola oil
2 garlic cloves, crushed, peeled
2 tablespoons coarsely chopped fresh ginger
1 jalapeño pepper, seeded, coarsely chopped
1 teaspoon packed brown sugar
1 lb. boneless skinless chicken breast halves, trimmed, cut into 1¼-inch chunks

10 cups mesclun salad mix
4 (½-inch-thick) slices fresh pineapple, cored, quartered
1 bunch green onions, stem ends and green tips trimmed, cut into 2-inch lengths
1 medium red bell pepper, cut into 1¼-inch chunks

❶ In blender, combine pineapple juice, soy sauce, vinegar, canola oil, garlic, ginger, jalapeño and brown sugar; blend until smooth. Reserve ¼ cup of pineapple juice mixture for basting; reserve ¼ cup for dressing salad.*

❷ Place chicken in shallow glass or large resealable plastic bag. Add ¼ cup of the remaining pineapple juice mixture; turn to coat. Cover; refrigerate at least 20 minutes or up to 2 hours.

❸ Heat grill.

❹ Place mesclun in large bowl. Thread chicken, pineapple, green onions (thread crosswise) and bell pepper onto four (12-inch) skewers.

❺ Lightly oil grill rack. Place kabobs on gas grill over medium-high heat or on charcoal grill 4 to 6 inches from medium-hot coals. Cover grill; cook kabobs 8 to 12 minutes or until chicken is no longer pink inside, turning occasionally, basting with reserved marinade.

❻ Toss greens with the ¼ cup of reserved pineapple juice dressing; mound on plates. Slide chicken, pineapple and vegetables off skewers; scatter over salads. Drizzle with remaining dressing. (Do not use marinade as dressing.*)

4 servings.
Preparation time: 20 minutes. Ready to serve: 1 hour.

Per serving: 270 calories, 5.5 g total fat (0.5 g saturated fat), 29 g protein, 27 g carbohydrate, 66 mg cholesterol, 467 mg sodium, 4 g fiber.
Star nutrients: Vitamin A (62%), Vitamin B6 (45%), Vitamin C (146%), Folate (33%), Niacin (70%), Phosphorus (29%). **Noteworthy nutrients:** Copper (18%), Fiber (17%), Magnesium (20%), Thiamin (19%).

FOOD SAFETY TIP *Do not use marinade that has been in contact with raw meat, poultry or fish for basting. If you plan to baste with marinade, reserve a little separately for this purpose.

Crispy Ham-&-Cheese-Stuffed Chicken Breasts

The trick to making crisp, juicy breaded chicken breasts is to brown them on one side in a skillet and then transfer them to a hot oven to finish cooking.

¼ cup (1 oz.) shredded Swiss, Monterey Jack or part-skim mozzarella cheese
2 tablespoons (¾ oz.) chopped ham
1 tablespoon low-fat mayonnaise
2 teaspoons Dijon mustard
⅛ teaspoon freshly ground pepper
4 boneless skinless chicken breast halves (1 to 1½ lb. total), trimmed
½ cup Italian-style bread crumbs
1 egg white
2 teaspoons olive oil

❶ Heat oven to 400°F. Coat baking sheet with nonstick cooking spray.

❷ In small bowl, mix cheese, ham, mayonnaise, mustard and pepper.

❸ Using small sharp knife, cut horizontal slit along the thin, long edge of a chicken breast half, cutting nearly through to opposite side. Open up breast; place about 1 tablespoon cheese mixture in center. Close breast over filling; press edges firmly together to seal. Repeat with remaining chicken breast halves and cheese mixture.

❹ Place bread crumbs in shallow glass dish. In medium bowl, lightly beat egg white with fork. Holding stuffed chicken breast together, dip each chicken breast half in egg white; coat with bread crumbs. (Discard any leftover bread crumbs.)

❺ In large nonstick skillet, heat olive oil over medium-high heat until hot. Add chicken breasts; cook about 2 minutes or until browned on one side. Using tongs, place chicken breasts, browned side up, on prepared baking sheet. Bake chicken 20 minutes or until no longer pink in center. An instant-read thermometer inserted in center should register 170°F.

4 servings. Preparation time: 25 minutes. Ready to serve: 50 minutes.

Per serving: 260 calories, 8.5 g total fat (2.5 g saturated fat), 32 g protein, 11 g carbohydrate, 76 mg cholesterol, 607 mg sodium, 1 g fiber. **Star nutrients:** Vitamin B6 (33%), Niacin (67%), Phosphorus (26%).

MAKE AHEAD Prepare chicken through Step 4. Cover and refrigerate for up to 8 hours.

TIMESAVING TIP Everyone loves the surprise of finding a nugget of cheesy filling in the center of a chicken breast, but if you are pressed for time, don't bother stuffing chicken breasts (skip Steps 2 and 3). Just bread chicken breasts (Step 4) and cook as directed in Step 5.

Sesame-Crusted Chicken

This oven-fried chicken makes a great family meal. Marinating the chicken in buttermilk keeps it moist and succulent. A light coating of flour, sesame seeds and spices forms an appealing crust during baking.

½ cup buttermilk
1 tablespoon Dijon mustard
2 garlic cloves, minced
1 teaspoon hot pepper sauce, such as Tabasco
2½ to 3 lb. bone-in chicken pieces of your choice, skin removed,* trimmed
½ cup all-purpose flour

1 tablespoon sesame seeds
1½ teaspoons baking powder
1½ teaspoons paprika
1 teaspoon dried thyme
Dash salt
Dash freshly ground pepper
Olive oil cooking spray

❶ In shallow glass dish, whisk buttermilk, mustard, garlic and hot pepper sauce until well blended. Add chicken; turn to coat. Cover; marinate in refrigerator at least 30 minutes or up to 8 hours.

❷ Heat oven to 425°F. Line baking sheet with aluminum foil. Set wire rack on baking sheet; coat with nonstick cooking spray.

❸ In small bowl, whisk flour, sesame seeds, baking powder, paprika, thyme, salt and pepper. Place flour mixture in paper bag or large resealable plastic bag. One at a time, place chicken pieces in bag; shake to coat. Shake off excess flour; place chicken on wire rack. (Discard any leftover flour mixture and marinade.) Spray chicken pieces with olive oil cooking spray. (Be sure to coat them evenly.)

❹ Bake chicken 40 to 50 minutes or until golden brown and no longer pink in center. An instant-read thermometer should register 170°F in breast pieces and 180°F in leg pieces.

4 servings.
Preparation time: 15 minutes.
Ready to serve: 1 hour, 30 minutes.

Per serving: 430 calories, 10.5 g total fat (2.5 g saturated fat), 64 g protein, 16 g carbohydrate, 200 mg cholesterol, 504 mg sodium, 1 g fiber. **Star nutrients:** Vitamin B6 (64%), Niacin (123%), Phosphorus (56%), Riboflavin (33%), Thiamin (25%), Zinc (33%). **Noteworthy nutrients:** Vitamin A (15%), Vitamin B12 (19%), Calcium (18%), Iron (22%), Magnesium (22%).

NUTRTION NOTE   *Removing skin from poultry saves you about 4 grams of fat per serving. To do this easily, grasp chicken skin with a piece of paper towel and pull skin away from flesh.

Turkey Burgers

When you are looking for a burger fix, lean ground turkey breast is a convenient alternative to traditional ground beef. Adding a little mayonnaise to ground turkey helps keep the patties moist, while grainy mustard and honey perk up flavor.

¼ cup grainy mustard, such as
   country-style Dijon
2 tablespoons honey
1½ teaspoons Worcestershire sauce
1 lb. ground turkey breast
1 tablespoon low-fat mayonnaise
1 garlic clove, minced

½ teaspoon salt
¼ teaspoon freshly ground pepper
4 hamburger rolls, preferably whole wheat
Optional garnishes: lettuce leaves, sliced tomato,
   sliced red or sweet onion, ketchup, low-fat
   mayonnaise (page 25)

❶ In medium bowl, stir together mustard, honey and Worcestershire sauce. Reserve 2 tablespoons of this mixture for glaze. Add ground turkey, mayonnaise, garlic, salt and pepper to mustard mixture remaining in bowl; mix with potato masher. Divide mixture into four portions; form each into ½-inch-thick patty.

❷ Heat grill.

❸ Lightly oil grill rack. Place patties on gas grill over medium-high heat or on charcoal grill 4 to 6 inches from medium-hot coals.* Cover grill; cook 4 minutes. Turn patties over; brush with reserved glaze. Cook, covered, 4 minutes. Turn patties again; brush with glaze. Cook an additional 2 to 4 minutes or until juices run clear and an instant-read thermometer inserted in center registers 165°F. Just before patties are cooked, place rolls on grill, cut-side down, 30 to 60 seconds or until lightly toasted.

❹ Place a patty in each roll. Garnish as desired.

4 servings.
Preparation time: 20 minutes. Ready to serve: 40 minutes.

Per serving (without garnishes): 360 calories, 5.5 g total fat (0.5 g saturated fat), 35 g protein, 41 g carbohydrate, 71 mg cholesterol, 788 mg sodium, 1 g fiber. **Star nutrients:** Vitamin B6 (36%), Niacin (49%), Phosphorus (33%). **Noteworthy nutrients:** Iron (21%), Magnesium (15%), Thiamin (23%), Zinc (15%).

MAKE AHEAD   Patties can be individually wrapped and refrigerated for up to 8 hours or frozen for up to 3 months. Thaw frozen patties in refrigerator before cooking.

TIP   *You can also broil patties, using the same cooking times.

NUTRITION NOTE   Ground turkey breast meat has just 1% fat, while regular ground turkey which contains a mixture of white and dark meat, has a fat content ranging from 7% to 15%. Check labels carefully.

Beef, Pork & Lamb

Red meat is not necessarily a villain. The following meat recipes feature lean cuts, utilize healthful cooking techniques and illustrate appropriate portion sizes.

Slow-Cooker Beef & Vegetable Stew

The trick to making a healthful, hearty meat stew is to include lots of vegetables and make a generous amount of full-bodied, low-fat gravy. Stew is easy to make in a slow-cooker; it keeps well and tastes even better the next day. Serve over rice, egg noodles or mashed potatoes. Two interesting variations appear on page 132.

1½ lb. cubed (1½ inch) boneless beef chuck
   stew meat, trimmed
½ teaspoon freshly ground pepper
¼ teaspoon salt
3 teaspoons olive oil, divided
1 medium onion, chopped (1 cup)
2 tablespoons all-purpose flour
4 garlic cloves, minced
1 cup dry red wine
1 (14½-oz.) can diced tomatoes, undrained

¾ cup reduced-sodium chicken broth
1 teaspoon Worcestershire sauce
1½ teaspoons dried thyme
2 bay leaves
2 cups (10 oz.) baby carrots
2 medium (12 oz.) white turnips,
   cut into 1x¾-inch chunks (2 cups)
1½ cups (6 oz.) frozen small whole onions
¼ cup chopped fresh parsley

❶ Pat beef dry with paper towels; sprinkle with pepper and salt. In large nonstick skillet, heat 2 teaspoons of the olive oil over medium-high heat until hot. Add half of the beef; cook 3 to 5 minutes or until browned, turning occasionally with tongs. Transfer to plate. Add remaining beef to skillet; brown in same manner. Transfer to plate.

❷ Add the remaining 1 teaspoon of the olive oil to skillet. Sauté chopped onion 1 to 2 minutes or until softened and light brown. Add flour and garlic; cook, 30 to 60 seconds, stirring. Add wine; bring to a boil, stirring to scrape up any browned bits clinging to skillet. Add tomatoes; mash with potato masher. Stir in broth, Worcestershire sauce, thyme and bay leaves; bring to a simmer.

❸ Place beef in 3½-quart slow-cooker. Spoon half of the tomato mixture over beef. Place carrots and turnips over tomato mixture; top with remaining tomato mixture. Cover; cook until beef and vegetables are very tender, 4 to 4½ hours at high setting or 7 to 8 hours at low setting.

❹ Shortly before stew is ready, cook whole onions according to package directions; add to stew. Discard bay leaves. Sprinkle with parsley.

8 (1-cup) servings.
Preparation time: 40 minutes. Ready to serve: 5 hours, 15 minutes.

Per serving: 235 calories, 8 g total fat (2.5 g saturated fat), 21 g protein, 14 g carbohydrate, 42 mg cholesterol, 371 mg sodium, 3 g fiber. **Star nutrients:** Vitamin A (111%), Vitamin B6 (26%), Vitamin B12 (50%), Vitamin C (42%), Zinc (34%).
Noteworthy nutrients: Calcium (17%), Iron (17%), Niacin (20%), Phosphorus (21%).

MAKE AHEAD Cover and refrigerate for up to 2 days or freeze for up to 3 months.

NUTRITION NOTE Chuck is not one of the leaner beef cuts, but it is still preferred for braising, as it remains moist during long, slow cooking.

Slow-Cooker Success

Slow-cookers, often known by the brand name "Crock Pot," became a popular appliance during the 1970s and '80s because they made it possible just to throw a few ingredients in the pot in the morning and return home to a meal. Slow-cookers are now making a comeback. The controlled low-temperature cooking is ideal for braises and beans. If you follow sound techniques, you can achieve excellent results from your slow-cooker. Here are some tips for slow-cooker success.

- Use a slow-cooker only for long-cooking recipes such as soups and stews; don't bother with fish and quickly cooked vegetables.

- Because little evaporation occurs in a slow-cooker, when adapting conventional recipes decrease liquids by about half. To prevent meat from drying out during early stages of cooking, place it in the bottom of the slow-cooker and cover with vegetables and sauce.

- For best flavor, brown meats before placing them in slow-cooker; caramelization improves flavor and color.

- For food safety reasons, do not attempt to cook a whole chicken or turkey in a slow-cooker. Use poultry pieces only and cook on High. If you are making a pot roast, it is important to brown it before slow-cooking. Searing effectively sterilizes the surface of the meat where bacteria are likely to develop.

- Just as in conventional cooking, food can become overcooked in a slow-cooker. Pay attention to cooking times.

Slow-Cooker Stew Variations
Try these variations to Slow-Cooker Beef & Vegetable Stew (page 130).

VARIATION **Lamb Stew with Spring Vegetables**

In Step 1, brown 1½ lb. trimmed, cubed lamb leg meat. In Step 2, substitute 1 cup dry white wine for red wine and 2 tablespoons chopped fresh rosemary for dried thyme. In Step 3, omit turnips. In Step 4, cook 1½ cups frozen small whole onions and 1½ cups frozen peas separately according to package directions; add to stew.

VARIATION **Pork Stew with Latin Flavors**

In Step 1, brown 1½ lb. trimmed, cubed boneless pork, such as top round. In Step 2, substitute 1 cup lager beer for red wine and 1 (14½-oz.) can mild green chile-seasoned tomatoes for diced tomatoes. Substitute 1½ teaspoons ground cumin and ¾ teaspoon dried oregano for thyme and bay leaves. In Step 3, omit carrots and turnips; instead use 1 medium sweet potato, peeled and cut into 1x¾-inch chunks. In Step 4, cook 1½ cups frozen small whole onions and 1½ cups frozen corn according to package directions; add to stew. Substitute fresh cilantro for parsley. Serve over rice with lime wedges and hot pepper sauce.

Spice-Rubbed Steak

A spice crust makes an easy and delicious fix-up for basic steak.

½ teaspoon ground cumin
½ teaspoon paprika
½ teaspoon chili powder
½ teaspoon freshly ground pepper
¼ teaspoon salt, preferably kosher (coarse) salt
1 (1-lb.) boneless sirloin steak, trimmed
1 garlic clove, halved

❶ Heat grill.

❷ In small bowl, mix cumin, paprika, chili powder, pepper and salt. Rub both sides of steak with cut sides of garlic. Sprinkle spice mixture evenly over both sides of steak. Press and rub spices into meat.

❸ Lightly oil grill rack.* Place steak on gas grill over high heat or on charcoal grill 4 to 6 inches from hot coals. Cook 4 to 5 minutes per side for medium-rare or to desired doneness. Transfer steak to cutting board; let rest 5 minutes. Slice steak thinly across the grain.

4 servings.
Preparation time: 5 minutes.
Ready to serve: 25 minutes (longer if using charcoal grill).

Per serving: 150 calories, 4.5 g total fat (1.5 g saturated fat), 24 g protein, 1 g carbohydrate, 54 mg cholesterol, 196 mg sodium, 0 g fiber. **Star nutrients:** Vitamin B6 (26%), Vitamin B12 (60%), Zinc (31%). **Noteworthy nutrients:** Iron (15%), Niacin (21%), Phosphorus (24%), Riboflavin (16%).

TIP   *If you prefer to cook the steak indoors, use a ridged grill pan or broiler.

Flank Steak with Coffee-Peppercorn Marinade

Coffee has a remarkable affinity for beef. In this marinade, the coffee is complemented by balsamic vinegar, garlic and crushed peppercorns. Serving the steak sliced across the grain makes an attractive presentation and helps control portion sizes.

3 tablespoons cold, strong brewed (or prepared instant) coffee
1 tablespoon balsamic vinegar
1 tablespoon packed brown sugar
1 tablespoon olive oil
2 garlic cloves, minced
1 teaspoon black peppercorns, crushed
½ teaspoon salt
1 lb. flank steak, trimmed

❶ In shallow glass dish (large to enough to hold steak flat), whisk coffee, vinegar, brown sugar, olive oil, garlic, peppercorns and salt. Add steak; turn to coat. Cover; refrigerate at least 1 hour or up to 8 hours.

❷ Heat grill.

❸ Remove steak from marinade; discard marinade. Lightly oil grill rack. Place steak on gas grill over high heat or on charcoal grill 4 to 6 inches from hot coals.* Cook 4 to 5 minutes per side for medium-rare (a little longer if you prefer your steak more well done). Transfer steak to cutting board; let rest 5 minutes. Slice steak thinly across the grain.

4 servings.
Preparation time: 10 minutes.
Ready to serve: 1 hour, 20 minutes (longer if using charcoal grill).

Per serving: 230 calories, 12 g total fat (4 g saturated fat), 25 g protein, 4 g carbohydrate, 46 mg cholesterol, 363 mg sodium, 0 g fiber. **Star nutrients:** Vitamin B12 (58%), Niacin (27%), Zinc (45%). **Noteworthy nutrients:** Vitamin B6 (25%), Phosphorus (21%).

TIP *If you prefer to cook the steak indoors, use a ridged grill pan or broiler.

Neapolitan Meatballs

This treasured family recipe has been passed down from my husband's mother, who was born in Naples. It takes a certain time commitment to put this dish together, but it will keep for several days in the refrigerator and it freezes well. Serve meatballs and sauce over spaghetti, then vary your menu on subsequent days by serving over instant polenta or mashed potatoes, in quick lasagna and in hot sandwiches.

½ cup bulgur, rinsed
3 teaspoons olive oil, divided
8 garlic cloves, cut into thin slivers
¾ teaspoon dried oregano
¼ teaspoon crushed red pepper
3 (28-oz.) cans diced tomatoes
2 cups cubed whole wheat country bread
  (two ½-inch-thick slices)
1 egg

1 egg white
1 lb. 93% lean ground beef
½ cup (1 oz.) freshly grated Parmesan cheese
1 teaspoon salt
½ teaspoon freshly ground pepper plus
  more to taste
¼ teaspoon ground cinnamon
½ teaspoon sugar (optional)

❶ In medium bowl, cover bulgur generously with hot water. Let soak 30 minutes or until bulgur is tender. Drain in fine-mesh sieve; press moisture from bulgur. Meanwhile, in Dutch oven, heat 2 teaspoons of the olive oil over medium-low heat until warm. Add garlic, oregano and crushed red pepper; cook 1 to 2 minutes or until softened but not browned, stirring. Add tomatoes; mash with potato masher. Increase heat to medium-high; bring to a simmer. Reduce heat to low. Partially cover; let simmer while preparing meatballs.

❷ In medium bowl, cover bread cubes with cold water. Let soak a few minutes. Remove bread cubes from water; squeeze out moisture. In large bowl, whisk egg and egg white. Add bulgur, bread cubes, ground beef, Parmesan cheese, salt, ½ teaspoon of the pepper and cinnamon. Mix well with potato masher or your hands. Form into 16 oval meatballs, each about 1¾ inches long.

❸ In large nonstick skillet, heat the remaining 1 teaspoon of the olive oil over medium-high heat. Add half of the meatballs; cook 3 to 4 minutes or until browned on all sides, turning occasionally. Transfer to paper towel-lined plate; blot with paper towels. Brown remaining meatballs in same manner.

❹ Add meatballs to simmering sauce. Partially cover; simmer over low heat for 50 minutes. Uncover; simmer an additional 10 to 15 minutes or until sauce has thickened to your liking. Taste sauce; add sugar, if it seems tart, and additional pepper, if desired.

8 servings (16 large meatballs). Preparation time: 1 hour. Ready to serve: 1 hour, 50 minutes.

Per serving: 310 calories, 11 g total fat (3.5 g saturated fat), 9 g protein, 24 g carbohydrate, 88 mg cholesterol, 1468 mg sodium, 4 g fiber. **Star nutrients:** Vitamin C (75%), Calcium (30%), Iron (66%). **Noteworthy nutrients:** Fiber (17%).

NUTRITION NOTE   By stretching ground meat with bulgur and whole wheat bread, you can significantly reduce fat and increase fiber and whole grain nutrients.

Picadillo

With an exquisite interplay of sweet, savory, tart and spicy flavors, picadillo, the Latin American dish of seasoned ground meat, makes an especially satisfying and easy supper. In this healthful adaptation, bulgur stands in for a portion of the ground beef, reducing saturated fat and contributing whole grain goodness. Serve this picadillo with warm flour tortillas and garnish with low-fat sour cream.

12 oz. 93% lean ground beef
2 teaspoons canola oil
2 medium onions, chopped (2 cups)
3 garlic cloves, minced
2 (14½-oz.) or 3 (10-oz.) cans mild green chile-seasoned diced tomatoes
¾ cup water
½ cup bulgur, rinsed
¼ cup raisins
1 tablespoon cider vinegar
¾ teaspoon ground cinnamon or ground cumin
½ teaspoon freshly ground pepper
¼ cup manzanilla olives stuffed with pimientos, rinsed, chopped

❶ In medium nonstick skillet, cook beef over medium-high heat 3 to 4 minutes or until browned, crumbling with wooden spoon. Drain in colander set over bowl.

❷ In Dutch oven, heat canola oil over medium-high heat until hot. Add onions; cook, stirring often, 3 to 4 minutes or until tender and lightly browned. Add garlic; cook 30 seconds, stirring. Add tomatoes, water, bulgur, raisins, vinegar, cinnamon, pepper and drained beef; bring to a simmer, stirring. Reduce heat to medium-low. Partially cover; simmer 20 to 25 minutes or until bulgur is tender and flavors have blended, stirring occasionally. Stir in olives.

6 (1-cup) servings.
Preparation time: 25 minutes.
Ready to serve: 50 minutes.

Per serving: 255 calories, 9 g total fat (2 g saturated fat), 3.8 g protein, 24 g carbohydrate, 57 mg cholesterol, 482 mg sodium, 5 g fiber. **Star nutrients:** Iron (63%). **Noteworthy nutrients:** Vitamin C (17%), Fiber (20%).

MAKE AHEAD Cover and refrigerate Picadillo for up to 2 days or freeze for up to 3 months.

Fennel-Crusted Pork Tenderloin

*With their subtle licorice flavor, fennel seeds pair with garlic to make a delicious crust for lean pork tenderloin.
Because pork tenderloin is in the oven for only a short time, it is important to brown it in a skillet before roasting.
An old-fashioned cast-iron skillet performs both functions beautifully. If you do not have an oven-safe skillet, use
your nonstick skillet to brown the pork, then transfer to a baking pan coated with nonstick cooking spray.*

1 tablespoon fennel seeds
3 garlic cloves, minced
½ teaspoon freshly ground pepper
¼ teaspoon salt
1 (¾- to 1-lb.) pork tenderloin, trimmed
2 teaspoons olive oil

½ cup dry white wine
1 cup reduced-sodium chicken broth
1 tablespoon water
2 teaspoons cornstarch
1 teaspoon Dijon mustard

❶ Heat oven to 425°F.

❷ In small bowl, mix fennel seeds, garlic, pepper and salt. Rub mixture evenly over pork, massaging
it into the crevices. Fold thin "tail" underneath; secure with butcher's string or toothpick.

❸ In large oven-safe skillet, such as cast-iron, heat olive oil over medium-high heat. Add pork;
cook about 1½ minutes or until lightly browned on one side. Turn pork over; transfer skillet to
oven. Bake about 20 minutes or until internal temperature registers 150°F. (Pork should be
juicy with just a trace of pink.) Transfer pork to carving board; cover loosely to let rest.

❹ Place skillet over medium-high heat. Add wine; bring to a boil, stirring to scrape up any
browned bits. Cook 2 to 3 minutes or until reduced by half. Add broth; return to a boil. Cook
2 to 3 minutes or until flavor is intensified. In small bowl, mix water and cornstarch; whisk
into simmering sauce. Cook about 1 minute or until slightly thickened, whisking constantly.
Whisk in mustard. Keep warm.

❺ Remove string or toothpick from pork. Carve into ⅜-inch-thick slices; serve with sauce.

4 servings.
Preparation time: 15 minutes.
Ready to serve: 45 minutes.

Per serving: 165 calories, 5 g total fat (1 g saturated fat), 21.5 g protein, 4 g carbohydrate, 50 mg cholesterol, 293 mg sodium,
1 g fiber. **Star nutrients:** Thiamin (56%). **Noteworthy nutrients:** Vitamin B6 (24%), Niacin (21%), Phosphorus (22%), Riboflavin (15%).

Maple-Mustard Glazed Pork Chops

The technique of browning pork chops on one side and then finishing cooking in the oven, yields a moist and succulent result. Pass on the monster-sized, extra-thick chops and look for ½- to ¾-inch-thick chops, which are more likely to be of appropriate portion size.

1½ tablespoons grainy mustard, such as country-style Dijon
1 tablespoon maple syrup
1½ teaspoons cider vinegar
4 (4-oz.) boneless pork loin chops, trimmed
1 garlic clove, halved
¼ teaspoon freshly ground pepper
2 teaspoons olive oil

❶ Heat oven to 400°F.

❷ In small bowl, mix mustard, maple syrup and vinegar. Rub pork chops with cut sides of garlic. Sprinkle with pepper.

❸ In large oven-safe skillet, such as cast-iron, heat olive oil over medium-high heat until hot.* Add pork chops; cook about 2 minutes or until browned on one side. Remove from heat. Turn pork chops over; spoon mustard mixture over top of chops. Transfer skillet to oven. Bake chops about 6 minutes or just until no longer pink in center.

4 servings.
Preparation time: 10 minutes.
Ready to serve: 20 minutes.

Per serving: 270 calories, 17 g total fat (5.5 g saturated fat), 23 g protein, 4 g carbohydrate, 76 mg cholesterol, 101 mg sodium, 0 g fiber. **Star nutrients:** Vitamin B6 (28%), Niacin (27%), Thiamin (84%). **Noteworthy nutrients:** Phosphorus (23%).

TIP   *If you do not have an oven-safe skillet, brown chops in large nonstick skillet. Turn over and transfer to nonstick cooking spray-coated baking sheet before baking.

Lamb Steaks with Mustard-Rosemary Marinade

Lamb with rosemary, mustard and lots of garlic is a time-honored combination. This simple marinade turns tender lamb into a special treat that you can assemble quickly. Many supermarkets now sell convenient slices of lamb leg labeled "lamb steaks" or "lamb cutlets." However, you can substitute 8 (3-oz.) lamb loin chops. Alternatively, double the marinade recipe and use it for a leg of lamb. I recommend that you seek out domestic lamb if you are splurging on a red meat meal. In my opinion, domestic lamb is much more delicate and delicious than Australian lamb.

3 tablespoons grainy mustard, such as country-style Dijon
2 tablespoons chopped fresh rosemary
2 tablespoons red wine vinegar
2 teaspoons olive oil
½ teaspoon Worcestershire sauce
4 garlic cloves, minced
¼ teaspoon salt
¼ teaspoon freshly ground pepper
1 lb. boneless lamb steaks (¾ inch thick), trimmed, cut into at least 4 portions

❶ In shallow glass dish, whisk mustard, rosemary, vinegar, olive oil, Worcestershire sauce, garlic, salt and pepper until blended. Add lamb steaks; turn to coat well. Cover; refrigerate at least 30 minutes or up to 4 hours.

❷ Heat grill.

❸ Lightly oil grill rack. Place lamb chops on gas grill over high heat or on charcoal grill 4 to 6 inches from hot coals. Cover grill; cook about 4 minutes per side for medium-rare (internal temperature of 140°F) or to desired doneness.

4 servings.
Preparation time: 10 minutes.
Ready to serve: 45 minutes.

Per serving: 205 calories, 10 g total fat (3 g saturated fat), 25 g protein, 3 g carbohydrate, 75 mg cholesterol, 294 mg sodium, 0 g fiber. **Star nutrients:** Vitamin B12 (42%), Niacin (38%), Phosphorus (25%), Zinc (26%). **Noteworthy nutrients:** Iron (15%), Riboflavin (16%).

Pork & Pineapple Kabobs

Because peeled fresh pineapple is now widely available in supermarkets and fruit markets, it is easier than ever to enjoy this tropical fresh fruit. Pineapple chunks are an interesting way to perk up a kabob, and they taste great with pork and a spicy molasses glaze.

¼ cup frozen pineapple juice concentrate, thawed
4 teaspoons apple cider vinegar
4 teaspoons molasses
1 teaspoon Worcestershire sauce
½ teaspoon hot pepper sauce, such as Tabasco
2 teaspoons canola oil
1 lb. center-cut, boneless pork loin chops (1¼ inch thick), trimmed, cut into 1¼-inch chunks
¼ teaspoon salt
¼ teaspoon freshly ground pepper
4 (⅜-inch-thick) slices fresh pineapple (about ¾ of small pineapple), each slice cut into 4 wedges
1 bunch green onions, white and light green parts only, cut into 2-inch lengths
Lime wedges

❶ In small bowl, whisk pineapple juice concentrate, vinegar, molasses, Worcestershire sauce, hot pepper sauce and canola oil.

❷ Heat grill.

❸ Sprinkle pork with salt and pepper. Thread a piece of pork, followed by a pineapple wedge, a piece of green onion (thread it crosswise) and another piece of pork onto a 10- or 12-inch skewer. Complete skewer in this manner, using a total of 5 pieces of pork, 4 pineapple wedges and 4 green onions. Repeat with remaining pork, pineapple and green onions to make a total of 4 kabobs.

❹ Lightly oil grill rack. Place kabobs on gas grill over medium-high heat or on charcoal grill 4 to 6 inches from medium-hot coals. Cover grill; cook 8 to 10 minutes or until pork is browned and just cooked through, turning occasionally and basting cooked sides with pineapple juice concentrate mixture. Garnish with lime wedges.

4 servings.
Preparation time: 40 minutes.
Ready to serve: 55 minutes.

Per serving: 360 calories, 18.5 g total fat (5.5 g saturated fat), 23 g protein, 25 g carbohydrate, 68 mg cholesterol, 218 mg sodium, 2 g fiber. **Star nutrients:** Vitamin B6 (32%), Vitamin C (40%), Niacin (30%), Thiamin (69%). **Noteworthy nutrients:** Magnesium (15%), Phosphorus (24%), Riboflavin (21%).

Greek Lamb Kabobs

Skewers of oregano-laced lamb, called souvlaki, are popular in restaurants in Greece and in Greek restaurants throughout America. These kabobs are easy to replicate in your kitchen.

3 tablespoons lemon juice
3 tablespoons dry white wine
1 tablespoon olive oil
1½ teaspoons dried oregano
1 garlic clove, minced
½ teaspoon salt
⅛ teaspoon freshly ground pepper
1¼ lb. boneless leg of lamb, trimmed, cut into 1¼-inch chunks

❶ In small bowl, whisk lemon juice, wine, olive oil, oregano, garlic, salt and pepper. Measure 3 tablespoons of mixture; reserve for basting. Place lamb in shallow glass dish. Add remaining marinade and turn to coat. Cover; refrigerate at least 20 minutes or up to 2 hours, turning occasionally.

❷ Heat grill.

❸ Thread lamb onto four (10- or 12-inch) skewers.*

❹ Lightly oil grill rack. Place skewers on gas grill over medium-high heat or on charcoal grill over medium-hot coals. Cover grill; cook 6 to 8 minutes or until lamb is browned and cooked to medium-rare, turning occasionally and basting with reserved marinade.

4 servings.
Preparation time: 20 minutes.
Ready to serve: 50 minutes.

Per serving: 225 calories, 10 g total fat (2.5 g saturated fat), 29 g protein, 2 g carbohydrate, 91 mg cholesterol, 380 mg sodium, 0 g fiber. **Star nutrients:** Vitamin B12 (64%), Niacin (44%), Phosphorus (28%), Zinc (36%). **Noteworthy nutrients:** Iron (16%), Riboflavin (21%).

TIP *If using wooden skewers, soak in cold water at least 30 minutes before using to prevent scorching.

Veal Stew with Mushrooms & Baby Onions

This elegant, creamy veal stew utilizes a generous quantity of baby onions and meaty mushrooms to extend a small amount of meat and help keep the saturated fat in check.

1½ lb. cubed (1½ inch) lean boneless stewing veal (from the leg), trimmed

¼ teaspoon salt

¼ teaspoon freshly ground pepper

4 teaspoons olive oil, divided

½ cup dry white wine

1 (14½-oz.) can reduced-sodium chicken broth

½ teaspoon dried thyme

1 bay leaf

1 medium onion, chopped (1 cup)

2 medium carrots, chopped (1 cup)

2 garlic cloves, minced

1½ cups (6 oz.) frozen small whole onions

1 (8- or 10-oz.) pkg. mushrooms, trimmed, quartered (3 cups)

2 tablespoons cornstarch

2 tablespoons water

⅓ cup low-fat sour cream

2 tablespoons chopped fresh parsley

2 teaspoons freshly grated lemon peel

1 to 2 teaspoons fresh lemon juice

❶ Heat oven to 300°F. Sprinkle veal with salt and pepper. In large nonstick skillet, heat 1 teaspoon of the olive oil over medium-high heat until hot. Add half of the veal; cook 3 to 4 minutes or until browned, turning occasionally. Transfer to plate. Add remaining veal; brown in same manner. Transfer to plate. Add wine to skillet; bring to a simmer. Add broth, thyme and bay leaf; bring to a simmer.

❷ In Dutch oven, heat 2 teaspoons of the olive oil over medium heat until hot. Add chopped onion and carrots; cook, stirring often, 2 to 3 minutes or until softened. Add garlic; cook 30 seconds, stirring. Add browned veal and broth mixture. Cover Dutch oven; place in oven.

❸ Bake 1½ to 2 hours or until veal is tender. After 1¼ hours, cook whole onions according to package directions; drain. In large nonstick skillet, heat the remaining 1 teaspoon of the olive oil over medium-high heat until hot. Add mushrooms; cook, stirring often, 4 to 5 minutes or until browned and tender.

❹ When veal is tender, pass braising liquid through a colander into medium saucepan. Discard bay leaf. Return solids to Dutch oven; cover to keep warm. Bring liquid in saucepan to a simmer over medium heat. In small bowl, mix cornstarch and water; add to braising liquid in saucepan. Cook 30 seconds or until slightly thickened, stirring constantly. Add sour cream; whisk until smooth and heated through. Add sauce to veal in Dutch oven. Add whole onions and mushrooms; heat through over medium heat. Stir in parsley, lemon peel and lemon juice to taste.

6 (1-cup) servings. Preparation time: 30 minutes. Ready to serve: 2 hours, 20 minutes.

Per serving: 280 calories, 13 g total fat (4.5 g saturated fat), 25 g protein, 12 g carbohydrate, 98 mg cholesterol, 318 mg sodium, 2 g fiber.
Star nutrients: Vitamin A (117%), Vitamin B6 (31%), Vitamin B12 (26%), Niacin (54%), Phosphorus (32%), Riboflavin (31%), Zinc (25%).
Noteworthy nutrients: Vitamin C (23%), Copper (17%).

MAKE AHEAD Cover and refrigerate stew for up to 2 days or freeze for up to 3 months.

Steakhouse Beef Salad

When you have leftover steak, roast beef or even deli roast beef on hand, you'll find that this French bistro-style salad gives beef leftovers a new lease on life. Accompany the salad with garlic-rubbed, grilled whole wheat country bread.

2 tablespoons wine vinegar
2 tablespoons extra-virgin olive oil
2 teaspoons Dijon mustard
½ teaspoon dried tarragon
¼ teaspoon salt
¼ teaspoon freshly ground pepper
8 cups mesclun salad mix or torn leaf lettuce
1 pint (2 cups) cherry tomatoes or grape tomatoes, halved
½ cup finely diced red onion (½ medium)
8 oz. cooked lean steak or roast beef, thinly sliced (1½ cups)
2 tablespoons drained capers, rinsed

❶ In small jar with tight-fitting lid or small bowl, combine vinegar, olive oil, mustard, tarragon, salt and pepper; shake or whisk to blend.

❷ In large bowl, combine mesclun, tomatoes and onion. Drizzle with 2 tablespoons of the dressing; toss to coat well. Divide salad among four plates. Top each serving with steak. Stir capers into remaining dressing; spoon over steaks.

4 (2-cup) servings.
Preparation time: 20 minutes.
Ready to serve: 20 minutes.

Per serving: 230 calories, 13.5 g total fat (3 g saturated fat), 19 g protein, 10 g carbohydrate, 49 mg cholesterol, 374 mg sodium, 3 g fiber. **Star nutrients:** Vitamin A (54%), Vitamin B12 (25%), Vitamin C (64%), Zinc (29%). **Noteworthy nutrients:** Iron (21%), Folate (19%), Niacin (18%), Phosphorus (19%), Riboflavin (17%).

VARIATION **Steakhouse Tuna Salad**
Substitute 1 (7-oz.) can water-packed tuna, drained and flaked, for the beef.

Fish & Seafood

The American Heart
Association recommends
that you eat at least
two servings of fish per
week. This chapter
offers many easy and
delicious options.

Oven-Poached Salmon Three Ways

Salmon fillets are wonderfully moist and succulent when poached in the oven with wine and shallots. To top them off, choose from one of the three sauce recipes that follow, here and on page 150.

1 lb. salmon fillet, cut into 4 portions
2 tablespoons dry white wine or water
¼ teaspoon salt
¼ teaspoon freshly ground pepper
2 tablespoons finely chopped
  shallot (1 medium)

1 recipe *Lemon-Dill Sauce, Parsley-Caper Sauce* or
  Light Remoulade Sauce (pages 148, 150)
Lemon wedges

❶ Heat oven to 425°F. Coat 9-inch glass pie plate with nonstick cooking spray.

❷ Place salmon, skin-side down, in pie plate. Sprinkle with wine, salt and pepper. Sprinkle with shallot. Cover with aluminum foil; bake 15 to 25 minutes or just until salmon flakes easily with fork.

❸ Meanwhile, prepare sauce of your choice.

❹ When salmon is ready, transfer pieces to dinner plates. Spoon any liquid remaining in pie plate over salmon. Serve with sauce. Garnish with lemon wedges.

4 servings. Preparation time: 20 minutes. Ready to serve: 30 minutes.

Per serving: 197 calories, 9 g total fat (1 g saturated fat), 23 g protein, 4 g carbohydrate, 60 mg cholesterol, 343 mg sodium, 0 g fiber. **Star nutrients:** Vitamin B12 (57%), Niacin (40%), Phosphorus (27%).

Lemon-Dill Sauce

This easy-to-make light, creamy sauce resembles hollandaise sauce and is also a nice way to dress up asparagus as well as Oven-Poached Salmon.

¼ cup low-fat mayonnaise
¼ cup low-fat (1%) milk
2 tablespoons chopped fresh dill
1 teaspoon freshly grated lemon peel

1 tablespoon fresh lemon juice
2 teaspoons Dijon mustard
¼ teaspoon freshly ground pepper

❶ Place mayonnaise in small saucepan. Gradually whisk in milk. Set saucepan over medium-low heat; cook, whisking constantly, until mixture is smooth and heated through but not bubbling, about 2 minutes. Remove from heat. Stir in dill, lemon peel, lemon juice, mustard and pepper. Serve warm.

½ cup (4 servings). Preparation time: 15 minutes. Ready to serve: 20 minutes.

Per serving: 56 calories, 5 g total fat (0 g saturated fat), 0 g protein, 3 g carbohydrate, 0 mg cholesterol, 121 mg sodium, 0 g fiber.

Parsley-Caper Sauce

An Italian classic, this piquant green sauce provides the perfect flourish for Oven-Poached Salmon, grilled chicken, turkey cutlets or fish steaks.

2 cups lightly packed fresh Italian parsley
¼ cup drained capers, rinsed
3 garlic cloves, crushed, peeled
2 tablespoons reduced-sodium chicken broth or
   vegetable broth
1 tablespoon extra-virgin olive oil

1 tablespoon low-fat mayonnaise
1 tablespoon fresh lemon juice
1 teaspoon Dijon mustard
½ teaspoon anchovy paste
⅛ teaspoon freshly ground pepper

❶ In food processor, combine parsley, capers and garlic; process until finely chopped. Add broth, olive oil, mayonnaise, lemon juice, mustard, anchovy paste and pepper; process until mixture forms smooth paste, stopping to scrape down sides of bowl several times.

½ cup (4 servings).
Preparation time: 15 minutes. Ready to serve: 15 minutes.

Per serving: 61 calories, 5 g total fat (0.5 g saturated fat), 1.5 g protein, 4 g carbohydrate, 0 mg cholesterol, 316 mg sodium, 1.5 g fiber.

MAKE AHEAD Place piece of plastic wrap directly on sauce's surface to prevent discoloration; refrigerate for up to 2 days. Serve at room temperature.

Light Remoulade Sauce

Here is a spiced-up mayonnaise that goes well with fish (such as Oven-Poached Salmon), shellfish, meat and poultry.

¼ cup low-fat mayonnaise
¼ cup nonfat plain yogurt
1 tablespoon grainy mustard, such as
   country-style Dijon
1 tablespoon fresh lemon juice

½ teaspoon anchovy paste
Dash cayenne pepper
4 teaspoons drained capers, rinsed
1 tablespoon chopped fresh parsley

❶ In small bowl, whisk mayonnaise, yogurt, mustard, lemon juice, anchovy paste and cayenne pepper until smooth. Stir in capers and parsley.

⅔ cup (4 servings). Preparation time: 15 minutes. Ready to serve: 15 minutes.

Per serving: 61 calories, 5 g total fat (0 g saturated fat), 1 g protein, 3.5 g carbohydrate, 0 mg cholesterol, 218 mg sodium, 0 g fiber.

MAKE AHEAD Cover and refrigerate for up to 2 days.

Focus on Fresh:
A Guide to Fish Cooking Techniques

So, you have resolved to eat more fish meals. You have selected a recipe and headed to the fish counter to purchase ingredients for tonight's dinner. But if the sole you have planned to cook looks dull and not very appealing, think about substituting another kind of fish. When it comes to preparing tasty fish, freshness is everything. Fortunately, most recipes can be made with several types of fish. The quality of different varieties varies day to day, depending on the season, where you live, fishing conditions and distribution systems. When purchasing fish, your best strategy is to be flexible and choose the fish that looks freshest at the market that day.

How can you tell if a fish is fresh? If you are purchasing whole fish, the eyes are a clue. They should be bright and not sunken. Fillets and steaks should be firm and shiny. Don't be shy about asking to smell the fish. The aroma should be fresh and reminiscent of the sea—not strong and "fishy."

Here is a guide to mixing and matching different varieties of fish with healthful cooking techniques:

Oven Poaching. Just a little bit of liquid is used for this method and the fish is cooked, covered, in the oven. It produces a particularly moist result and is well suited to a variety of fish. It is an excellent technique for moderately firm, rich fish like salmon and Arctic char, as well as delicate fish, such as sole, haddock, cod or orange roughy.

Grilling. When you are cooking over direct heat, choose firm-textured fish such as tuna, swordfish, halibut and monkfish. Salmon fillets and steaks are also great for grilling. If you would like to cook a delicate fish like sole or cod on your outdoor grill, your best bet is to enclose the fish in a foil packet.

Broiling. This simple method works well for almost all fish, and it is particularly successful for rich fish like salmon. If you are broiling lean, delicate fish such as sole or flounder, baste the fish often to prevent it from drying out.

Roasting. This oven-cooking technique is ideal for moderately firm fish such as sea bass, mahimahi and red snapper.

Braising. Opt for firm fish when you are simmering fish in flavorful liquid to make a stew. Good choices for braising include halibut, monkfish and swordfish.

Sautéing. This is a good method for delicate fish such as sole, flounder, cod and orange roughy. Dredge the fish lightly in flour to ensure a nice crisp crust, and use a nonstick skillet to minimize the amount of oil needed for cooking.

Mahimahi Mediterranean-Style

Firm-textured fish like mahimahi tastes great when quickly roasted in a piquant tomato sauce. When shopping for fish, be flexible and select whatever looks freshest that day. You can also use halibut, swordfish or tuna in this recipe.

2 teaspoons olive oil
1 small onion, thinly sliced (½ cup)
2 garlic cloves, minced
½ teaspoon dried oregano
Dash crushed red pepper
1 (14½-oz.) can diced tomatoes, undrained
1 tablespoon drained capers, rinsed
1 lb. mahimahi fillet, cut into 4 portions
⅛ teaspoon salt
⅛ teaspoon freshly ground pepper

❶ Heat oven to 450°F. Coat glass pie plate or small baking dish with nonstick cooking spray.

❷ In medium saucepan, heat olive oil over medium heat. Add onion; cook, stirring often, 3 to 4 minutes or until softened and lightly browned. Add garlic, oregano and crushed red pepper; cook 30 seconds, stirring. Add tomatoes; mash with potato masher. Bring to a simmer. Cook 5 minutes. Stir in capers.

❸ Place mahimahi, skin-side down, in single layer in pie plate. Sprinkle with salt and pepper. Spoon tomato sauce over mahimahi. Bake, uncovered, 20 to 25 minutes or until fish flesh flakes and is opaque in center.

4 servings.
Preparation time: 15 minutes.
Ready to serve: 45 minutes.

Per serving: 145 calories, 3 g total fat (0.5 g saturated fat), 22 g protein, 6 g carbohydrate, 83 mg cholesterol, 568 mg sodium, 1 g fiber. **Star nutrients:** Vitamin B6 (25%), Vitamin C (28%), Niacin (35%). **Noteworthy nutrients:** Phosphorus (17%).

Roasted Fish & Potatoes

As illustrated by the long-term popularity of fish and chips, the pairing of fish and potatoes is timeless. But instead of deep-frying fish and potatoes, try roasting them. Roasting is a much more healthful cooking technique, and the juices from the fish flavor the bed of sliced potatoes.

1½ lb. all-purpose potatoes (4 to 5 medium), such as Yukon Gold, peeled, sliced ¼ inch thick*
4 teaspoons olive oil, divided
4 teaspoons chopped fresh rosemary or 1 teaspoon dried, divided
½ teaspoon salt, divided
¼ teaspoon freshly ground pepper, divided
1 tablespoon fresh lemon juice
1 lb. striped bass, sea bass, red snapper or halibut fillet, cut into 4 portions
1 tablespoon chopped fresh chives or parsley (optional)
Lemon wedges

❶ Heat oven to 450°F. Coat 9x13-inch baking dish with nonstick cooking spray.

❷ In baking dish, toss potatoes with 2 teaspoons of the olive oil, 2 teaspoons of the rosemary, ¼ teaspoon of the salt and ⅛ teaspoon of the pepper. Cover; bake 25 minutes. Meanwhile, in small bowl, stir together lemon juice, the remaining 2 teaspoons of the olive oil, the remaining 2 teaspoons of the rosemary, the remaining ¼ teaspoon of the salt and the remaining ⅛ teaspoon of the pepper.

❸ Lay fish pieces, skin-side down, over potatoes. Spoon lemon juice mixture over fish. Return to oven; bake, uncovered, an additional 10 to 20 minutes (depending on thickness of fish) or until fish flakes easily with fork and potatoes are tender.

❹ Sprinkle with chives, if desired; serve with lemon wedges.

4 servings.
Preparation time: 15 minutes.
Ready to serve: 40 minutes.

Per serving: 285 calories, 7.5 g total fat (1 g saturated fat), 24 g protein, 31 g carbohydrate, 91 mg cholesterol, 379 mg sodium, 3 g fiber. **Star nutrients:** Vitamin B6 (39%), Vitamin B12 (72%), Vitamin C (57%), Niacin (25%), Phosphorus (30%). **Noteworthy nutrients:** Copper (24%), Magnesium (21%), Thiamin (18%).

TIP   *To ensure uniform, thin potato slices and to save time, use a food processor fitted with medium slicing disc to slice potatoes.

Grilled Swordfish Steaks with Salsa

Swordfish steaks are great for grilling, but purchase whichever firm fish looks best at the fish market. Halibut and tuna steaks are also good grilling choices. You can also broil fish or use a ridged grill pan.

1 tablespoon lemon juice
1 tablespoon extra-virgin olive oil
2 garlic cloves, minced
¼ teaspoon salt

¼ teaspoon freshly ground pepper
⅛ teaspoon crushed red pepper
4 (4- to 5-oz.) swordfish steaks (¾ inch thick)
1 recipe *Tomato-Olive Salsa* (recipe follows)

❶ In shallow glass dish, whisk lemon juice, olive oil, garlic, salt, ground pepper and crushed red pepper. Add swordfish steaks; turn to coat. Cover; refrigerate 20 to 30 minutes.

❷ Meanwhile, heat grill. Prepare Tomato-Olive Salsa.

❸ Lightly oil grill rack. Place swordfish on gas grill over medium-high heat or on charcoal grill 4 to 6 inches from medium-hot coals. Cook 3 to 5 minutes per side or until fish flakes easily with fork. Top with Tomato-Olive Salsa.

4 servings. Preparation time: 30 minutes. Ready to serve: 40 minutes.

Per serving: 200 calories, 10.5 g total fat (2 g saturated fat), 23 g protein, 3 g carbohydrate, 44 mg cholesterol, 362 mg sodium, 1 g fiber.
Star nutrients: Vitamin B12 (33%), Niacin (53%), Phosphorus (31%). **Noteworthy nutrients:** Vitamin B6 (21%), Vitamin C (22%).

Tomato-Olive Salsa

1 medium tomato, seeded, diced (1 cup)
½ cup diced cucumber
2 tablespoons chopped green onions
2 tablespoons chopped pitted Kalamata olives*
2 tablespoons chopped fresh Italian parsley

1½ teaspoons extra-virgin olive oil
1½ teaspoons wine vinegar
Dash salt
Dash freshly ground pepper

❶ In medium bowl, combine tomato, cucumber, green onions, olives, parsley, olive oil, vinegar, salt and pepper; toss gently to mix. Serve within 1 hour.

1½ cups (4 servings). Preparation time: 15 minutes. Ready to serve: 15 minutes.

Per serving: 50 calories, 2.5 g total fat (0.5 g saturated fat), 0 g protein, 3 g carbohydrate, 0 mg cholesterol, 114 mg sodium, 1 g fiber.

TIMESAVING TIP *Look for pitted Kalamata olives in the deli section of your supermarket. If you can't find them already pitted, here is an easy away to pit them: Place olive on cutting board. Set flat side of chef's knife on olive. Tap knife with fist of your free hand. The olive will split and it will be easy to remove pit.

Sole with Mushrooms & Tomato

Here is proof that "less is more." A tiny bit of butter is all you need to give this simple fish dish an exquisite finish.

2 teaspoons olive oil
2 cups (6 oz.) sliced mushrooms
¼ cup chopped shallot (1 large)
1 medium tomato, seeded, diced
¼ cup dry white wine
1 teaspoon dried tarragon
¼ teaspoon salt
⅛ teaspoon freshly ground pepper
1 lb. sole, flounder or orange roughy fillets
2 teaspoons butter, cut into small pieces
2 tablespoons chopped fresh parsley

❶ Heat oven to 425°F. Coat 8x11½-inch (or similar) baking dish with nonstick cooking spray.

❷ In large nonstick skillet, heat olive oil over medium-high heat. Add mushrooms; cook, stirring often, 4 to 5 minutes or until lightly browned. Add shallot; cook 1 minute, stirring. Add tomato, wine, tarragon, salt and pepper; bring to a simmer. Remove from heat.

❸ Fold fish fillets in thirds; place, folded ends down, in baking dish. Spoon mushroom mixture over fillets. Dot with butter. Cover loosely with aluminum foil. Bake 20 to 30 minutes or until fish is opaque in center and flakes when poked with knife. Sprinkle with parsley.

4 servings.
Preparation time: 20 minutes.
Ready to serve: 45 minutes.

Per serving: 165 calories, 6.5 g total fat (2 g saturated fat), 21 g protein, 5 g carbohydrate, 57 mg cholesterol, 262 mg sodium, 1 g fiber. **Star nutrients:** Vitamin B12 (170%), Phosphorus (41%). **Noteworthy nutrients:** Vitamin C (16%), Niacin (21%), Riboflavin (17%).

Shrimp & Scallop Curry

Coconut milk balances the spices in a curry and contributes a delightful creaminess. However, coconut milk is high in saturated fat, so it should be used sparingly. Light coconut milk, which is available in most supermarkets, is a good alternative to full-fat coconut milk; stretching it with chicken broth reduces fat further. Serve this simple curry over basmati rice or rice noodles.

2 teaspoons canola oil
1 medium onion, chopped (1 cup)
2 teaspoons minced fresh ginger
2 garlic cloves, minced
1 jalapeño pepper, seeded, minced (1 tablespoon)
2 teaspoons curry powder
¾ cup light unsweetened coconut milk
¾ cup reduced-sodium chicken broth
1 teaspoon tomato paste
¼ teaspoon salt
8 oz. uncooked medium shrimp, peeled, deveined
8 oz. sea scallops, halved
2 tablespoons chopped fresh cilantro
Lime wedges

❶ In Dutch oven, heat canola oil over medium heat until hot. Add onion; cook 2 to 3 minutes or until softened. Add ginger, garlic, jalapeño and curry powder; cook 30 to 60 seconds or until fragrant, stirring. Add coconut milk, broth, tomato paste and salt; bring to a simmer. Cook, uncovered, 5 minutes.

❷ Add shrimp and scallops; reduce heat to low. Cover; cook about 5 minutes or until shrimp turns pink and scallops are opaque in the center. Stir in cilantro. Garnish with lime wedges.

4 (¾-cup) servings.
Preparation time: 15 minutes.
Ready to serve: 35 minutes.

Per serving: 210 calories, 9.5 g total fat (5.5 g saturated fat), 23 g protein, 9 g carbohydrate, 105 mg cholesterol, 427 mg sodium, 1 g fiber. **Star nutrients:** Vitamin B12 (26%), Phosphorus (27%). **Noteworthy nutrients:** Vitamin C (21%), Vitamin D (22%), Magnesium (16%).

Warm Salad of Shrimp, White Beans & Arugula

During the heat of summer, warm salads are especially satisfying because they combine the refreshing crunch of a salad with enough protein to make the meal substantial.

2 garlic cloves, crushed, peeled
¼ teaspoon salt
¼ teaspoon crushed red pepper
¼ cup plus 1 teaspoon extra-virgin olive oil, divided
3 tablespoons lemon juice
¼ teaspoon freshly ground pepper
1 (15½- or 19-oz.) can cannellini beans, drained, rinsed
⅓ cup finely diced red onion
6 cups arugula (one 6-oz. pkg. or 1 bunch), torn into bite-size pieces
12 oz. uncooked medium shrimp, peeled, deveined

❶ Using mortar and pestle or side of chef's knife, mash garlic, salt and crushed red pepper into a paste. Transfer to small bowl, if necessary. Add ¼ cup of the olive oil, lemon juice and pepper; whisk to blend.

❷ In medium bowl, combine beans and onion. Add 2 tablespoons of the lemon dressing, tossing to coat well. Place arugula in large bowl.

❸ In large nonstick skillet, heat the remaining 1 teaspoon of the olive oil over medium-high heat until hot. Add shrimp; cook about 3 minutes or until they turn pink. Immediately add shrimp to arugula. Add bean mixture and remaining lemon dressing; toss to coat well.

4 servings.
Preparation time: 20 minutes.
Ready to serve: 25 minutes.

Per serving: 320 calories, 17.5 g total fat (2.5 g saturated fat), 23 g protein, 20 g carbohydrate, 129 mg cholesterol, 508 mg sodium, 5 g fiber. **Star nutrients:** Vitamin D (32%). **Noteworthy nutrients:** Vitamin A (17%), Vitamin C (21%), Fiber (20%), Iron (23%), Phosphorus (20%).

Mustard-Glazed Salmon with Lentils

Salmon with lentils may sound like an unlikely combo, but it is actually a French bistro classic. This shortcut version utilizes canned lentil soup instead of dried lentils.

2 (19-oz.) cans lentil soup
1 lb. salmon fillet, cut into 4 portions
¼ teaspoon freshly ground pepper
3 tablespoons grainy mustard, such as country-style Dijon
2 teaspoons olive oil
1 bunch green onions, trimmed, chopped (about ⅔ cup)
½ teaspoon dried thyme
1 tablespoon fresh lemon juice
Lemon wedges

❶ Heat oven to 450°F. Line small baking pan with aluminum foil. Coat with nonstick cooking spray.

❷ Place lentil soup in sieve set over bowl; set aside to drain several minutes.

❸ Place salmon, skin-side down, in baking pan. Sprinkle with pepper. Spread mustard over top of salmon pieces. Bake 12 to 15 minutes or until salmon flakes easily with fork.*

❹ Meanwhile, in medium saucepan, heat olive oil over medium heat. Add green onions; cook 1 to 2 minutes or until softened, stirring. Add drained lentil soup and thyme; heat through. Stir in lemon juice. Spoon lentils onto plates. Top each serving with a piece of salmon. Garnish with lemon wedges.

4 servings.
Preparation time: 10 minutes.
Ready to serve: 25 minutes.

Per serving: 330 calories, 9.5 g total fat (1 g saturated fat), 34 g protein, 28 g carbohydrate, 59 mg cholesterol, 981 mg sodium, 9 g fiber. **Star nutrients:** Vitamin B12 (57%), Fiber (34%), Iron (31%), Niacin (48%), Phosphorus (29%). **Noteworthy nutrients:** Vitamin A (22%), Thiamin (24%).

TIP *To cook salmon in microwave, place in microwave-safe dish; cover with wax paper. Microwave at High for 5 to 7 minutes.

Shrimp Kabobs with Spanish Red Pepper Sauce

Until recently, people with cholesterol concerns avoided shrimp because of its high cholesterol content. However, shrimp are very low in calories and fat. It is believed that cholesterol in food does not raise blood cholesterol as much as saturated fat does. As long as shrimp are not deep-fried, enjoy them in moderation. In this recipe, they taste great quickly broiled and served with a Mediterranean-flavored dipping sauce.

1 recipe *Spanish Red Pepper Sauce* (page 162)
1 tablespoon olive oil
1 garlic clove, minced
¼ teaspoon salt
¼ teaspoon freshly ground pepper
1½ lb. uncooked extra-jumbo shrimp (16 to 20 count), peeled, deveined
Lemon wedges

❶ Prepare Spanish Red Pepper Sauce.

❷ Heat broiler. Coat broiler pan or baking sheet with nonstick cooking spray.

❸ In large bowl, combine olive oil, garlic, salt and pepper. Add shrimp; toss to coat well. Thread shrimp onto four (10- or 12-inch) skewers, connecting tail and head portion of each shrimp.*

❹ Broil kabobs 3 to 4 minutes per side or until shrimp turn pink. Serve with Spanish Red Pepper Sauce. Garnish with lemon wedges.

6 servings.
Preparation time: 30 minutes.
Ready to serve: 1 hour.

Per serving: 230 calories, 10.5 g total fat (1.5 g saturated fat), 26 g protein, 8 g carbohydrate, 172 mg cholesterol, 843 mg sodium, 2 g fiber. **Star nutrients:** Vitamin C (41%), Vitamin D (43%). **Noteworthy nutrients:** Vitamin B12 (22%), Copper (23%), Iron (21%), Magnesium (18%), Niacin (19%), Phosphorus (29%).

TIP   *If using wooden skewers, soak them in cold water at least 30 minutes before using to prevent scorching.

Spanish Red Pepper Sauce

This sauce for Shrimp Kabobs is also delicious with grilled tuna, chicken and vegetables.

⅓ cup (1¼ oz.) slivered almonds, toasted*
1 (½-inch-thick) baguette slice, lightly toasted
1 garlic clove, crushed, peeled
¼ teaspoon salt
1 (7-oz.) jar roasted red bell peppers, drained, rinsed
1 medium tomato, seeded, cut into chunks (1 cup)
1 tablespoon extra-virgin olive oil
1 tablespoon wine vinegar
½ teaspoon paprika
¼ teaspoon crushed red pepper
¼ teaspoon freshly ground pepper
3 tablespoons chopped fresh parsley

❶ In food processor, combine almonds, baguette slice, garlic and salt; process until finely ground. Add roasted bell peppers, tomato, olive oil, vinegar, paprika, crushed red pepper and pepper; process until smooth. Transfer to bowl; stir in parsley. Serve at room temperature.

1½ cups (6 servings).
Preparation time: 20 minutes.
Ready to serve: 20 minutes.

Per serving: 90 calories, 6.5 g total fat (0.5 g saturated fat), 3 g protein, 6 g carbohydrate, 0 mg cholesterol, 578 mg sodium, 2 g fiber.

MAKE AHEAD Cover and refrigerate for up to 2 days.

TIP *To toast almonds, place in a dry skillet. Cook, stirring constantly, over medium-low heat 2 minutes or until light golden and fragrant. Transfer to a small bowl to cool.

Provençal Fish Stew

Fennel seeds and a hint of orange peel give this simple fish stew a distinctive flavor. Accompany with orzo.

2 teaspoons olive oil
1½ cups sliced leeks* (2 medium)
3 garlic cloves, minced
1 teaspoon fennel seeds
⅛ teaspoon crushed red pepper
½ cup dry white wine
1 (14½-oz.) can diced tomatoes, undrained
2 (3-inch-long) strips orange peel
1 lb. halibut fillet, monkfish fillet or swordfish, trimmed, cut into 1¼-inch chunks
2 tablespoons chopped fresh parsley
⅛ teaspoon freshly ground pepper

❶ In large nonstick skillet, heat olive oil over medium-low heat. Add leeks; cook, stirring often, 4 to 6 minutes or until softened but not browned. Add garlic, fennel and crushed red pepper; cook 30 seconds, stirring. Add wine; increase heat to medium-high. Bring to a simmer. Cook about 1½ minutes or until most of the liquid has evaporated. Add tomatoes; mash with potato masher. Add orange peel; bring to a simmer.

❷ Add fish; reduce heat to medium-low. Cover; cook about 10 minutes or until fish is opaque in center. Discard orange peel. Stir in parsley and pepper.

4 (1-cup) servings.
Preparation time: 20 minutes.
Ready to serve: 30 minutes.

Per serving: 210 calories, 5 g total fat (0.5 g saturated fat), 25 g protein, 10 g carbohydrate, 36 mg cholesterol, 402 mg sodium, 2 g fiber. **Star nutrients:** Vitamin B6 (25%), Vitamin C (39%), Vitamin D (170%), Magnesium (28%), Niacin (34%), Phosphorus (27%). **Noteworthy nutrients:** Vitamin B12 (22%), Calcium (15%).

TIP *Leeks harbor a fair amount of grit between their layers, so it is important to clean them thoroughly. Trim the fuzzy root end and green stems. Use only the white and pale green portions. With a sharp knife, cut several incisions in the leek's stem end to open it up like a fan. Soak the leek in a large bowl of water several minutes, then swish to dislodge dirt. Repeat this process until the water runs clear and no trace of grit remains between layers.

Sole Florentine

The term Florentine simply means "with spinach." Setting fish on a bed of spinach and topping with a Parmesan-flavored "cream" sauce is an easy way to dress up delicate fish fillets such as sole or haddock. It is also a great way to slip an extra vegetable serving into your dinner.

1 teaspoon freshly grated lemon peel*
1¾ cups low-fat (1%) milk, divided
3 tablespoons all-purpose flour
1 cup (2 oz.) freshly grated Parmesan cheese, divided
¼ teaspoon salt
⅛ teaspoon freshly ground pepper
Dash cayenne pepper

1 (16-oz.) or 1½ (10-oz.) pkg. frozen spinach
1 lb. sole, haddock, flounder or orange roughy fillets
2 teaspoons fresh lemon juice
3 tablespoons Italian-style bread crumbs
1 teaspoon olive oil

❶ Heat oven to 425°F. Coat 8x11½-inch (2-quart) baking dish with nonstick cooking spray; sprinkle with lemon peel.

❷ In small bowl, whisk ¼ cup of the milk and flour until smooth. In heavy medium saucepan, heat the remaining 1½ cups milk over medium heat until steaming. Add flour mixture; cook 2 to 3 minutes or until sauce bubbles and thickens, whisking constantly. Remove from heat. Stir in ¾ cup of the Parmesan cheese, salt, pepper and cayenne pepper.

❸ Meanwhile, cook spinach according to package directions. Drain; refresh under cold running water. Press out excess moisture.

❹ Spread spinach over bottom of baking dish. Arrange fish fillets, slightly overlapping, over spinach. Sprinkle with lemon juice. Spoon Parmesan cheese sauce evenly over fish. Sprinkle the remaining ¼ cup of the Parmesan cheese over sauce. In small bowl, mix bread crumbs and olive oil; sprinkle over top of sauce.

❺ Bake fish 30 to 35 minutes or until golden and bubbly and fish flakes when poked with small, sharp knife.

4 servings.
Preparation time: 30 minutes.
Ready to serve: 1 hour.

Per serving: 330 calories, 11.5 g total fat (6 g saturated fat), 38 g protein, 19 g carbohydrate, 76 mg cholesterol, 986 mg sodium, 4 g fiber. **Star nutrients:** Vitamin A (185%), Vitamin B12 (182%), Vitamin C (51%), Calcium (62%), Folate (41%), Magnesium (32%), Phosphorus (71%), Riboflavin (32%. **Noteworthy nutrients:** Fiber (16%), Iron (22%), Niacin (16%), Thiamin (17%), Zinc (16%).

TIP   *Sprinkling the baking dish with freshly grated lemon peel will contribute a delightful and subtle lemon fragrance to the dish.

Broiled Teriyaki Salmon

Salmon is most likely one of the most popular fish in America today. High-quality salmon is widely available in supermarkets and fish markets across the country. And as awareness of the benefits of omega-3 fatty acids has increased, salmon has become a standby for family meals. It is useful to have a good repertoire of salmon recipes. One of the easiest ways to cook salmon is to marinate it and then run it under the broiler.

3 tablespoons reduced-sodium soy sauce
1 tablespoon sugar
1 tablespoon medium-dry sherry or orange juice
1 teaspoon toasted sesame oil or canola oil
1½ teaspoons minced fresh ginger

1 garlic clove, minced
1 lb. salmon fillet, cut into 4 portions
2 tablespoons chopped green onions
1 tablespoon sesame seeds, toasted*
Lime or lemon wedges

❶ In small bowl, combine soy sauce, sugar, sherry, sesame oil, ginger and garlic; stir to dissolve sugar. Place salmon in shallow glass dish. Spoon 2 tablespoons of the soy sauce mixture over salmon; turn to coat. Cover; refrigerate 20 to 30 minutes. Reserve remaining soy sauce mixture.

❷ Heat broiler. Line broiler pan or baking sheet with aluminum foil; coat with nonstick cooking spray.

❸ Place salmon, skin-side down, on broiler pan. Broil, 4 to 6 inches from heat source, 8 to 10 minutes or until salmon is opaque in center and flakes when poked with knife. If salmon pieces are thick, carefully turn them onto each side to cook for a few minutes. Drizzle reserved soy sauce mixture over salmon. Sprinkle with green onions and sesame seeds. Garnish with lime wedges.

4 servings.
Preparation time: 15 minutes.
Ready to serve: 55 minutes.

Per serving: 185 calories, 6 g total fat (1 g saturated fat), 24 g protein, 6 g carbohydrate, 59 mg cholesterol, 456 mg sodium, 0 g fiber. **Star nutrients:** Vitamin B12 (57%), Niacin (40%), Phosphorus (28%). **Noteworthy nutrients:** Thiamin (15%).

TIP   *To toast sesame seeds, heat small skillet over medium-low heat. Add sesame seeds; stir continuously until seeds are lightly browned, 2 to 3 minutes.

VARIATION   **Broiled Lemon-&-Garlic Salmon**

In shallow glass dish, combine 2 tablespoons lemon juice, 1 tablespoon olive oil, ½ teaspoon honey, 2 cloves minced garlic, ¼ teaspoon salt and ¼ teaspoon freshly ground pepper. Add 1 lb. salmon, cut into 4 portions; turn to coat. Cover; refrigerate 20 to 30 minutes. Broil salmon 8 to 10 minutes or until opaque in center. Sprinkle with 2 tablespoons snipped fresh chives or chopped fresh parsley. Garnish with lemon wedges.

Meatless Main Dishes

An occasional vegetarian meal can be a delicious way to help you toward your goal of eating more plant foods. The hearty vegetarian recipes in this chapter, featuring tofu, beans, legumes and whole grains, are high in plant proteins and prepared in ways that will surprise, delight and satisfy you.

Tofu "Steaks" with Greek Flavors

Tofu gets a bad rap because of its bland flavor. But when tofu absorbs the flavors of a marinade, it undergoes an extraordinary transformation. The trick to making delicious tofu is to marinate it and serve it with a flavorful sauce. Tofu is often paired with Asian seasonings, but it is also delicious with assertive Mediterranean flavors. During the colder months, cook tofu in the skillet and serve it with a hot tomato sauce; throughout summer, grill it and top with a chunky tomato salad.

¼ cup lemon juice
1 tablespoon plus 1 teaspoon extra-virgin olive oil, divided
4 garlic cloves, minced
2 teaspoons dried oregano
½ teaspoon salt
¼ teaspoon freshly ground pepper
1 (14- or 16-oz.) pkg. firm regular tofu, drained, patted dry
1 recipe *Quick Tomato Sauce with Olives* (page 170)

❶ In small bowl, whisk lemon juice, 1 tablespoon of the olive oil, garlic, oregano, salt and pepper. Cut tofu in half crosswise; cut each piece in half horizontally. Pat each piece thoroughly dry; place in shallow glass dish. Pour lemon juice mixture over tofu; turn to coat. Cover; refrigerate 1 hour or up to 8 hours.

❷ Meanwhile, prepare Quick Tomato Sauce with Olives.

❸ Remove tofu from marinade, reserving marinade. In large nonstick skillet, heat the remaining 1 teaspoon of the olive oil over medium-high heat. Add tofu pieces to pan; cook 3 to 4 minutes per side or until nicely browned, basting occasionally with reserved marinade. Serve tofu "steaks" topped with sauce.

4 servings.
Preparation time: 20 minutes.
Ready to serve: 1 hour, 20 minutes.

Per serving: 180 calories, 11.5 g total fat (1.5 g saturated fat), 11 g protein, 9 mg carbohydrate, 0 mg cholesterol, 670 mg sodium, 2 g fiber. **Star nutrients:** Vitamin C (46%). **Noteworthy nutrients:** Calcium (23%).

> VARIATION   **Grilled Tofu "Steaks" with Tomato-Olive Salsa**
>
> Use the same marinade, but substitute Tomato-Olive Salsa (page 154) for Quick Tomato Sauce with Olives. In Step 3, heat grill. Lightly oil grill rack. Place tofu pieces on gas grill over medium-high heat or on charcoal grill 4 to 6 inches from medium-hot coals. Cover grill; cook tofu 3 to 4 minutes per side or until nicely browned, basting occasionally with reserved marinade. Serve tofu "steaks" topped with salsa.

Quick Tomato Sauce with Olives

This simple sauce for Tofu "Steaks" with Greek Flavors is also good with fish or pasta.

2 teaspoons olive oil
2 garlic cloves, minced
Dash crushed red pepper
1 (14½-oz.) can diced tomatoes, undrained

2 tablespoons coarsely chopped pitted
  Kalamata olives
3 tablespoons chopped fresh Italian parsley
⅛ teaspoon freshly ground pepper

❶ In medium saucepan, heat olive oil over low heat until warm. Add garlic and crushed red pepper; cook, stirring frequently, 1 to 2 minutes or until garlic is softened and fragrant, but not colored. Add tomatoes; mash with potato masher. Bring to a simmer. Cook, uncovered, over medium-low heat 10 minutes or until slightly thickened, stirring and mashing occasionally. Add olives; simmer 1 minute. Remove from heat; stir in parsley and pepper.

1½ cups (4 servings).
Preparation time: 10 minutes. Ready to serve: 20 minutes.

Per serving: 185 calories, 11 g total fat (1.5 g saturated fat), 4 g protein, 18 g carbohydrate, 0 mg cholesterol, 1476 mg sodium, 4 g fiber.

MAKE AHEAD Cover and refrigerate for up to 2 days.

Cilantro-Parsley Sauce

This versatile North African sauce is great with Roasted Vegetables and also complements grilled fish and poultry.

1½ cups lightly packed fresh cilantro leaves
1½ cups lightly packed fresh Italian parsley leaves
3 garlic cloves, peeled, crushed
1 tablespoon ground cumin
2 teaspoons paprika
¾ teaspoon salt

Dash cayenne pepper
½ cup reduced-sodium chicken broth or
  vegetable broth
⅓ cup low-fat firm silken tofu
2 tablespoons lemon juice
1 tablespoon extra-virgin olive oil

❶ In food processor, combine cilantro, parsley, garlic, cumin, paprika, salt and cayenne pepper; process until finely chopped. Add broth, tofu, lemon juice and olive oil; process until mixture forms creamy sauce, stopping to scrape down sides of bowl several times. Place sauce in small saucepan; heat over medium heat, stirring, until heated through but not bubbling.

1 cup (4 servings). Preparation time: 15 minutes. Ready to serve: 15 minutes.

Per serving: 275 calories, 17.5 g total fat (2.5 g saturated fat), 14 g protein, 18 g carbohydrate, 0 mg cholesterol, 2038 mg sodium, 7 g fiber.

MAKE AHEAD Prepare recipe. Place piece of plastic wrap directly on sauce's surface to prevent discoloration; refrigerate for up to 2 days.

Roasted Vegetables with Cilantro-Parsley Sauce & Couscous

This elegant entree features roasted vegetables and a spicy herb sauce that is sure to please both meat lovers and vegetarians alike.

1 small eggplant (¾ lb.), cut into ⅜-inch-thick slices
1 medium red bell pepper, cut lengthwise into 12 wedges
1 medium zucchini, cut into ⅜-inch-thick ovals
1 large red onion, cut into ⅜-inch-thick slices
6 plum tomatoes, cored, halved lengthwise
2 teaspoons olive oil
¼ teaspoon salt
¼ teaspoon freshly ground pepper
1 recipe *Cilantro-Parsley Sauce* (page 170)
1 cup couscous, preferably whole wheat
⅓ cup (1¼ oz.) slivered almonds, toasted*

❶ Heat oven to 450°F. Coat large roasting pan or rimmed baking sheet with nonstick cooking spray.

❷ In pan, toss eggplant, bell pepper, zucchini, onion and tomatoes with olive oil, salt and pepper. Bake 25 to 30 minutes or until vegetables are tender and start to brown, stirring several times.

❸ Meanwhile, prepare Cilantro-Parsley Sauce.

❹ Prepare couscous according to package directions. Mound warm couscous in center of individual plates; surround with roasted vegetables. Drizzle sauce over vegetables and couscous. Sprinkle with almonds.

4 servings.
Preparation time: 30 minutes.
Ready to serve: 45 minutes.

Per serving: 445 calories, 14 g total fat (1.5 g saturated fat), 17 g protein, 70 g carbohydrate, 0 mg cholesterol, 670 mg sodium, 16 g fiber. **Star nutrients:** Vitamin A (96%), Vitamin C (237%), Fiber (65%), Folate (27%), Iron (39%), Magnesium (23%), Riboflavin (26%). **Noteworthy nutrients:** Vitamin B6 (22%), Vitamin E (21%), Calcium (17%), Copper (21%), Phosphorus (19%), Thiamin (19%).

TIP *To toast almonds, place in a dry skillet. Cook, stirring constantly, over medium-low heat 2 minutes or until light golden and fragrant. Transfer to a small bowl to cool.

Quick Vegetarian Chili

The combination of beans and barley makes this easy chili rich in fiber.

2 teaspoons canola oil
1 medium onion, chopped (1 cup)
1 medium red bell pepper, diced (1½ cups)
3 garlic cloves, minced
1 (4½-oz.) can chopped mild green chiles
2 teaspoons chili powder
1 teaspoon ground cumin
1 teaspoon dried oregano
1 (14½-oz.) can reduced-sodium chicken broth or 1¾ cups vegetable broth
¼ cup water
1 (14½-oz.) can diced tomatoes, undrained
1 (15½- or 19-oz.) can black beans, drained, rinsed
⅔ cup quick-cooking barley
3 tablespoons chopped fresh cilantro
Optional garnishes: salsa, preferably green; reduced-fat sour cream; Baked Tortilla Crisps (page 26) or
  commercial low-fat baked tortilla chips; lime wedges

❶ In Dutch oven, heat canola oil over medium-high heat. Add onion and bell pepper; cook about
   3 minutes or until softened, stirring often. Add garlic, green chiles, chili powder, cumin and
   oregano; cook 1 minute or until fragrant, stirring. Add broth, water, tomatoes, beans and
   barley; bring to a simmer. Cover; reduce heat to low. Simmer about 20 minutes or until barley
   is tender and chili has thickened. Stir in cilantro. Serve with your choice of garnishes.

6 (1-cup) servings.
Preparation time: 20 minutes.
Ready to serve: 40 minutes.

MAKE AHEAD Cover and refrigerate for up to 2 days or freeze for up to 3 months.

Per serving (without garnishes): 175 calories, 3 g total fat (0 g saturated fat), 8 g protein, 30 g carbohydrate, 0 mg cholesterol, 627 mg sodium, 8 g fiber. **Star nutrients:** Vitamin A (32%), Vitamin C (100%), Fiber (33%). **Noteworthy nutrients:** Iron (15%).

How to Cook Dried Beans

Canned beans are certainly convenient, but it is more economical to cook dried beans from scratch. Furthermore, canned beans are high in sodium; you take control when you cook them yourself. And since beans absorb the flavor of the onion, garlic and herbs in the cooking liquid, home-cooked results are more flavorful. The lengthy cooking time required prevents most of us from enjoying home-cooked beans regularly, but they require very little attention during cooking. Here are instructions for cooking them on the stovetop and in a slow-cooker.

To prepare beans: Soak 2 cups dried black beans, kidney beans, great northern beans, navy beans or pinto beans in cold water at least 6 hours or overnight. Alternatively, use the quick-soak method: Place beans in large pot with enough water to cover by 2 inches. Bring to a boil over medium-high heat. Remove from heat; let stand 1 hour.

To cook beans on the stovetop: Drain beans; place in Dutch oven. Add 1 chopped onion, 4 cloves minced garlic, 1 teaspoon dried thyme and 1 bay leaf. Pour in 5 cups boiling water. Cook, covered, over low heat 1½ hours. Add ½ teaspoon salt. Cook, covered, an additional 15 to 30 minutes or until beans are tender. Drain; reserve cooking liquid for soups if desired. Discard bay leaf.

To cook beans in a slow-cooker: Drain beans; place in 3½-quart slow-cooker. Add 1 chopped onion, 4 cloves minced garlic, 1 teaspoon dried thyme and 1 bay leaf. Pour in 5 cups boiling water. Cook, covered, on High for about 3½ hours. Add ½ teaspoon salt; cook an additional 15 to 30 minutes or until beans are tender. Drain; reserve cooking liquid for soups if desired. Discard bay leaf.

Makes 5 cups cooked beans.

MAKE AHEAD Cover and refrigerate cooked beans for up to 2 days or freeze for up to 3 months.

TIP If you are using home-cooked beans in a recipe that calls for canned beans, substitute 1½ cups cooked beans for 1 (15-oz.) can beans and 1¾ cups cooked beans for 1 (19-oz.) can beans.

Black Bean & Sweet Potato Burritos

Rich-tasting sweet potato binds the bean and vegetable filling in this vegetarian burrito. The dish is very flavorful and satisfying—no one will miss the meat.

10 (7-inch) flour tortillas
2 teaspoons canola oil
1 medium onion, chopped (1 cup)
2 garlic cloves, minced
4 teaspoons ground cumin
½ teaspoon dried oregano
¾ cup vegetable broth or reduced-sodium chicken broth
1 medium sweet potato, peeled, diced (3 cups)
1 (14½-oz.) can mild green chile-seasoned diced tomatoes, undrained
1 (15½- or 19-oz.) can black beans, drained, rinsed
¾ cup frozen corn
¼ cup chopped fresh cilantro
1 tablespoon fresh lime juice
⅛ teaspoon freshly ground pepper
⅔ cup (2 oz.) grated pepper Jack or Monterey Jack cheese
⅓ cup low-fat sour cream

❶ Heat oven to 325°F. Wrap tortillas in aluminum foil; heat in oven 15 to 20 minutes or until steaming.

❷ Meanwhile, in large nonstick skillet, heat canola oil over medium heat. Add onion; cook, stirring often, 2 to 3 minutes or until softened. Add garlic, cumin and oregano; cook 30 seconds, stirring. Add broth and sweet potato; bring to a simmer. Cover; cook 5 minutes.

❸ Add tomatoes, beans and corn; return to a simmer. Cover; cook an additional 5 to 10 minutes or until sweet potato is tender. Use potato masher to mash about one-fourth of the vegetable mixture in skillet. (This will thicken burrito filling and make it cohesive.) Stir mashed and unmashed portions together. Stir in cilantro, lime juice and pepper.

❹ To serve, spoon about ½ cup of the sweet potato filling down center of each warm tortilla. Sprinkle with about 1 tablespoon cheese. Fold in edges of tortilla, then fold one side over filling and wrap up burrito. Serve with sour cream for dipping.

5 servings.
Preparation time: 20 minutes. Ready to serve: 40 minutes.

Per serving: 450 calories, 13 g total fat (4.5 g saturated fat), 16 g protein, 67 g carbohydrate, 16 mg cholesterol, 1041 mg sodium, 10 g fiber. **Star nutrients:** Vitamin A (120%), Vitamin C (33%), Calcium (26%), Fiber (39%), Folate (23%), Iron (27%).
Noteworthy nutrients: Vitamin B6 (15%), Copper (17%), Niacin (19%), Phosphorus (20%), Riboflavin (20%).

Lentil & Orzo Casserole

Combining lentils and orzo makes this meatless casserole particularly satisfying, and good for feeding a crowd.

CASEROLE

2 teaspoons olive oil
2 medium onions, chopped (2 cups)
2 medium carrots, diced (1 cup)
6 garlic cloves, minced
Dash crushed red pepper
1 cup brown lentils, rinsed, sorted
1 teaspoon dried thyme
3 cups reduced-sodium chicken broth or
  vegetable broth
1 cup (6 oz.) orzo
1 (14½-oz.) can diced tomatoes, undrained
¼ teaspoon salt
¼ teaspoon freshly ground pepper
1¼ cups boiling water

TOPPING

⅓ cup Italian-style bread crumbs
2 tablespoons chopped fresh parsley
1 teaspoon olive oil
½ cup (1 oz.) freshly grated Parmesan cheese

❶ In large saucepan, heat 2 teaspoons of the olive oil over medium-high heat until hot. Add onions and carrots; cook, stirring often, 4 to 6 minutes or until onions are softened. Add garlic and crushed red pepper; cook 30 seconds, stirring. Add lentils and thyme; stir to coat. Add broth; bring to a simmer. Reduce heat to low. Cover; cook 20 minutes.

❷ Meanwhile, heat oven to 350°F. Coat 3-quart deep casserole with nonstick cooking spray.

❸ Transfer lentil mixture to casserole. Add orzo, tomatoes, salt and pepper; mix well. Pour in boiling water. Cover with aluminum foil. Bake 30 minutes or until lentils and orzo are almost tender.

❹ Meanwhile, in small bowl, stir together bread crumbs, parsley and 1 teaspoon olive oil.

❺ Uncover casserole; stir to redistribute ingredients. Sprinkle with Parmesan cheese, then bread crumb mixture. Bake, uncovered, an additional 15 to 20 minutes or until bubbly and crusty.

8 servings. Preparation time: 15 minutes. Ready to serve: 1 hour, 35 minutes.

Per serving: 265 calories, 4.5 g total fat (1.5 g saturated fat), 15 g protein, 41 g carbohydrate, 5 mg cholesterol, 580 mg sodium, 10 g fiber. **Star nutrients:** Vitamin A (89%), Vitamin C (35%), Fiber (40%), Folate (41%), Thiamin (27%). **Noteworthy nutrients:** Calcium (16%), Copper (16%), Iron (22%), Niacin (16%), Phosphorus (23%).

MAKE AHEAD Casserole can be made ahead through Step 4. Cover and refrigerate for up to 2 days. Reheat on stovetop, adding enough water to achieve stew-like consistency. Return to casserole and proceed as directed in Step 5.

Vegetable Stew with Poached Eggs

Using basic ingredients that you might already have on hand, this easy vegetable stew with poached eggs makes a great supper or brunch dish. Serve with grilled or toasted whole wheat country bread, rubbed with garlic and drizzled with olive oil.

2 teaspoons olive oil
3 cups frozen pepper stir-fry vegetables
4 garlic cloves, minced
⅛ teaspoon crushed red pepper
1 (28-oz.) or 2 (14½-oz.) cans diced tomatoes, undrained
1 (15½- or 19-oz.) can garbanzo beans, drained, rinsed
⅛ teaspoon freshly ground pepper
4 eggs
Dash paprika

❶ In large nonstick skillet, heat olive oil over medium-high heat until hot. Add stir-fry vegetables; cook, stirring often, 4 to 6 minutes or until softened. Add garlic and crushed red pepper; cook 30 seconds, stirring. Add tomatoes, garbanzo beans and pepper; bring to a simmer. Cook, uncovered, about 10 minutes or until slightly thickened, stirring occasionally.

❷ Crack eggs; drop each into separate quadrant of the stew, taking care not to break yolks. Cover skillet; cook over medium-low heat 5 to 7 minutes or until eggs are set. Sprinkle eggs with paprika. With slotted spoon or egg lifter, transfer an egg with vegetable mixture to each plate. Spoon additional vegetable mixture and sauce around eggs.

4 servings.
Preparation time: 10 minutes.
Ready to serve: 30 minutes.

Per serving: 280 calories, 8.5 g total fat (2 g saturated fat), 18 g protein, 32 g carbohydrate, 213 mg cholesterol, 1,025 mg sodium, 7 g fiber. **Star nutrients:** Vitamin C (108%), Fiber (28%). **Noteworthy nutrients:** Vitamin A (23%), Calcium (21%), Iron (16%), Riboflavin (15%).

Falafel with Flaxseeds

Vegetarian patties called falafel were popular in the Middle East long before commercial veggie burgers were introduced in this country. In the following version, flaxseeds help bind the patties, contributing a nutty flavor and appealing crunch. Traditionally, the patties are deep-fried. However, to create a crispy crust without deep-frying, brown patties on one side in a nonstick skillet, flip them over onto a baking sheet and finish them in a hot oven.

⅓ cup plus 1 tablespoon flaxseeds, divided
1 (15½- or 19-oz.) can garbanzo beans, drained, rinsed
¼ cup chopped fresh parsley
2 garlic cloves, minced
1 teaspoon ground cumin
¼ teaspoon ground coriander
½ teaspoon salt
¼ teaspoon cayenne pepper

2 tablespoons lemon juice
¼ cup fine dry bread crumbs
1 egg white
2 teaspoons olive oil
1 recipe *Mediterranean Chopped Salad* (page 180)
4 (6-inch) whole wheat pita breads
8 lettuce leaves
½ cup plain nonfat yogurt

❶ Heat oven to 450°F. Coat baking sheet with nonstick cooking spray. In clean dry coffee grinder or blender, grind ⅓ cup of the flaxseeds.

❷ In food processor, pulse garbanzo beans several times just until coarsely chopped. Add parsley, garlic, cumin, coriander, salt, cayenne pepper, lemon juice and ground flaxseeds; pulse until mixture is cohesive, but still retains some texture. Using scant ¼ cup per patty, form mixture into 8 (½-inch-thick) oval patties.

❸ In shallow dish, combine bread crumbs and the remaining 1 tablespoon of the flaxseeds. In medium bowl, beat egg white with fork until frothy. Dip each patty into egg white; coat with bread crumb mixture.

❹ In large nonstick skillet, heat olive oil over medium-high heat until hot. Add patties; cook about 2 minutes or until underside is browned. Turn patties over onto baking sheet. Bake patties 15 to 20 minutes or until golden brown on both sides and heated through. Meanwhile, prepare Mediterranean Chopped Salad.

❺ To serve, cut each pita in half to form 2 pockets. Line each pocket with lettuce leaf and fill with a patty. Garnish falafel with Mediterranean Chopped Salad and yogurt.

4 servings. Preparation time: 25 minutes. Ready to serve: 45 minutes.

Per serving: 465 calories, 14.5 g total fat (1.5 g saturated fat), 20 g protein, 69 g carbohydrate, 1 mg cholesterol, 1,208 mg sodium, 16 g fiber. **Star Nutrients:** Vitamin C (40%), Fiber (63%), Folate (28%), Magnesium (33%), Phosphorus (29%). **Noteworthy nutrients:** Vitamin A (16%), Vitamin B6 (23%), Calcium (19%), Copper (23%), Thiamin (24%), Zinc (16%).

MAKE AHEAD Prepare patties through Step 4. Cover and refrigerate for up to 2 days.

Mediterranean Chopped Salad

This versatile salad is full of texture and flavor. Use it to jazz up any pita sandwich, or to top grilled fish.

1 small tomato, diced
½ cup diced cucumber
1 green onion, chopped
1 jalapeño pepper, seeded, minced
2 tablespoons chopped fresh cilantro or parsley
2 teaspoons lemon juice
2 teaspoons extra-virgin olive oil
¼ teaspoon salt
⅛ teaspoon freshly ground pepper

❶ In medium bowl, combine tomato, cucumber, green onion, jalapeño, cilantro, lemon juice, olive oil, salt and pepper; toss gently to mix. Serve within 1 hour.

1⅓ cups.
Preparation time: 10 minutes.
Ready to serve: 10 minutes.

Per serving: 32 calories, 2.5 g total fat (0.5 g saturated fat), 1 g protein, 3 g carbohydrate, 0 mg cholesterol, 150 mg sodium, 1 g fiber.

Grilled Polenta with White Bean Salad

Keep a tube of prepared polenta on hand so you can put together this speedy summer supper at a moment's notice. A simple salad, made with canned white beans, tomatoes and fresh basil, rounds out the meal and boosts protein in this vegetarian entree.

2 tablespoons plus 2 teaspoons extra-virgin olive oil, divided
2 tablespoons wine vinegar
¼ teaspoon salt
⅛ teaspoon freshly ground pepper
1 (19-oz.) can cannellini beans, drained, rinsed
2 medium tomatoes, seeded, diced
1 bunch green onions, trimmed, chopped (⅔ cup)
⅓ cup chopped fresh basil
¼ cup pitted Kalamata olives, chopped
1 (16-oz.) tube prepared polenta,* cut into ½-inch-thick slices

❶ Heat grill.

❷ In large bowl, whisk 2 tablespoons of the olive oil, vinegar, salt and pepper. Add beans, tomatoes, green onions, basil and olives; toss to coat.

❸ Place polenta slices on baking sheet. Brush the remaining 2 teaspoons of the olive oil over both sides of polenta. Lightly oil grill rack. Place polenta slices on gas grill over high heat or on charcoal grill 4 to 6 inches from hot coals. Cover grill; cook polenta 3 to 5 minutes per side or until lightly browned. Divide white bean salad among four plates. Arrange grilled polenta slices over salad.

4 servings.
Preparation time: 20 minutes.
Ready to serve: 30 minutes.

Per serving: 290 calories, 10 g total fat (1.5 g saturated fat), 8 g protein, 39 g carbohydrate, 0 mg cholesterol, 856 mg sodium, 7 g fiber. **Star nutrients:** Vitamin C (35%), Fiber (30%). **Noteworthy nutrients:** Vitamin A (18%), Iron (17%).

INGREDIENT NOTE *You can find logs of prepared polenta in a refrigerated case, usually in the produce department, in large supermarkets, specialty stores and Italian markets.

North African Squash Stew with Couscous

This combination of squash, garbanzo beans, greens and spices makes a particularly satisfying and nutritious meatless dish.

2 teaspoons olive oil
2 medium onions, slivered (2 cups)
3 garlic cloves, minced
¾ teaspoon ground ginger
¾ teaspoon ground turmeric
2 (14½-oz.) cans reduced-sodium chicken broth or 3½ cups vegetable broth
2 lb. butternut squash* (1 medium), seeded, peeled, cut into ¾-inch cubes (5 cups)
1 (19-oz.) can garbanzo beans, drained, rinsed

Dash saffron threads, crumbled, or ⅛ teaspoon ground turmeric
1 cinnamon stick
1 (14½-oz.) can diced tomatoes, undrained
1 (1-lb.) bunch Swiss chard, stems trimmed, cut into ½-inch-wide ribbons (6 cups)
½ cup raisins
1 cup couscous, preferably whole wheat
¼ teaspoon freshly ground pepper

❶ In Dutch oven, heat olive oil over medium heat until hot. Add onions; cook 3 to 5 minutes or until softened and light golden, stirring often. Add garlic, ginger and ¾ teaspoon turmeric; cook, 30 seconds, stirring. Add broth, squash, garbanzo beans, saffron and cinnamon stick; bring to a simmer. Reduce heat to low. Cover; simmer 8 minutes or until squash is almost tender.

❷ Add tomatoes, Swiss chard and raisins. Increase heat to medium. Cook, covered, 5 to 15 minutes or until squash is tender and Swiss chard has wilted, stirring once or twice.

❸ Meanwhile, prepare couscous according to package directions. When stew is ready, discard cinnamon stick. Stir in pepper. Serve stew over couscous.

8 (1½-cup) servings.
Preparation time: 15 minutes. Ready to serve: 50 minutes.

Per serving: 295 calories, 3 g total fat (0.5 g saturated fat), 12 g protein, 61 g carbohydrate, 0 mg cholesterol, 659 mg sodium, 11 g fiber. **Star nutrients:** Vitamin A (216%), Vitamin C (98%), Fiber (43%). **Noteworthy nutrients:** Vitamin B6 (16%), Calcium (17%), Iron (23%), Magnesium (23%).

MAKE AHEAD This stew reheats well; be careful not to overcook the vegetables. Cover and refrigerate for up to 2 days.

TIMESAVING TIP *Purchase cubed, peeled squash in the produce section of your supermarket. In some stores you can find frozen, cubed squash (packaged in a plastic bag rather than frozen in a block) in the freezer section. Both are convenient options; use 5 cups.

Mediterranean-Flavored Lentil Burgers

These savory veggie burgers are rich in fiber and folic acid. Arborio rice has a sticky quality when cooked, so it does an excellent job of binding the patties. Because the lentils take a little while to cook, it is worth making a batch of patties when you have time and storing extras in the refrigerator or freezer.

6 teaspoons olive oil, divided
1 medium onion, chopped (1 cup)
2 garlic cloves, minced
½ teaspoon dried oregano
⅛ teaspoon crushed red pepper
1 (14½-oz.) can reduced-sodium chicken broth
    or 1¾ cups vegetable broth
½ cup water
⅔ cup brown lentils, rinsed, sorted
¼ cup dry-packed, sun-dried tomatoes, chopped
⅓ cup Arborio rice

½ cup (2 oz.) crumbled feta cheese
½ cup grated carrot (1 medium)
½ cup Italian-style bread crumbs
3 tablespoons coarsely chopped pitted
    Kalamata olives
¼ cup chopped fresh parsley
¼ teaspoon freshly ground pepper
8 whole wheat hamburger rolls, split
Optional garnishes: Yogurt-Garlic Sauce
    (page 25) or nonfat plain yogurt; ketchup;
    lettuce leaves; sliced tomatoes; sliced red onion

❶ In medium saucepan, heat 2 teaspoons of the olive oil over medium heat until hot. Add onion; cook, stirring often, 2 to 3 minutes or until softened. Add garlic, oregano and crushed red pepper; cook 30 seconds, stirring. Add broth, water, lentils and sun-dried tomatoes; bring to a simmer. Reduce heat to low; cover. Simmer 15 minutes.

❷ Add rice to lentil mixture. Cover; cook 20 to 25 minutes or until lentils and rice are tender. If any liquid remains in pan, drain it off. Spread lentil mixture in shallow dish; let cool completely, at least 30 minutes.

❸ Transfer lentil mixture to food processor. Add feta cheese, carrot, bread crumbs, olives, parsley and pepper; pulse several times or until mixture is cohesive. Using about ½ cup per patty, form mixture into 8 (½-inch-thick) patties.

❹ In large nonstick skillet, heat 2 teaspoons of the olive oil over medium heat. Add 4 of the patties; cook 2½ to 3 minutes per side or until nicely browned. Repeat with the remaining 2 teaspoons of the olive oil and the remaining 4 patties. Meanwhile, toast rolls. Set patties on rolls; garnish as desired.

8 servings. Preparation time: 30 minutes. Ready to serve: 1 hour, 45 minutes.

Per serving (without garnishes): 255 calories, 7 g total fat (2 g saturated fat), 11 g protein, 39 g carbohydrate, 6 mg cholesterol, 471 mg sodium, 8 g fiber. **Star nutrients:** Vitamin A (42%), Fiber (32%). **Noteworthy nutrients:** Vitamin C (17%), Folate (22%), Iron (18%), Phosphorus (18%), Thiamin (15%).

MAKE AHEAD Prepare patties through Step 3. Cover; refrigerate for up to 2 days or wrap individually and freeze for up to 4 months. Thaw frozen patties in refrigerator before cooking.

Teriyaki Tofu & Vegetable Kabobs

Tofu takes well to the grill. Like a sponge, it soaks up the marinade's flavors beautifully. Brief cooking on the grill caramelizes the outside for a delicious result.

⅓ cup reduced-sodium soy sauce
2 tablespoons sugar
2 tablespoons medium-dry sherry or orange juice
1 tablespoon canola oil
1 tablespoon minced fresh ginger
2 garlic cloves, minced
1 (1-lb.) pkg. extra-firm regular tofu, drained, blotted dry, cut into 1¼-inch cubes
1 medium red bell pepper, cut into 1¼-inch pieces
1 bunch green onions, trimmed, cut into 1½-inch lengths
1 tablespoon sesame seeds, toasted*

❶ In small bowl or measuring cup, stir together soy sauce, sugar, sherry, canola oil, ginger and garlic. Reserve 3 tablespoons of this mixture for basting. Place tofu in shallow glass dish. Pour remaining soy sauce mixture over tofu; turn to coat. Cover; refrigerate at least 1 hour or up to 8 hours, turning several times.

❷ Heat grill.

❸ Thread tofu, bell pepper and green onions (thread crosswise) onto four (10- or 12-inch) skewers. Lightly oil grill rack. Place kabobs on gas grill over medium-high heat or on charcoal grill 4 to 6 inches from medium-hot coals. Cover grill; cook 6 to 8 minutes or until lightly browned on all sides, turning and basting occasionally with reserved marinade. Sprinkle with sesame seeds.

4 servings.
Preparation time: 20 minutes.
Ready to serve: 1 hour, 30 minutes.

Per serving: 225 calories, 10.5 g total fat (1.5 g saturated fat), 15 g protein, 15 g carbohydrate, 0 g cholesterol, 712 mg sodium, 2 g fiber. **Star nutrients:** Vitamin A (35%), Vitamin C (101%). **Noteworthy nutrients:** Thiamin (15%).

TIP *To toast sesame seeds, heat small skillet over medium-low heat. Add sesame seeds; stir continuously until seeds are lightly browned, 2 to 3 minutes.

Curried Vegetable Stew

Other than mincing the aromatic garlic, ginger and jalapeños, there are no vegetables to chop for this vegetarian curry—all the vegetables are frozen or canned. This is a handy recipe for those evenings when you end up foraging in the freezer for dinner. Serve over brown rice.

1 teaspoon canola oil
2 cups frozen pepper stir-fry vegetables
1 tablespoon minced fresh ginger
3 garlic cloves, minced
2 jalapeño peppers, seeded, minced
2 teaspoons curry powder
1 (14½-oz.) can diced tomatoes, undrained
1 (14-oz.) can light unsweetened coconut milk
2 tablespoons reduced-sodium soy sauce
2 teaspoons packed brown sugar
1 (16-oz.) pkg. frozen cauliflower
1 (10-oz.) pkg. frozen spinach or 4 cups individually quick frozen spinach
Lime wedges

❶ In Dutch oven, heat canola oil over medium heat until hot. Add stir-fry vegetables; cook, stirring often, 3 to 4 minutes or until softened. Add ginger, garlic, jalapeños and curry powder; cook about 30 seconds or until fragrant, stirring. Add tomatoes, coconut milk, soy sauce and brown sugar; bring to a simmer. Add cauliflower; return to a simmer. Reduce heat to medium-low. Cover; cook 10 minutes or until cauliflower is tender.

❷ Meanwhile, cook spinach according to package directions. Drain; press out excess moisture. Stir spinach into stew. Garnish with lime wedges.

6 (1-cup) servings.
Preparation time: 10 minutes.
Ready to serve: 30 minutes.

Per serving: 165 calories, 9 g total fat (7.5 g saturated fat), 7 g protein, 17 g carbohydrate, 0 mg cholesterol, 482 mg sodium, 5 g fiber. **Star nutrients:** Vitamin A (81%), Vitamin C (129%), Folate (27%). **Noteworthy nutrients:** Fiber (19%).

Pasta & Rice

All too often, pasta dishes are richer than they need to be. This chapter demonstrates how to replace heavy cream sauces with vegetable-based pasta sauces. In addition, you will find an easy whole grain paella and a light risotto recipe.

Macaroni & Cheese with Spinach

This updated recipe illustrates how you can lower the saturated fat, without sacrificing the rich cheesy taste, in classic macaroni and cheese. A layer of spinach in the center adds nutritional value.

1¾ cups low-fat (1%) milk, divided
3 tablespoons all-purpose flour
2 cups (6 oz.) grated extra-sharp cheddar cheese
1 cup low-fat (1%) cottage cheese
½ teaspoon salt

¼ teaspoon freshly ground pepper
⅛ teaspoon ground nutmeg
1 (10-oz.) pkg. frozen spinach
8 oz. (2 cups) elbow macaroni
¼ cup toasted wheat germ

❶ Heat oven to 400°F. Coat 8-inch (2-quart) square baking dish with nonstick cooking spray. In small bowl, whisk ¼ cup of the cold milk with flour until smooth; set aside. In heavy medium saucepan, heat the remaining 1½ cups of the milk over medium heat until steaming. Add flour mixture; cook 2 to 3 minutes or until sauce boils and thickens, whisking constantly. Remove from heat; add cheddar cheese, stirring until melted. Stir in cottage cheese, salt, pepper and nutmeg.

❷ Cook spinach according to package directions; drain. Refresh under cold water; press out excess moisture.

❸ Cook macaroni in large pot of lightly salted boiling water, 4 to 5 minutes or until not quite tender, stirring often. (Macaroni will continue to cook while baking.) Drain; rinse with cold water. Drain again.

❹ In large bowl, mix cheese sauce with macaroni. Spread half of the macaroni mixture in baking dish. Spoon spinach over top. Spread remaining macaroni mixture over spinach layer. Sprinkle with wheat germ.

❺ Bake 35 to 45 minutes or until bubbly and golden.

6 (1⅓-cup) servings. Preparation time: 25 minutes. Ready to serve: 1 hour, 10 minutes.

Per serving: 355 calories, 12 g total fat (7 g saturated fat), 22 g protein, 41 g carbohydrate, 34 mg cholesterol, 597 mg sodium, 3 g fiber. **Star nutrients:** Vitamin A (83%), Calcium (38%), Folate (43%), Phosphorus (39%), Riboflavin (34%), Thiamin (40%). **Noteworthy nutrients:** Vitamin B6 (19%), Vitamin B12 (18%), Vitamin C (20%), Copper (16%), Iron (18%), Magnesium (19%), Niacin (19%), Zinc (17%).

TIMESAVING TIP Begin heating water for pasta at Step 1.

MAKE AHEAD Prepare recipe through Step 4. Cover and refrigerate for up to 2 days or freeze for up to 2 months. Thaw in the refrigerator before baking.

VARIATION Southwestern Macaroni & Cheese & Peppers

In Step 1, substitute a mixture of 1 cup grated pepper Jack cheese and 1 cup grated extra-sharp cheddar cheese for 2 cups cheddar cheese. Omit nutmeg; add 1 (4½-oz.) can chopped mild green chiles, ⅓ cup chopped fresh cilantro and dash cayenne pepper to cheese sauce. In Step 2, omit spinach. Instead, sauté 2 cups frozen pepper stir-fry vegetables in 1 teaspoon olive oil, 3 to 4 minutes or until tender. In Step 4, spoon pepper mixture over bottom macaroni layer.

Getting Your Lycopene Fix

Lycopene, a phytochemical found in tomatoes, has been getting a lot of attention recently because of its potential for protecting against prostate cancer. Tomatoes release more lycopene when they are cooked. In addition, a little bit of fat aids in absorption. Hence, tomato sauce made with a little olive oil makes sense as a delicious way to get the benefits of lycopene. A light tomato sauce is also a terrific alternative to rich, creamy pasta sauces. Here is an ultra-simple recipe for tomato sauce. For a satisfying meal, toss with pasta and steamed vegetables; top with a sprinkling of Parmesan cheese or feta cheese.

20-Minute Tomato Sauce. Heat 2 teaspoons olive oil in large heavy saucepan over medium-low heat until warm. Add 4 cloves minced garlic, 1 teaspoon dried oregano and ⅛ teaspoon crushed red pepper; cook 30 to 60 seconds or until fragrant but not colored, stirring. Add 2 (14-oz.) cans undrained diced tomatoes; mash with potato masher. Bring to a simmer. Cook, uncovered, over medium-low heat about 20 minutes or until thickened, stirring and mashing occasionally. Stir in ⅛ teaspoon freshly ground pepper. Makes about 2¼ cups, enough for 4 servings or 12 oz. pasta (weighed before cooking).

Pasta with Lentil & Mushroom Sauce

Lentils make a great meat substitute in a hearty pasta sauce. Curly pasta shapes are an excellent choice for this dish, because the flavorful braised lentils become trapped in the ridges.

2 teaspoons olive oil
8 to 10 oz. mushrooms, stem ends trimmed, quartered (3 cups)
1 large or 2 medium onions, chopped (2 cups)
3 garlic cloves, minced
1 teaspoon dried oregano
Dash crushed red pepper
1/3 cup brown lentils, rinsed, sorted
1 1/4 cups reduced-sodium chicken broth or vegetable broth
1 (14 1/2-oz.) can diced tomatoes, undrained
4 oz. baby spinach or leaf spinach, stems trimmed (6 cups)
1/4 teaspoon freshly ground pepper
12 oz. fusilli or rotini
3/4 cup (1 1/2 oz.) freshly grated Parmesan cheese

❶ In large nonstick skillet, heat olive oil over medium-high heat. Add mushrooms; cook 3 to 5 minutes or until browned, stirring occasionally. Add onion; cook, stirring frequently, 2 to 3 minutes or until softened. Add garlic, oregano and crushed red pepper; cook 30 seconds, stirring. Add lentils and broth; bring to a simmer. Reduce heat to low; cover skillet with lid or aluminum foil. Simmer 30 minutes or until lentils are almost tender.

❷ Add tomatoes to lentil mixture; return to a simmer. Cook, covered, an additional 10 to 15 minutes or until lentils are tender and flavors have blended. Stir in spinach; cook, covered, 3 to 4 minutes or until spinach has wilted. Stir in pepper.

❸ Meanwhile, cook pasta according to package directions. Drain; toss with lentil sauce. Serve with Parmesan cheese.

4 (2-cup) servings.
Preparation time: 30 minutes.
Ready to serve: 1 hour.

Per serving: 515 calories, 8.5 g total fat (2.5 g saturated fat), 25 g protein, 86 g carbohydrate, 8 mg cholesterol, 694 mg sodium, 12 g fiber.
Star nutrients: Vitamin A (34%), Vitamin C (56%), Calcium (28%), Copper (34%), Fiber (50%), Folate (71%), Iron (44%), Niacin (49%), Phosphorus (40%), Riboflavin (45%), Thiamin (73%). **Noteworthy nutrients:** Vitamin B6 (22%), Magnesium (24%), Zinc (16%).

Quick Sausage & Spinach Lasagna

Lasagna is a crowd-pleasing favorite. This recipe trims the fat but keeps the flavor.

1 (4-oz.) link hot Italian turkey sausage,
  casing removed
1 (26-oz.) jar marinara sauce (3 cups)
1 teaspoon dried oregano
¼ teaspoon crushed red pepper
1 (16-oz.) or 1½ (10-oz.) pkg. frozen spinach
1 egg
1 (15-oz.) container light ricotta cheese

½ cup (1 oz.) freshly grated Parmesan
  cheese, divided
¼ teaspoon freshly ground pepper
⅛ teaspoon ground nutmeg
1 (8-oz.) pkg. oven-ready lasagna noodles
  (12 noodles)
1⅓ cups (4 oz.) grated part-skim
  mozzarella cheese, divided

❶ Heat oven to 400°F. Coat 9x13-inch baking dish with nonstick cooking spray. In small nonstick skillet, cook sausage over medium heat 2 to 4 minutes or until browned, crumbling sausage with wooden spoon. Blot sausage with paper towel. Transfer to medium bowl; stir in marinara sauce, oregano and crushed red pepper.

❷ Cook spinach according to package directions. Drain; refresh with cold running water. Drain well; press out moisture. In medium bowl, whisk egg and ricotta cheese until smooth. Add spinach, ¼ cup of the Parmesan cheese, pepper and nutmeg; mix well.

❸ In deep dish or bowl, cover 3 of the lasagna noodles with warm water; let soak while you assemble lasagna. Spread about ¾ cup marinara mixture in baking dish. Place 3 of the remaining unsoaked noodles crosswise over sauce. Spread about 1 cup spinach mixture over noodles. Spoon ½ cup marinara mixture over spinach mixture. Sprinkle with ⅓ cup of the mozzarella cheese. Add another layer of unsoaked noodles; repeat layering with spinach mixture, marinara mixture and mozzarella cheese two more times. Lift soaked noodles from water. Shake off excess water; arrange over lasagna. Spread remaining marinara mixture evenly over final layer of noodles.

❹ Cover lasagna with aluminum foil; bake 35 minutes. Sprinkle with the remaining ¼ cup of the Parmesan cheese and the remaining ⅓ cup of the mozzarella cheese. Bake, uncovered, an additional 10 to 15 minutes or until noodles are tender and lasagna is bubbly. Let stand 5 minutes before serving.

6 servings. Preparation time: 30 minutes. Ready to serve: 1 hour, 30 minutes.

Per serving: 400 calories, 18.5 g total fat (8 g saturated fat), 24 g protein, 34 g carbohydrate, 82 mg cholesterol, 986 mg sodium, 5 g fiber. **Star nutrients:** Vitamin A (138%), Vitamin C (47%), Calcium (48%), Folate (28%), Phosphorus (28%). **Noteworthy nutrients:** Fiber (20%), Iron (21%), Magnesium (22%), Niacin (16%), Riboflavin (24%), Thiamin (23%).

MAKE AHEAD Prepare recipe through Step 3. Cover and refrigerate for up to 2 days or freeze for up to 3 months. Thaw in refrigerator before continuing with Step 4.

Pasta Pie with Broccoli

Made with a few staple ingredients, this simple pasta pie makes a satisfying homemade supper on those evenings when the refrigerator seems bare.

5 tablespoons Italian-style bread crumbs, divided
2 teaspoons olive oil, divided
1 medium onion, chopped (1 cup)
1 cup (6 oz.) ditalini pasta
4 eggs
¾ cup low-fat (1%) milk
1 teaspoon hot pepper sauce, such as Tabasco
½ teaspoon salt
¼ teaspoon freshly ground pepper
1 cup (3 oz.) grated cheddar, Monterey Jack or part-skim mozzarella cheese
1 (10-oz.) pkg. frozen chopped broccoli (3 cups), rinsed under cold water to thaw

❶ Heat oven to 350°F. Coat 9-inch (1½-quart) deep-dish pie plate with nonstick cooking spray. Sprinkle with 2 tablespoons of the bread crumbs, tilting to coat evenly. In small bowl, mix the remaining 3 tablespoons of the bread crumbs with 1 teaspoon of the olive oil.

❷ In medium nonstick skillet, heat the remaining 1 teaspoon of the olive oil over medium heat. Add onion; cook, stirring often, 3 to 4 minutes or until tender and light golden.

❸ Meanwhile, cook pasta according to package directions. Drain; rinse with cold water.

❹ In large bowl, whisk eggs, milk, hot pepper sauce, salt and pepper. Add cheese, onion, broccoli and pasta; mix with rubber spatula. Pour into pie plate, spreading evenly. Sprinkle evenly with reserved bread crumb mixture.

❺ Bake 30 to 40 minutes or until light golden and set. (The tip of a knife inserted in center should come out clean.) Let cool slightly; cut into wedges. Serve hot.

6 servings.
Preparation time: 25 minutes.
Ready to serve: 1 hour, 10 minutes.

Per serving: 250 calories, 10.5 g total fat (4.5 g saturated fat), 14 g protein, 25 g carbohydrate, 158 mg cholesterol, 447 mg sodium, 3 g fiber. **Star nutrients:** Vitamin A (28%), Vitamin C (48%), Folate (25%), Riboflavin (26%). **Noteworthy nutrients:** Calcium (20%), Phosphorus (22%), Thiamin (20%).

Pasta with Broccoli Rabe & Cannellini Beans

Cannellini beans provide a comforting contrast to assertive broccoli rabe in this simple, satisfying pasta dish.

12 oz. broccoli rabe,* about 1 inch trimmed from stems (6 cups)
1 tablespoon olive oil
6 garlic cloves, minced
¼ teaspoon crushed red pepper
1¼ cups reduced-sodium chicken broth or vegetable broth
¼ cup dry-packed, sun-dried tomatoes, diced
1 (19-oz.) can cannellini beans, drained, rinsed
1 cup canned crushed tomatoes
¼ teaspoon salt
¼ teaspoon freshly ground pepper
12 oz. gnocchi or orrechietti pasta
¾ cup (1½ oz.) freshly grated Parmesan cheese

❶ Drop broccoli rabe into large pot of lightly salted boiling water; stir to immerse. Cook, uncovered, 3 to 4 minutes or until water returns to a boil. Drain; refresh under cold running water. Press out excess moisture. Transfer to cutting board; cut into ½-inch lengths.

❷ In large nonstick skillet, heat olive oil over medium-low heat. Add garlic and crushed red pepper; cook, stirring constantly, 1 to 2 minutes or until garlic is softened and fragrant but not colored. Add broccoli rabe; increase heat to medium-high. Cook 2 minutes, stirring. Add broth and sun-dried tomatoes; bring to a simmer. Reduce heat to medium-low. Cook, uncovered, 5 minutes or until broccoli rabe is tender. Add beans and crushed tomatoes; return to a simmer. Cook 5 minutes or until flavors have blended. Season with salt and pepper.

❸ Meanwhile, cook pasta according to package directions. Drain; toss with broccoli rabe sauce. Serve with Parmesan cheese.

4 (1¾-cup) servings.
Preparation time: 25 minutes. Ready to serve: 30 minutes.

Per serving: 415 calories, 8.5 g total fat (3 g saturated fat), 20 g protein, 67 g carbohydrate, 13 mg cholesterol, 1,260 mg sodium, 12 g fiber. **Star nutrients:** Vitamin A (37%), Vitamin C (155%), Calcium (26%), Fiber (47%), Iron (29%), Niacin (28%). **Noteworthy nutrients:** Vitamin B6 (19%), Copper (15%), Folate (19%), Phosphorus (21%), Thiamin (21%).

INGREDIENT NOTE *You can find broccoli rabe in most supermarkets these days. Also known as rapini, this vegetable resembles broccoli, but the flavor is much more pungent and bitter. This bitterness is tamed by blanching in boiling water for a few minutes. Garlic and hot peppers complement its assertive taste. Broccoli rabe is popular in Italy and you will find it used in many classic Italian recipes.

Linguine with Tuna & Capers

This is a great standby dish for those evenings when you must scrounge a quick, satisfying dinner from your pantry. Every time I tell my husband we are having pasta with tuna and tomato sauce for dinner, he expresses skepticism about the combination. But at the end of dinner, he inevitably exclaims, "That was good!"

2 teaspoons olive oil
4 garlic cloves, minced
⅛ teaspoon crushed red pepper
1 (28-oz.) or 2 (14½-oz.) cans diced tomatoes, undrained
1 (6-oz.) or 2 (3½-oz.) cans water-packed tuna, drained, flaked
2 tablespoons drained capers, rinsed
1 teaspoon freshly grated lemon peel
⅛ teaspoon freshly ground pepper
2 tablespoons chopped fresh parsley (optional)
12 oz. linguine or spaghetti

❶ In large heavy saucepan, heat olive oil over medium-low heat until warm. Add garlic and crushed red pepper; cook, stirring constantly, 30 to 60 seconds or until softened and fragrant, but not colored. Add tomatoes; mash with potato masher. Increase heat to medium-high; bring to a simmer. Reduce heat to medium-low. Cook, uncovered, about 20 minutes or until thickened, stirring and mashing occasionally.

❷ Stir tuna, capers, lemon peel and pepper into tomato sauce. Cook 2 to 3 minutes or until heated through. Stir in parsley, if desired.

❸ Meanwhile, cook linguine according to package directions. Drain; toss with tuna sauce.

4 servings.
Preparation time: 15 minutes.
Ready to serve: 30 minutes.

Per serving: 435 calories, 5 g total fat (1 g saturated fat), 23 g protein, 72 g carbohydrate, 18 mg cholesterol, 934 mg sodium, 4 g fiber. **Star nutrients:** Vitamin C (56%), Folate (50%), Iron (26%), Niacin (45%), Riboflavin (25%), Thiamin (60%). **Noteworthy nutrients:** Calcium (15%), Magnesium (15%), Phosphorus (23%).

Pasta Shells with Black-Eyed Peas & Artichokes

This unusual pasta dish relies primarily on pantry staples. Artichokes, black-eyed peas, caraway seeds and smoky cheese make an intriguing combination.

1 (15½-oz.) can black-eyed peas, drained, rinsed
2 teaspoons olive oil
1 medium red onion, chopped (1 cup)
4 garlic cloves, minced
1 to 1½ teaspoons caraway seeds, lightly crushed*
⅛ teaspoon crushed red pepper
1 (14-oz.) can artichoke hearts, drained, rinsed, coarsely chopped

2 cups reduced-sodium chicken broth or vegetable broth
¼ teaspoon salt
⅓ cup chopped fresh parsley
1 to 2 teaspoons cider vinegar
¼ teaspoon freshly ground pepper
12 oz. medium pasta shells
1 cup (3 oz.) grated smoked mozzarella cheese or smoked cheddar cheese

❶ In small bowl, mash ¼ cup of the black-eyed peas with fork; set mashed and whole black-eyed peas aside.

❷ In large nonstick skillet, heat olive oil over medium-high heat until hot. Add onion; cook, stirring often, 3 to 5 minutes or until softened. Add garlic, caraway seeds and crushed red pepper; cook 30 seconds, stirring. Stir in artichokes and whole and mashed black-eyed peas; stir to coat. Add broth and salt; bring to a simmer. Reduce heat to medium-low. Cook, uncovered, 10 minutes. Stir in parsley, vinegar and pepper.

❸ Meanwhile, cook pasta according to package directions. Drain; toss with artichoke sauce and mozzarella cheese.

4 servings.
Preparation time: 20 minutes.
Ready to serve: 30 minutes.

Per serving: 535 calories, 7 g total fat (2.5 g saturated fat), 26 g protein, 89 g carbohydrate, 12 mg cholesterol, 909 mg sodium, 6 g fiber. **Star nutrients:** Vitamin C (37%), Folate (53%), Iron (37%), Niacin (36%), Phosphorus (35%), Riboflavin (30%), Thiamin (64%). **Noteworthy nutrients:** Calcium (22%), Copper (15%), Fiber (24%).

TIMESAVING TIP Begin heating water for pasta at Step 1.

TIP *Crushing caraway seeds brings out their flavor. To crush them, place seeds on a cutting board and use bottom of a heavy saucepan to crush lightly. Alternatively, use a mortar and pestle.

Penne alla Vodka on the Lighter Side

This simple dish fills the bill when you crave a creamy pasta dish. The base is a meaty tomato sauce, which is enriched with low-fat sour cream. To prevent curdling, toss pasta with sour cream before adding tomato sauce. The starch in the pasta stabilizes the sour cream.

4 strips (2 oz.) reduced-fat bacon or turkey bacon, diced
1 medium onion, chopped (1 cup)
2 garlic cloves, minced
⅛ teaspoon crushed red pepper
1 (14½-oz.) can diced tomatoes, undrained
1 cup water
3 tablespoons vodka
½ teaspoon freshly ground pepper
12 oz. penne or ziti pasta
¼ cup reduced-fat sour cream
¼ cup (½ oz.) freshly grated Parmesan cheese

❶ In large nonstick skillet, cook bacon over medium heat, stirring often, 3 to 5 minutes or until crisp. Transfer to paper towel-lined plate to drain. Pour off fat from skillet if necessary.

❷ Add onion to skillet; cook 2 to 3 minutes or until softened and lightly browned. Add garlic and crushed red pepper; cook 30 seconds, stirring. Add tomatoes; mash with potato masher. Add water and cooked bacon. Cook, uncovered, over medium heat about 15 minutes or until thickened and saucy, stirring and mashing tomatoes occasionally. Stir in vodka and pepper.

❸ Meanwhile, cook penne according to package directions. Drain; place in large warm bowl. Add sour cream, tossing to coat well. Add tomato sauce; toss again. Serve with Parmesan cheese.

4 (1½-cup) servings.
Preparation time: 15 minutes.
Ready to serve: 30 minutes.

Per serving: 455 calories, 7.5 g total fat (3 g saturated fat), 17 g protein, 72 g carbohydrate, 21 mg cholesterol, 655 mg sodium, 3 g fiber. **Star nutrients:** Vitamin C (31%), Folate (52%), Niacin (32%), Riboflavin (26%), Thiamin (60%). **Noteworthy nutrients:** Calcium (19%), Iron (21%), Phosphorus (21%).

Risotto with Asparagus & Lemon

Because it requires close surveillance during cooking, home cooks who are pressed for time often avoid risotto. However, there is very little preparation involved. Besides, standing by the stove to stir and cook a risotto can be very relaxing, and it only takes 20 minutes. Risotto is also a nice way to highlight vegetables; by precooking them in the broth used in the risotto, you add even more flavor.

2 (14½-oz.) cans reduced-sodium chicken broth
1 cup water
1 lb. asparagus, tough ends snipped off, stems
   peeled if desired, cut into 1-inch pieces
   (2 cups)
1 tablespoon olive oil
⅔ cup trimmed, chopped green onions
   (1 bunch)

1 cup Arborio rice*
½ cup (1 oz.) freshly grated Parmesan cheese
2 tablespoons chopped fresh parsley
2 teaspoons freshly grated lemon peel
1 tablespoon fresh lemon juice
Dash salt
¼ teaspoon freshly ground pepper

❶ In medium saucepan, combine broth and water; bring to a simmer over medium heat. Drop in asparagus; cook, uncovered, 2 to 4 minutes or until just tender. With slotted spoon, transfer asparagus to plate; set aside. Reduce heat to low; keep broth at a bare simmer.

❷ In Dutch oven, heat olive oil over medium heat. Add green onions; cook about 1 minute or until softened, stirring. Add rice; cook 30 seconds, stirring. Add about 1 cup of the hot broth; cook, stirring constantly, 1 to 1½ minutes or until most of the liquid has been absorbed. Continue to simmer and stir almost constantly, adding broth about ½ cup at a time, waiting until most of it has been absorbed before adding more, about 20 minutes or until rice is tender and risotto is creamy.

❸ Add asparagus; stir about 1 minute or until heated through. Remove risotto from heat; stir in Parmesan cheese, parsley, lemon peel, lemon juice, salt and pepper.

4 (1¼-cup) servings.
Preparation time: 45 minutes.
Ready to serve: 45 minutes.

Per serving: 285 calories, 7.5 g total fat (3 g saturated fat), 13 g protein, 42 g carbohydrate, 10 mg cholesterol, 639 mg sodium, 5 g fiber. **Star nutrients:** Vitamin C (56%). **Noteworthy nutrients:** Vitamin A (19%), Calcium (22%), Fiber (19%), Phosphorus (19%).

INGREDIENT NOTE   *Arborio, a medium-grain rice from Italy, has a high starch content, which is needed to produce the characteristic creamy texture in risotto. You can find Arborio in specialty stores and most supermarkets. Sometimes, it is simply labeled "Risotto Rice."

Pasta with Pesto, Potatoes & Green Beans

Silken tofu is an effective replacement for much of the olive oil in traditional pesto. The addition of vegetables makes this simple pasta dish more substantial and nutritious. As a bonus, the vegetable steaming water produces a flavorful vegetable broth, which is perfect for thinning and warming the pesto.

1½ cups lightly packed fresh basil leaves
¼ cup (1½ oz.) pine nuts, toasted*
1 garlic clove, minced
½ teaspoon salt, plus more to taste
⅛ teaspoon freshly ground pepper
Dash crushed red pepper
½ cup (4 oz.) low-fat firm silken tofu
1 tablespoon extra-virgin olive oil
½ cup (½ oz.) freshly grated Parmesan cheese
12 oz. small red potatoes (about 4), cut into ¾-inch chunks
4 oz. green beans, tough ends trimmed, cut in half crosswise (1 cup)
12 oz. penne or ziti

❶ In food processor, combine basil, pine nuts, garlic, ½ teaspoon of the salt, ground pepper and crushed red pepper; process until finely chopped. Add tofu and olive oil; process until smooth and creamy, stopping to scrape down sides of bowl several times. Add Parmesan cheese; pulse several times to blend.

❷ Place potatoes and green beans in steamer basket over boiling water; sprinkle with salt to taste. Cover; steam until tender, 8 to 10 minutes for beans, 10 to 12 minutes for potatoes. (Be careful not to let water run dry.) Transfer vegetables to large bowl to keep warm. Stir ⅓ cup of the water remaining in bottom of steamer into basil pesto.

❸ Meanwhile, cook pasta according to package directions. Drain; toss with vegetables and pesto.

4 servings.
Preparation time: 25 minutes.
Ready to serve: 40 minutes.

Per serving: 515 calories, 11.5 g total fat (2.5 g saturated fat), 20 g protein, 84 g carbohydrate, 5 mg cholesterol, 448 mg sodium, 5 g fiber. **Star nutrients:** Vitamin C (40%), Copper (32%), Folate (58%), Iron (32%), Magnesium (26%), Niacin (42%), Phosphorus (31%), Riboflavin (30%), Thiamin (71%). **Noteworthy nutrients:** Vitamin A (17%), Vitamin B6 (19%), Calcium (16%), Fiber (21%), Zinc (15%).

TIP *To toast pine nuts, place in a dry skillet. Cook, stirring constantly, over medium-low heat 2 minutes or until golden brown. Transfer to a small bowl to cool.

Quick & Easy Paella

Paella, the signature Spanish dish of rice, chicken, seafood and vegetables, makes a satisfying one-pot meal and is easy to make. This version, using instant brown rice, blends the nutritional benefits of whole grains with convenience.

1½ cups reduced-sodium chicken broth

¼ teaspoon saffron threads,* crumbled, or dash powdered saffron

8 oz. boneless skinless chicken breasts, trimmed, cut into ¾-inch chunks

¼ teaspoon salt

⅛ teaspoon freshly ground pepper

3 teaspoons olive oil, divided

1 medium onion, chopped (1 cup)

2 garlic cloves, minced

⅛ teaspoon crushed red pepper

1 (14½-oz.) can diced tomatoes, undrained

1½ cups instant brown rice

8 oz. cooked medium shrimp (thawed if frozen), tails removed

1 cup frozen green peas, rinsed under cold running water to thaw

⅓ cup diced bottled roasted red bell peppers, rinsed (half 7-oz. jar)**

❶ In glass measuring cup or small saucepan, combine chicken broth and saffron; bring to a simmer in microwave or on stovetop. Remove from heat. Cover; keep warm.

❷ Sprinkle chicken with salt and pepper. In large nonstick skillet, heat 2 teaspoons of the olive oil over medium heat. Add chicken; cook about 5 minutes or until browned and no longer pink in center. Transfer to plate.

❸ Add the remaining 1 teaspoon of the olive oil to skillet. Add onion; cook over medium heat, stirring often, 3 to 4 minutes or until softened and lightly browned. Add garlic and crushed red pepper; cook 30 seconds, stirring. Add tomatoes; mash with potato masher. Bring to a simmer; cook 5 minutes.

❹ Add rice; stir to coat well. Add broth mixture; bring to a simmer. Reduce heat to medium-low. Cover; cook 5 minutes. Add shrimp, peas, roasted bell peppers and cooked chicken; mix well with rubber spatula. Return to a simmer. Re-cover skillet; remove from heat. Let stand 10 minutes.***

4 (1½-cup) servings. Preparation time: 20 minutes. Ready to serve: 50 minutes.

Per serving: 475 calories, 7 g total fat (1.5 g saturated fat), 35 g protein, 67 g carbohydrate, 143 mg cholesterol, 987 mg sodium, 6 g fiber. **Star nutrients:** Vitamin B6 (44%), Vitamin C (64%), Iron (25%), Magnesium (38%), Niacin (63%), Phosphorus (48%), Thiamin (30%). **Noteworthy nutrients:** Vitamin B12 (18%), Copper (22%), Fiber (24%), Zinc (21%).

TIP *Saffron, the distinctive seasoning in paella, is available in the spice section of most supermarkets, but it is expensive. To cut costs for this dish, substitute 1 teaspoon paprika.

TIP ** Store leftover bottled roasted red peppers, covered, in the refrigerator for up to 4 days or in the freezer for up to 4 months. Use roasted red peppers to perk up sandwiches and salads.

TIP ***This instant rice paella must stand to allow rice to absorb liquid after a brief cooking period. Retain heat by placing covered skillet in a warm place, such as on warming tray or in 200°F oven with door ajar.

Whole Wheat Spaghetti with Cabbage & Pinto Beans

Here is a stick-to-your-ribs dish that will warm your soul on a cold evening. Nutty whole wheat spaghetti is a perfect complement to the deceptively rich-tasting cabbage and bean sauce.

1 (15-oz.) can pinto beans, drained, rinsed	¼ teaspoon salt
2 teaspoons olive oil	2½ cups reduced-sodium chicken broth or
1 medium onion, slivered (1 cup)	vegetable broth
4 cups shredded green cabbage, preferably	2 teaspoons balsamic vinegar
Savoy (½ medium)	¼ teaspoon freshly ground pepper
1 cup diced carrots (2 to 4 carrots)	12 oz. whole wheat spaghetti*
4 garlic cloves, minced	1 cup (3 oz.) grated fontina or
1 teaspoon dried thyme	Monterey Jack cheese

❶ In small bowl, mash ¼ cup of the beans with fork; set mashed and whole beans aside.**

❷ In large nonstick skillet, heat olive oil over medium-high heat until hot. Add onion; cook, stirring often, 2 to 3 minutes or until softened. Add cabbage, carrots, garlic, thyme and salt; cook, stirring often, 3 to 4 minutes or until cabbage has wilted. Add broth and reserved mashed and whole beans; bring to a simmer. Reduce heat to medium-low; simmer, uncovered, 10 to 15 minutes or until cabbage is tender, stirring occasionally. Stir in vinegar and pepper.

❸ Meanwhile, cook spaghetti according to package directions. Drain; toss with cabbage sauce and cheese.

4 servings.
Preparation time: 25 minutes.
Ready to serve: 1 hour.

Per serving: 555 calories, 11 g total fat (5 g saturated fat), 27 g protein, 93 g carbohydrate, 24 mg cholesterol, 902 mg sodium, 16 g fiber. **Star nutrients:** Vitamin A (192%), Vitamin B6 (28%), Vitamin C (66%), Calcium (25%), Copper (34%), Fiber (65%), Folate (46%), Iron (32%), Magnesium (46%), Niacin (30%), Phosphorus (47%), Thiamin (42%), Zinc (26%). **Noteworthy nutrients:** Riboflavin (17%).

INGREDIENT NOTE *Whole wheat spaghetti can be found in the natural food section of supermarkets and at health food stores. If you cannot find it, substitute regular spaghetti or linguine.

TIMESAVING TIPS Begin heating water for pasta at Step 1. Substitute 5 cups prepared coleslaw mix for the cabbage and carrots.

TIP **When making sauces and soups with beans, mash a portion of the beans. This is an easy way to add body to the dish.

Desserts & Treats

Desserts can—and should—be part of a healthy diet. They are an excellent way to enjoy an extra serving of fruit. This chapter offers a selection of simple fruit desserts. You will also find cookies and bars featuring whole grains—and low-fat ways to satisfy a sweet tooth.

Pear & Dried Cranberry Gratin

Fruit baked in a rich-tasting almond cream makes a homey yet elegant dessert. Silken tofu stands in for much of the butter in the almond cream. This is a versatile concept, as you will see in the following variations.

⅓ cup dried cranberries
2 tablespoons brandy or cranberry juice
⅓ cup (1¼ oz.) slivered almonds, toasted*
¼ cup plus 2 teaspoons sugar, divided
1 tablespoon all-purpose flour
Dash salt
1 egg
1 egg white

½ cup (4 oz.) low-fat firm silken tofu
1 tablespoon butter, softened
2 teaspoons freshly grated lemon peel
1 teaspoon vanilla extract
3 firm ripe pears, such as Anjou or Bosc
1 lemon, cut in half
Powdered sugar for dusting

❶ Heat oven to 375°F. Coat 9-inch pie plate with nonstick cooking spray.

❷ In small bowl, combine dried cranberries and brandy. Cover with vented plastic wrap; microwave at High 1 minute. Set aside to plump and cool.

❸ In food processor, combine almonds, ¼ cup of the sugar, flour and salt; process until almonds are ground. Add egg, egg white, tofu, butter, lemon peel and vanilla; process until smooth. Scrape into pie plate, spreading evenly. Scatter cranberries over tofu mixture.

❹ Peel, halve and core pears. Rub flesh with cut sides of lemon halves to prevent discoloration. Set pear halves, flat-side down, on cutting board. Leaving pear halves intact, cut crosswise into ¼-inch-thick slices. Slide metal spatula under a pear half; press gently with palm of your hand to fan it slightly. Set pear half, stem-end toward center, on top of tofu mixture. Repeat with remaining pear halves, making circular pattern. Press pears gently into almond cream. Sprinkle the remaining 2 teaspoons of the sugar over pears.

❺ Bake gratin 30 to 40 minutes or until pears are tender and almond cream is golden. Let cool slightly. Dust with powdered sugar. Serve warm or at room temperature.

6 servings.
Preparation time: 35 minutes. Ready to serve: 1 hour, 30 minutes.

Per serving: 220 calories, 7 g total fat (2 g saturated fat), 5 g protein, 34 g carbohydrate, 41 mg cholesterol, 108 mg sodium, 4 g fiber. **Star nutrients:** Vitamin C (30%). **Noteworthy nutrients:** Fiber (17%).

TIP *To toast almonds, place in small baking sheet; bake at 375°F 6 minutes or until golden brown.

VARIATION Cherry Gratin

Substitute Bing cherries for dried cranberries and pears.

- Skip Step 2. In Step 3, combine ⅓ cup toasted almonds, ⅓ cup sugar, 1 tablespoon all-purpose flour and dash salt in food processor; process until almonds are ground. Add 1 egg, 1 egg white, ½ cup low-fat firm silken tofu, 1 tablespoon softened butter and ¼ teaspoon almond extract; process until smooth. Do not spread tofu mixture in pie plate.
- In Step 4, spread 3 cups pitted Bing cherries (fresh or frozen and partially thawed) in prepared pie plate. Spoon tofu mixture evenly over cherries. Omit remaining 2 teaspoons sugar.
- In Step 5, bake gratin 30 to 40 minutes or until golden. Let cool slightly. Dust with powdered sugar. Serve warm or at room temperature.

VARIATION Mixed Berry Gratin

Follow instructions for Cherry Gratin through Step 3.

- In Step 4, spread 3 cups mixed berries, such as raspberries, blackberries and blueberries (fresh or frozen and partially thawed) in prepared pie plate. Spoon tofu mixture evenly over berries. Omit remaining 2 teaspoons sugar. Bake as directed in Step 5 above. Let cool slightly. Dust with powdered sugar. Serve warm or at room temperature.

Broiled Mangoes

Here is an incredibly simple but elegant dessert with a taste of the tropics. The final squeeze of lime juice gives the mangoes a fresh finish. To round out the dessert, serve with toasted low-fat pound cake slices.

2 mangoes
4 teaspoons packed brown sugar

4 teaspoons rum
1 lime, cut into wedges

❶ Heat broiler. Place a mango on cutting board with narrow side facing you. With sharp knife, slice off one side of mango, sliding knife alongside long, flat seed; repeat on other side. With paring knife, make crisscross cuts through flesh, leaving skin intact. Repeat with second mango.

❷ Sprinkle 1 teaspoon brown sugar over each mango half; drizzle each with 1 teaspoon rum. Set mango halves, flesh-side up, on broiler pan or baking sheet. Broil mangoes 5 to 7 minutes or until tops are light golden. Garnish with lime wedges.

4 servings (1 serving = ½ mango). Preparation time: 10 minutes. Ready to serve: 18 minutes.

Per serving: 100 calories, 0.5 g total fat (0 g saturated fat), 1 g protein, 24 g carbohydrate, 0 mg cholesterol, 4 mg sodium, 2 g fiber.
Star nutrients: Vitamin A (81%), Vitamin C (56%).

MAKE AHEAD Prepare recipe through Step 1. Set mangoes aside, covered, at room temperature for up to 1 hour or in refrigerator for up to 4 hours.

Orange & Pomegranate Salad

If you have never tried a pomegranate, you are in for a treat. Pomegranates are in season late fall and early winter. It is actually the seeds that you eat. They have an exquisite, tart flavor and make a festive garnish for a fruit salad.

2 tablespoons orange liqueur, such as Grand Marnier or Cointreau, or orange juice
1 tablespoon sugar
3 medium-large navel oranges
½ pomegranate

❶ In medium bowl, stir together orange liqueur and sugar. With paring knife, peel oranges, removing white pith. Quarter and slice oranges. Add orange segments to bowl with orange liqueur; toss to coat. Scoop seeds from pomegranate half into small bowl, discarding membrane. Sprinkle seeds over oranges.

6 (½-cup) servings. Preparation time: 15 minutes. Ready to serve: 15 minutes.

Per serving: 65 calories, 0 g total fat (0 g saturated fat), 1 g protein, 14 g carbohydrate, 0 mg cholesterol, 0 mg sodium, 2 g fiber.
Star nutrients: Vitamin C (59%).

MAKE AHEAD Cover and refrigerate salad for up to 8 hours.

Simple Fruit Finales

Everyone looks forward to dessert. And besides, dessert is a good excuse for eating more fruit. The following are some no-fuss ways to finish your meals with fruit.

Fruit Fondue. Prepare Quick Chocolate-Hazelnut Sauce (page 218). Arrange assorted fruit such as strawberries, sliced bananas, sliced kiwi fruit and pineapple wedges on platter or individual plates. Serve with warm chocolate sauce. Provide skewers or fondue forks for dipping.

Chocolate-Dipped Strawberries or Dried Apricots. Melt semisweet chocolate in double boiler. Dip strawberries or dried apricots in chocolate, covering half of each fruit. Set on wire rack over wax paper; let stand until hardened.

Pears with Cheese & Walnuts. Serve ripe pears, accompanied by a flavorful cheese such as Gorgonzola, Parmesan or goat cheese, and walnuts.

Instant Strawberry Frozen Yogurt. Place 1 (16-oz.) pkg. unsweetened frozen strawberries and ½ cup sugar in food processor; pulse until coarsely chopped. Mix ½ cup nonfat plain yogurt and 1 tablespoon orange juice in measuring cup. With food processor running, gradually pour yogurt mixture through feed tube. Process until smooth and creamy, stopping once or twice to scrape down sides of bowl. Serve directly from food processor. Makes 6 (½-cup) servings.

Grilled Fruit. Heat grill. Brush peeled, pitted peach halves, pitted nectarine halves, pitted plum halves or ½-inch-thick pineapple slices with lemon juice. Spray fruit lightly with nonstick cooking spray. Lightly oil grill rack. Place fruit, cut-side down, on grill rack. Cook 4 to 6 minutes or until grill marks appear. Turn fruit over; cook 3 to 4 minutes longer or until heated through.

Fruit Salad. Toss assorted fresh fruit, such as pineapple wedges, orange segments, hulled strawberries, grapes and melon chunks, with sprinkling of sugar and squeeze of lemon juice.

Apple-Cranberry Crumble

An old-fashioned crumble showcases fruit in a satisfying dessert. To reduce saturated fat, moisten the crumbs with canola oil and apple juice concentrate; just a little butter lends incomparable flavor to the topping.

5 cups sliced peeled apples
   (4 to 5 medium or 1½ lb.)
1 cup fresh cranberries
⅓ cup sugar
⅔ cup whole wheat flour
½ cup old-fashioned rolled oats
½ cup packed light brown sugar
2 teaspoons ground cinnamon

Dash salt
1 tablespoon butter, cut into small pieces
1 tablespoon canola oil
3 tablespoons frozen apple juice concentrate
1 tablespoon (¼ oz.) chopped walnuts
⅔ cup Vanilla Cream (page 25) or 1½ cups
   low-fat vanilla ice cream or nonfat frozen
   vanilla yogurt (optional)

❶ Heat oven to 375°F. Coat 8-inch (2-quart) square baking dish with nonstick cooking spray.

❷ In baking dish, combine apples, cranberries and sugar; toss to mix. Cover with aluminum foil; bake 20 minutes. (If using some frozen fruit, bake 25 minutes.)

❸ Meanwhile, in medium bowl, mix flour, oats, brown sugar, cinnamon and salt with fork. Add butter; crumble with pastry blender or your fingertips until well blended. Add canola oil; stir with fork to coat. Add apple juice concentrate; stir and toss until dry ingredients are moistened.

❹ When crumble has baked 20 minutes, sprinkle flour mixture evenly over fruit. Sprinkle with walnuts. Bake, uncovered, an additional 20 to 30 minutes or until fruit is bubbly and tender and topping is lightly browned. Let cool at least 10 minutes before serving warm or at room temperature with Vanilla Cream, if desired.

6 (¾-cup) servings.
Preparation time: 20 minutes. Ready to serve: 1 hour, 25 minutes.

Per serving: 430 calories, 13 g total fat (6 g saturated fat), 7 g protein, 76 g carbohydrate, 31 mg cholesterol, 131 mg sodium, 6 g fiber. **Star nutrients:** Fiber (25%). **Noteworthy nutrients:** Phosphorous (20%).

VARIATION **Peach-Raspberry Crumble**

- In Step 2, combine 5 cups sliced peeled peaches (2 lb.), 1 cup raspberries, 2 tablespoons sugar and 1 tablespoon lemon juice in prepared baking dish; toss to mix. Cover with aluminum foil; bake 20 minutes. (If using some frozen fruit, bake 25 minutes.)
- In Step 3, mix ⅔ cup whole wheat flour, ½ cup old-fashioned rolled oats, ½ cup packed light brown sugar, 1 teaspoon ground cinnamon and dash salt with fork. Add 1 tablespoon butter; crumble with pastry blender or your fingertips until well blended. Add 1 tablespoon canola oil; stir with fork to coat. Add 3 tablespoons frozen orange juice concentrate; stir and toss until dry ingredients are moistened.
- In Step 4, sprinkle flour mixture evenly over fruit. Sprinkle with 1 tablespoon chopped slivered almonds. Bake 20 to 30 minutes.

VARIATION Rhubarb-Blackberry Crumble

- In Step 2, combine 5 cups diced (½ inch) rhubarb (1½ lb. before trimming), 1 cup blackberries and ½ cup sugar in baking dish; toss to mix. Cover with aluminum foil; bake 20 minutes. (If using some frozen fruit, bake 25 minutes.)
- In Step 3, mix ⅔ cup whole wheat flour, ½ cup old-fashioned rolled oats, ½ cup packed light brown sugar, 1 teaspoon ground cinnamon and dash salt with fork. Add 1 tablespoon butter; crumble with pastry blender or your fingertips until well blended. Add 1 tablespoon canola oil; stir with fork to coat. Add 3 tablespoons frozen orange juice concentrate; stir and toss until dry ingredients are moistened.
- In Step 4, sprinkle flour mixture evenly over fruit. Sprinkle with 1 tablespoon chopped slivered almonds. Bake 20 to 30 minutes.

Maple-Walnut Roasted Pears

Throughout the colder months, pears are an excellent choice in fruit. Roasting pears with maple syrup brings out their inherent sweetness and creates an elegant yet simple dessert. Bay leaves contribute a delicate citrus note to the syrup and make an attractive garnish.

½ cup maple syrup
¼ cup apple cider or apple juice
2 teaspoons butter
2 large or 3 small Bosc or Anjou pears
½ lemon
4 bay leaves (optional)
¼ cup (1 oz.) chopped walnuts
¼ cup low-fat vanilla yogurt

❶ Heat oven to 400°F. Coat 8x11-inch (or similar) baking dish with nonstick cooking spray.

❷ In small saucepan, combine maple syrup, apple cider and butter; bring to a simmer, stirring.

❸ Core and quarter pears. Rub and squeeze lemon half over each cut side of pear. Place pears in baking dish. Spoon maple syrup mixture over pears. Scatter bay leaves over pears, if desired. Cover with aluminum foil.

❹ Bake pears 30 minutes. Baste pears to coat with syrup. Sprinkle with walnuts. Bake, uncovered, an additional 20 to 30 minutes or until pears are tender and glazed, basting pears several times. Let cool slightly. Divide pears among four dessert dishes, spooning syrup over pears. Serve with vanilla yogurt. Garnish each serving with bay leaf, if desired.

4 servings.
Preparation time: 10 minutes.
Ready to serve: 1 hour, 5 minutes.

Per serving: 240 calories, 7 g total fat (1.5 g saturated fat), 3 g protein, 43 g carbohydrate, 6 mg cholesterol, 35 mg sodium, 3 g fiber.

Updated Old-Fashioned Date Squares

These lower-fat date squares are an energy-boosting treat.

FILLING
1 (8-oz.) pkg. chopped pitted dates (1¾ cups)
⅓ cup orange juice
⅓ cup water

CRUST & TOPPING
1 cup whole wheat flour
½ cup all-purpose flour
½ cup old-fashioned rolled oats
1½ cups packed light brown sugar
¼ teaspoon baking soda
⅛ teaspoon salt
⅓ cup canola oil
¼ cup frozen orange juice concentrate
2 teaspoons butter, softened

❶ In small saucepan, combine dates, orange juice and water; bring to a simmer over medium-high heat. Reduce heat to low. Cook, uncovered, 5 to 8 minutes or until dates are tender and filling has thickened, stirring often. Remove from heat; let cool completely.

❷ Heat oven to 350°F. Coat 8-inch square pan with nonstick cooking spray. In medium bowl, combine whole wheat flour, all-purpose flour, oats, brown sugar, baking soda and salt; blend with fork. Add canola oil; toss with fork to coat. Add orange juice concentrate; blend with your fingertips until moistened and crumbly.

❸ Measure ½ cup flour mixture into small bowl; set aside for topping. Pat remaining flour mixture firmly in bottom of pan. Drop spoonfuls of date filling over bottom crust; gently spread into even layer with bottom of spoon or offset spatula. Add butter to reserved topping; blend with your fingertips until crumbly. Sprinkle topping over filling. Bake 25 to 30 minutes or until golden. Let cool completely in pan on wire rack. Cut into 16 squares.

16 servings. Preparation time: 20 minutes. Ready to serve: 1 hour, 30 minutes.

Per serving: 215 calories, 5.5 g total fat (0.5 g saturated fat), 2 g protein, 42 g carbohydrate, 1 mg cholesterol, 52 mg sodium, 2 g fiber.

VARIATION   **Updated Old-Fashioned Apricot Squares**

In Step 1, combine 1¾ cups chopped dried apricots, ¾ cup orange juice and ¾ cup water in small saucepan; bring to a simmer over medium-high heat. Reduce heat to low. Cover; cook, stirring occasionally, 25 to 30 minutes or until dried apricots are tender and filling has thickened. Let cool.

VARIATION   **Updated Old-Fashioned Dried Cranberry Crumble Squares**

In Step 1, combine 1 cup dried cranberries, ¾ cup raisins, 1 cup orange juice and 1 cup water in small saucepan; bring to a simmer over medium-high heat. Reduce heat to low. Cover; cook, stirring occasionally, 45 to 50 minutes or until dried cranberries and raisins are tender and filling has thickened. Let cool.

Dried Fruit Compote

Because it is easily stored in the pantry, dried fruit is particularly handy to have on hand. An assortment of dried fruits is delicious when plumped in a spiced syrup made with brewed tea. Serve this compote for dessert over vanilla frozen yogurt, or for breakfast (without the brandy) with yogurt and a sprinkling of toasted wheat germ. Either way, the fragrance of this simmering compote will make you feel all warm inside.

4 cups water
4 black tea bags
2 (2-inch-long) strips orange peel
2 cinnamon sticks
¼ cup sugar
1 cup (6 oz.) pitted dried plums (prunes)
1 cup (6 oz.) dried apricots
¾ cup (4 oz.) dried peaches or dried pears, cut into quarters or dried pineapple wedges
2 tablespoons brandy (optional)

❶ In large saucepan, bring water to a boil. Remove from heat. Add tea bags, orange peel and cinnamon sticks; cover. Let steep 5 minutes. Remove tea bags.

❷ Add sugar to tea; stir to dissolve. Add dried plums, dried apricots and dried peaches; bring to a simmer over medium-high heat. Reduce heat to medium-low. Cover; cook 15 to 20 minutes or until fruit is tender.

❸ With slotted spoon, transfer fruit to medium bowl; discard orange peel and cinnamon sticks. Increase heat to medium-high. Simmer cooking liquid, uncovered, 5 minutes to thicken slightly and intensify flavor. Pour syrup over reserved fruit. Stir in brandy, if desired. Serve warm or chilled.

8 (½-cup) servings.
Preparation time: 10 minutes.
Ready to serve: 40 minutes.

Per serving: 160 calories, 0.5 g total fat (0 g saturated fat), 2 g protein, 39 g carbohydrate, 0 mg cholesterol, 7 mg sodium, 4 g fiber. **Star nutrients:** Vitamin A (39%). **Noteworthy nutrients:** Fiber (17%).

MAKE AHEAD Cover and refrigerate compote for up to 4 days.

Peach-Blackberry Compote

Blackberries provide beautiful color contrast to sweet peaches in this simple summer fruit dessert.

¼ cup sugar
3 tablespoons dry white wine
2 (2-inch-long) strips orange peel
1 cinnamon stick
3 cups sliced peeled* peaches (3 to 4 medium or 1½ lb.)
1 cup fresh blackberries
1 tablespoon lemon juice
Fresh mint sprigs

❶ In small saucepan, combine sugar and wine. Bring to a simmer. Remove from heat. Add orange peel and cinnamon stick. Cover; let steep 30 minutes.

❷ Discard orange peel and cinnamon stick. Place peaches, blackberries and lemon juice in large bowl. Add syrup; toss gently to coat. Garnish with mint.

4 (1-cup) servings.
Preparation time: 20 minutes.
Ready to serve: 50 minutes.

Per serving: 145 calories, 0.5 g total fat (0 g saturated fat), 1 g protein, 36 g carbohydrate, 0 mg cholesterol, 1 mg sodium, 4 g fiber. **Star nutrients:** Vitamin C (35%). **Noteworthy nutrients:** Fiber (16%).

TIP   *To peel peaches, dip them into boiling water for a few seconds, then slip off skin.

Mixed Berry Sundaes

Take advantage of the jewels of summer to enjoy a refreshing and colorful dessert. Crushing a small portion of the berries gives the berry compote extra body and intensifies flavor.

3 cups mixed fresh berries, such as raspberries, blueberries, blackberries and sliced strawberries, rinsed
2 tablespoons crème de cassis or black currant syrup
1 tablespoon lemon juice
1 tablespoon sugar
1 pint (2 cups) raspberry sorbet or lemon sorbet, slightly softened*

❶ In medium bowl, crush ¼ cup of the berries with fork. Add crème de cassis, lemon juice and sugar, stirring until sugar has dissolved. Add the remaining 2¾ cups of the berries; stir gently to coat. Place scoop of sorbet in each of four dessert dishes. Spoon berry mixture over sorbet.

4 servings.
Preparation time: 10 minutes.
Ready to serve: 10 minutes.

Per serving: 210 calories, 0.5 g total fat (0 g saturated fat), 1 g protein, 52 g carbohydrate, 0 mg cholesterol, 5 mg sodium, 6 g fiber.
Star nutrients: Vitamin C (55%), Fiber (25%).

TIP *To soften sorbet, place container in the refrigerator for 20 to 30 minutes. Alternatively, microwave at Defrost for 30 to 60 seconds.

Caramelized Banana-Chocolate Sundaes

Running sweetened banana slices under the broiler makes them absolutely delicious. Add a scoop of light vanilla ice cream, an easy chocolate sauce and some toasted nuts, and in just a few minutes you have a sensational dessert.

¼ cup *Quick Chocolate-Hazelnut Sauce* (recipe follows)
2 firm bananas
2 teaspoons sugar
1 cup low-fat, reduced-calorie vanilla ice cream or nonfat frozen vanilla yogurt
2 tablespoons (½ oz.) chopped hazelnuts, toasted*

❶ Prepare Quick Chocolate-Hazelnut Sauce.

❷ Heat broiler. Coat baking sheet with nonstick cooking spray.

❸ Peel bananas; cut into ⅜-inch-thick diagonal slices. Place on baking sheet; sprinkle with sugar. Broil 3 to 4 minutes or until tops are golden. Place small scoop of ice cream in each dessert dish. Surround ice cream with caramelized banana slices; drizzle with chocolate sauce. Sprinkle with hazelnuts.

4 servings. Preparation time: 10 minutes. Ready to serve: 10 minutes.

Per serving: 195 calories, 6 g total fat (1.5 g saturated fat), 3 g protein, 36 g carbohydrate, 5 mg cholesterol, 43 mg sodium, 2 g fiber. **Noteworthy nutrients:** Vitamin B6 (19%).

TIP *To toast hazelnuts, spread on baking sheet; bake at 375°F about 10 minutes or until lightly browned. Cool.

Quick Chocolate-Hazelnut Sauce

It is amazing how a little bit of chocolate-hazelnut spread can transform prepared fat-free chocolate syrup into a luxurious chocolate sauce. This sauce is also great as a dip for fruit.

⅔ cup fat-free chocolate syrup
⅓ cup chocolate-hazelnut spread, such as Nutella

❶ In small saucepan, combine chocolate syrup and chocolate-hazelnut spread; heat over low heat, stirring occasionally, until smooth and warm.

1 cup (16 servings). Preparation time: 2 minutes. Ready to serve: 5 minutes.

MAKE AHEAD Cover and refrigerate sauce for up to 2 weeks.

Per serving: 60 calories, 2 g total fat (0 g saturated fat), 1 g protein, 12 g carbohydrate, 0 mg cholesterol, 14 mg sodium, 0 g fiber.

Wholesome Chocolate Chip Cookies

Their name sounds like an oxymoron doesn't it? But this recipe for America's all-time favorite cookie is lower in fat than standard recipes. Tofu successfully replaces much of the butter, while a moderate quantity of chocolate chips delivers a satisfying hit of chocolate. A few nuts strategically placed on top gives the cookies a rich-tasting finish.

1 cup plus 3 tablespoons all-purpose flour
1 cup whole wheat flour
1 teaspoon baking soda
¼ teaspoon salt
⅔ cup low-fat firm silken tofu
1 egg
1 egg white

⅔ cup sugar
⅔ cup packed light brown sugar
⅓ cup canola oil
2 tablespoons butter, softened
1 teaspoon vanilla extract
¾ cup chocolate chips
⅓ cup (1½ oz.) chopped walnuts

❶ Heat oven to 375°F. Coat 2 or 3 baking sheets with nonstick cooking spray.

❷ In medium bowl, whisk all-purpose flour, whole wheat flour, baking soda and salt.

❸ In food processor, puree tofu. Add egg, egg white, sugar, brown sugar, canola oil, butter and vanilla; process until smooth, stopping once or twice to scrape down sides of bowl. Scrape mixture into bowl with flour mixture; mix with rubber spatula until well blended. Stir in chocolate chips.

❹ Drop batter by scant tablespoonfuls, about 2½ inches apart, onto baking sheets. Sprinkle cookies with walnuts. Bake, one sheet at a time, 12 to 14 minutes or until golden brown. Transfer cookies to wire racks to cool.

3 dozen cookies.
Preparation time: 20 minutes.
Ready to serve: 1 hour.

Per cookie: 110 calories, 4.5 g total fat (1.5 g saturated fat), 2 g protein, 16 g carbohydrate, 8 mg cholesterol, 67 mg sodium, 1 g fiber.

NUTRTION NOTE This recipe has about half the fat of a traditional chocolate chip cookie recipe.

Rolled Sugar Cookies

Most recipes for crisp sugar cookies start off with at least a stick of butter. Tofu is a highly successful stand-in for butter in this updated version. Some whole wheat flour adds a pleasant nuttiness and further improves nutrition. These make fine holiday cookies when cut into your favorite shapes and decorate as desired, but they also make great additions to your everyday cookie jar. Enjoy them with afternoon tea, too.

COOKIES
1½ cups all-purpose flour
¾ cup whole wheat flour
1 teaspoon baking powder
¼ teaspoon salt
⅓ cup low-fat firm silken tofu
1 egg
1 cup sugar

¼ cup canola oil
1 tablespoon butter, softened
2 teaspoons vanilla extract

GLAZE
2 tablespoons sugar
½ teaspoon ground cinnamon
1 egg white, lightly beaten

❶ In medium bowl, whisk all-purpose flour, whole wheat flour, baking powder and salt.

❷ In food processor, puree tofu. Add egg, 1 cup sugar, canola oil, butter and vanilla; process until smooth, stopping once or twice to scrape down sides of bowl. Add flour mixture; pulse several times just until dough clumps together. Transfer to lightly floured surface; knead several times. Divide dough in half; press each piece into a round. Dust rounds with flour; wrap in plastic wrap. Refrigerate at least 2 hours or overnight.

❸ Heat oven to 350°F. Coat several baking sheets with nonstick cooking spray. In small bowl, mix 2 tablespoons sugar and cinnamon.

❹ Working with one piece at a time, on lightly floured surface, roll out dough to ⅛-inch thickness. Using cookie cutter, cut out shapes. Place cookies, about ½ inch apart, on baking sheets. Brush cookies with egg white; sprinkle with cinnamon-sugar mixture. Gather scraps; re-roll.

❺ Bake cookies, one sheet at a time, 12 to 15 minutes or until light golden around edges. Transfer cookies to wire rack to cool completely.

3 dozen cookies.
Preparation time: 45 minutes. Ready to serve: 3 hours.

Per cookie: 70 calories, 2 g total fat (0.5 g saturated fat), 1 g protein, 12 g carbohydrate, 7 mg cholesterol, 36 mg sodium, 0 g fiber.

NUTRITION NOTE This recipe contains one-third less fat than a traditional sugar cookie.

Almond Biscotti

Biscotti, imports from Italy now popular in coffee bars and bakeries throughout America, are twice-baked biscuits. Most biscotti recipes are low in saturated fat, so they are generally a healthful choice for a cookie or snack. Biscotti are easy to make at home. And, because they are dried, biscotti are great keepers.

1 cup plus 2 tablespoons all-purpose flour	1 cup sugar
1 cup whole wheat flour	1 teaspoon vanilla extract
1 teaspoon baking powder	¾ teaspoon almond extract
½ teaspoon baking soda	¾ cup (3 oz.) slivered almonds, toasted,*
¼ teaspoon salt	chopped
3 eggs	

❶ Heat oven to 350°F. Coat baking sheet with nonstick cooking spray.

❷ In medium bowl, whisk all-purpose flour, whole wheat flour, baking powder, baking soda and salt.

❸ In large bowl, combine eggs and sugar; beat with electric mixer at high speed 3 to 4 minutes or until thickened and pale. Blend in vanilla and almond extract. Add reserved flour mixture; mix with rubber spatula until dry ingredients are moistened. Stir in almonds.

❹ Using half of the batter, drop large spoonfuls in a row along one long side of baking sheet. Repeat with remaining batter, placing it about 3 inches from first row of batter on other side of baking sheet. Lightly moisten hands; smooth each row of batter into 12x2½-inch log.

❺ Bake logs 20 to 25 minutes or until lightly browned and tops spring back when touched lightly. Loosen logs with metal spatula; transfer to wire rack to cool completely (at least 20 minutes). Reduce oven temperature to 300°F.

❻ Using serrated knife, slice logs diagonally into ¾-inch-thick slices. Place wire cooling rack on baking sheet. Lay biscotti on their sides on rack. Return to oven; bake 20 to 25 minutes or until lightly toasted. Let cool completely.

30 biscotti. Preparation time: 30 minutes. Ready to serve: 1 hour, 15 minutes.

Per biscotti: 85 calories, 2.5 g total fat (0.5 g saturated fat), 2 g protein, 14 g carbohydrate, 21 mg cholesterol, 60 mg sodium, 1 g fiber.

MAKE AHEAD Store biscotti in airtight container for up to 1 month.

TIP *To toast almonds, place in a dry skillet. Cook, stirring constantly, over medium-low heat 2 minutes or until light golden and fragrant. Transfer to a small bowl to cool.

VARIATION Hazelnut Biscotti
Substitute ¾ cup toasted chopped hazelnuts for almonds. Omit almond extract. Increase vanilla extract to 1½ teaspoons.

Better-For-You Brownies

Dates, the secret ingredient in these lower-fat brownies, replace butter and have a remarkable affinity with chocolate. Ground walnuts give these brownies a rich background flavor.

½ cup unsweetened cocoa
½ cup chopped pitted dates
1 teaspoon instant coffee granules
½ cup boiling water
⅔ cup whole wheat flour
½ teaspoon baking powder
¼ teaspoon salt

⅓ cup (1½ oz.) walnuts, toasted*
1 egg
1 egg white
1 cup plus 1 tablespoon sugar, divided
2 tablespoons canola oil
1 teaspoon vanilla extract
¼ cup semisweet chocolate chips

❶ Heat oven to 350°F. Coat 8x11½-inch (or similar) baking dish with nonstick cooking spray. In medium bowl, combine cocoa, dates and coffee. Add boiling water; stir until cocoa has dissolved. Let stand about 10 minutes or until completely cooled.

❷ In food processor, combine flour, baking powder, salt and walnuts; process until walnuts are ground. Transfer to large bowl.

❸ Scrape cooled cocoa mixture into food processor. Add egg, egg white, 1 cup of the sugar, canola oil and vanilla; process until smooth, stopping once or twice to scrape down sides of bowl.

❹ Add cocoa mixture to reserved flour mixture; mix with rubber spatula just until dry ingredients are moistened. Stir in chocolate chips. Scrape batter into baking dish, spreading evenly. Sprinkle the remaining 1 tablespoon of the sugar evenly over top.

❺ Bake brownies 22 to 25 minutes or until top is firm around edges and just set in center. Let cool in pan on wire rack. Cut into bars.**

12 servings. Preparation time: 20 minutes. Ready to serve: 1 hour, 15 minutes.

Per serving: 185 calories, 6.5 g total fat (1.5 g saturated fat), 3 g protein, 32 g carbohydrate, 18 mg cholesterol, 77 mg sodium, 3 g fiber.

TIP *To toast walnuts, place in a dry skillet. Cook, stirring constantly, over medium-low heat 3 minutes or until fragrant. Transfer to a small bowl to cool.

TIP **To prevent brownies from sticking to the knife, spray it with nonstick cooking spray before cutting into the bars.

NUTRITION NOTE The added bonus of this brownie recipe is fiber. It provides 3 grams of fiber per serving, while a traditional brownie recipe has just 1 gram.

Pumpkin Custards

These custards make deliciously healthful alternatives to the traditional Thanksgiving pie, but they are so easy to make you can enjoy them for everyday desserts, too. Vanilla soymilk makes exceptionally rich-tasting, low-fat custards. If you do not have any soymilk on hand, substitute low-fat (1%) milk and increase vanilla to 1 teaspoon.

2 eggs
2 egg whites
⅔ cup sugar
¾ cup canned unseasoned pumpkin puree
1½ teaspoons ground cinnamon
½ teaspoon ground nutmeg
¼ teaspoon salt
½ teaspoon vanilla extract
1½ cups vanilla soymilk
⅓ cup Vanilla Cream (page 25)

❶ Heat oven to 325°F. Line roasting pan with folded kitchen towel. Put kettle of water on to boil for water bath.

❷ In large bowl, whisk eggs, egg whites and sugar until smooth. Add pumpkin, cinnamon, nutmeg, salt and vanilla; whisk until blended. Gently whisk in soymilk.

❸ Divide mixture among six 6-oz. (¾-cup) custard cups. Skim foam from surface of custards. Place custard cups in pan. Pour enough boiling water into pan to come halfway up sides of custard cups. Place pan in oven; bake, uncovered, 50 to 55 minutes or until custards are just set. Transfer custard cups to wire rack to cool. Cover custards; refrigerate at least 1 hour or until chilled.

❹ Meanwhile, prepare Vanilla Cream. Top each custard with dollop of Vanilla Cream just prior to serving.

6 servings.
Preparation time: 15 minutes.
Ready to serve: 2 hours, 40 minutes.

Per serving: 255 calories, 10 g total fat (5 g saturated fat), 9 g protein, 35 g carbohydrate, 96 mg cholesterol, 192 mg sodium, 2 g fiber. **Star nutrients:** Vitamin A (143%). **Noteworthy nutrients:** Calcium (15%), Phosphorus (17%), Riboflavin (20%).

MAKE AHEAD Cover and refrigerate custards for up to 2 days.

Menus

A well planned menu presents an appealing variety of colors and textures, is well suited to the season, and provides nutritional balance. The following menus will help you use the recipes in Cooking for Health & Flavor *and provide inspiration for putting together healthful meals.*

Spring

Grab-&-Go Breakfast
Banana-Berry Smoothie (page 30)
Whole Wheat Banana-Bran Muffin (page 65)

This menu provides 2 servings fruits and vegetables, 1 serving whole grain.

Elegant & Easy Dinner
Oven-Poached Salmon with Light Remoulade Sauce (page 148)
Quinoa Pilaf (page 93)
Spinach. Cook frozen spinach according to package directions or wilt fresh spinach (see page 98)
Raspberry sorbet with fresh raspberries

This menu provides 2 servings fruits and vegetables, 1 serving whole grain.

Spring Celebration
Asparagus Salad with Orange-Sesame Dressing (page 74)
Broiled Lemon-&-Garlic Salmon (page 166)
Boiled red potatoes. Boil potatoes about 20 minutes, toss with parsley.
Green peas. Cook frozen peas according to package directions.
Mixed Berry Gratin (page 207)

This menu provides 4 servings fruits and vegetables.

Saint Patrick's Day Dinner
Irish Soda Bread (page 64)
Lamb Steaks with Mustard-Rosemary Marinade (page 141)
Garlic Mashed Potatoes with Greens (page 110)
Steamed carrots. Steam carrot sticks or mini carrots 4 to 6 minutes.
Fresh green grapes

This menu provides 3 servings fruits and vegetables, 1 serving whole grain.

Evening in Provençe
Spinach Salad with Orange Segments & Olives (page 82)
Provençal Fish Stew (page 163)
Orzo. Cook according to package directions.
Fresh pears

This menu provides 2 servings fruits and vegetables.

Paella Olé
Quick & Easy Paella (page 203)
Tossed green salad with Balsamic Vinaigrette (page 79)
Fresh pineapple wedges

This menu provides 3 servings fruits and vegetables, 1 serving whole grain.

Company Fare

Herbed Edamame Spread (page 42) with whole wheat crackers
Veal Stew with Mushrooms & Baby Onions (page 145)
Egg noodles. Cook according to package directions.
Steamed carrots. Steam carrot sticks or mini carrots 4 to 6 minutes.
Green peas. Cook frozen green peas according to package directions.
Rhubarb-Blackberry Crumble (page 211)

This menu provides 4 servings fruits and vegetables, 1 serving whole grain.

A Taste of Spring

Sole with Mushrooms & Tomato (page 156)
Brown rice. Cook according to package directions.
Steamed asparagus. Steam asparagus 4 to 6 minutes.
Fresh strawberries

This menu provides 2½ servings fruits and vegetables, 1 serving whole grain.

Brown Bag Lunch in the Park

Tuna sandwich with whole wheat bread and Carrot Salad with Lemon & Dill (page 83)
Cherry tomatoes or grape tomatoes
Fresh pear
Cranberry juice

This menu provides 3 servings fruits and vegetables, 1 serving whole grain.

Simple Spring Supper

Turkey Cutlets with Dried Apricot & Mint Sauce (page 112)
Brown rice. Cook according to package directions.
Sugar snap peas. Cook frozen sugar snap peas according to package directions.
Mixed Berry Sundaes (page 216)

This menu provides 2 servings fruits and vegetables, 1 serving whole grain.

Light & Easy

Salad of arugula & toasted walnuts with Balsamic Vinaigrette (page 79)
Risotto with Asparagus & Lemon (page 200)
Chocolate-Dipped Strawberries (page 209)

This menu provides 3 servings fruits and vegetables.

Presto Pesto

Pasta with Pesto, Potatoes & Green Beans (page 202)
Salad of mesclun greens with French Dressing (page 73)
Fruit Salad (page 209)

This menu provides 3 servings fruits and vegetables.

Summer

Breakfast Buffet for Guests

Freshly squeezed orange juice
Muesli (page 30)
Irish Soda Bread (page 64)
Reduced-fat cream cheese, assorted fruit preserves
Fresh melon wedges
Coffee and tea

This menu provides 3 servings fruits and vegetables, 2 servings whole grain.

Beach Picnic

Sandwiches made with Asian Peanut Dip (page 41) grated carrots, sliced cucumber & lettuce on whole wheat bread
Nectarines
Wholesome Chocolate Chip Cookies (page 219)
Lemonade

This menu provides 3 servings fruits and vegetables, 1 serving whole grain.

Carefree Summer Barbecue

Flank Steak with Coffee-Peppercorn Marinade (page 134)
Roasted red potatoes (page 109)
Grilled Cherry Tomatoes (page 108)
Corn on the cob. Steam husked corncobs 4 to 6 minutes.
Peaches

This menu provides 4 servings fruits and vegetables.

Mediterranean Evening

Grilled Swordfish Steaks with Salsa (page 154)
Grilled zucchini (page 109)
New potatoes. Steam or boil potatoes 15 to 20 minutes.
Fresh melon slices

This menu provides 4 servings fruits and vegetables.

Supper for a Sultry Evening

Warm Salad with Grilled Vegetables & Garlic Croutons (page 80)
White Bean Spread with Rosemary (page 44)
Peach-Blackberry Compote (page 215)

This menu provides 3 servings fruits and vegetables.

Outdoor Concert Picnic

Fruity Tabbouleh (page 77)
Sliced cold chicken breast. To cook chicken, see page 123 or purchase supermarket rotisserie chicken.
Assorted crudités (carrots, celery, cherry tomatoes, etc.)
Whole Wheat Pita Bread. Use recipe on page 60 or purchase ready-made pitas.
Cherries

This menu provides 3 servings fruits and vegetables, 2 servings whole grain.

Taverna Night

Roasted Red Pepper-Walnut Spread (page 38)
Whole Wheat Pita Crisps (page 26)
Greek Lamb Kabobs (page 144)
Bulgur Pilaf with Raisins & Pine Nuts (page 90)
Grilled Cherry Tomatoes (page 108)
Tossed green salad with Balsamic Vinaigrette (page 79)
Peach-Blackberry Compote (page 215)

This menu provides 3 servings fruits and vegetables, 1 serving whole grain.

When It's Too Hot to Cook

Chicken Salad with Dill (page 118)
Spinach Salad with Orange Segments & Olives (page 82)
Whole wheat country bread
Iced mint tea
Plums

This menu provides 2 servings fruits and vegetables, 1 serving whole grain.

Latino Grill

Baked Tortilla Crisps (page 26) with salsa
Pork & Pineapple Kabobs (page 142)
Beans & Rice (page 96)
Carrot Salad with Cumin & Lemon (page 83)
Broiled Mangoes (page 208)

This menu provides 2½ servings fruits and vegetables, 1 serving whole grain.

Vegetarian Kabobs

Teriyaki Tofu & Vegetable Kabobs (page 185)
Brown rice. Cook according to package directions.
Coleslaw with Asian Flavors (page 88)
Peach-Blackberry Compote (page 215)

This menu provides 2½ servings fruits and vegetables, 1 serving whole grain.

Summer Grazing Menu

Grilled Whole Wheat Flatbreads (page 58)
Herbed Edamame Spread (page 42)
Yogurt-Garlic Sauce (page 25)
Salad of tomatoes, cucumbers, sweet onions, feta cheese & olives with Greek Lemon Dressing (page 73)
Fresh melon wedges

This menu provides 3 servings fruits and vegetables, 1 serving whole grain.

Vegetarian Grill

Grilled Polenta with White Bean Salad (page 181)
Tossed green salad with Balsamic Vinaigrette (page 79)
Grilled whole wheat country bread
Grilled peaches (page 209)
Almond Biscotti (page 222)

This menu provides 3 servings fruits and vegetables, 1 serving whole grain.

Autumn

Cozy Fireside Supper

Spinach salad with Creamy Buttermilk Dressing (page 73)
Turkey Cutlets with Port & Dried Cranberry Sauce (page 112)
Quick barley. Prepare according to package directions.
Citrus-Scented Squash Puree (page 95)
Maple-Walnut Roasted Pears (page 212)

This menu provides 4 servings fruits and vegetables, 1 serving whole grain.

Steakhouse Supper

Spice-Rubbed Steak (page 133)
Baked potatoes. Bake russet potatoes at 450°F about 50 minutes.
Cajun Corn Sauté (page 95)
Sliced tomatoes
Fresh grapes

This menu provides 4 servings fruits and vegetables.

Kid- (and Adult-) Pleasing Dinner

Sesame-Crusted Chicken (page 127)
Two-Potato Oven Fries (page 103)
Steamed broccoli. Steam fresh broccoli florets 5 to 8 minutes or cook frozen broccoli according to package directions.
Better-For-You Brownies (page 223) with light vanilla ice cream and Quick Chocolate-Hazelnut Sauce (page 218)

This menu provides 2 servings fruits and vegetables.

Sunday Dinner

Roasted Chicken & Vegetables (page 116)
Swiss Chard with Red Peppers & Olives (page 104)
Pear & Dried Cranberry Gratin (page 206)

This menu provides 3 servings fruits and vegetables.

Fall Foliage Picnic

Sandwiches made with Asian Peanut Dip (page 41), grated carrots, sliced cucumber and lettuce
Apples
Updated Old-Fashioned Date Squares (page 213)
Thermos of hot apple cider

This menu provides 2 servings fruits and vegetables, 1 serving whole grain.

Seafood Supper for a Frosty Night

Shrimp Kabobs with Spanish Red Pepper Sauce (page 160)
Rice & Noodle Pilaf with Toasted Flaxseeds (page 92)
Spinach. Cook frozen spinach according to package directions.
Fresh pineapple

This menu provides 2½ servings fruits and vegetables.

Harvest Season Dinner

Cider House Chicken (page 122)
Spinach. Cook frozen spinach according to package directions.
Acorn squash. Quarter squash and remove seeds. Microwave, partially covered, 15 to 20 minutes or until tender.
Orzo. Cook according to package directions.
Fresh apples and pears

This menu provides 3 servings fruits and vegetables.

Dinner Party for Vegetarians & Nonvegetarians Alike

Herbed Edamame Spread (page 42)
Whole Wheat Pita Crisps (page 26)
Roasted Vegetables with Cilantro-Parsley Sauce & Couscous (page 171)
Chicken. Grill boneless chicken breasts (see page 123) or purchase rotisserie chicken.
Tossed green salad with Orange-Flaxseed Dressing (page 82)
Pumpkin Custards (page 224)

This menu provides 2½ servings fruits and vegetables, 1 serving whole grain.

Soup Supper for a Frosty Night

Hearty Bean & Barley Soup (page 46)
Toasted whole wheat country bread
Tossed green salad with French Dressing (page 73)
Fresh pears

This menu provides 3 servings fruits and vegetables, 1 serving whole grain.

Middle Eastern Menu

Falafel with Flaxseeds (page 178)
Green salad with Apricot-Ginger Dressing (page 76)
Orange & Pomegranate Salad (page 208)

This menu provides 3 servings fruits and vegetables, 1 serving whole grain.

It's a Wrap

Black Bean & Sweet Potato Burritos (page 174)
Tossed green salad with Creamy Buttermilk Dressing (page 73)
Instant Strawberry Frozen Yogurt (page 209)

This menu provides 4 servings fruits and vegetables.

Weekend Brunch Menu

Grilled Whole Wheat Flatbreads (page 58)
Vegetable Stew with Poached Eggs (page 177)
Fruit Salad (page 209)
Rolled Sugar Cookies (page 221)
Sparkling apple cider
Coffee and tea

This menu provides 3 servings fruits and vegetables, 1 serving whole grain.

Lazy Sunday Breakfast

Cranberry juice cocktail
Multi-Grain Pancakes (page 35)
Dried Fruit Compote (page 214)
Yogurt
Coffee or tea

This menu provides 2 servings fruits and vegetables, 1 serving whole grain.

Winter

Hearty Après-Ski Supper

Romaine salad with Creamy Buttermilk Dressing (page 73)
Slow-Cooker Beef & Vegetable Stew (page 130)
Egg noodles. Cook according to package directions.
Crusty whole wheat country bread
Orange & Pomegranate Salad (page 208)

This menu provides 3 servings fruits and vegetables, 1 serving whole grain.

New Year's Good Luck Dinner

Sautéed chicken breasts (page 123)
Braised Mustard Greens with Black-Eyed Peas & Bacon (page 100)
Brown rice. Cook according to package directions.
Broiled Mangoes (page 208)

This menu provides 2 servings fruits and vegetables, 1 serving whole grain.

Weeknight Family Dinner

Maple-Mustard Glazed Pork Chops (page 140)
Garlic Mashed Potatoes with Greens (page 110)
Steamed carrots. Steam carrot sticks or mini carrots 4 to 6 minutes.
Caramelized Banana-Chocolate Sundaes (page 218)

This menu provides 3 servings fruits and vegetables, 1 serving whole grain.

Holiday Brunch

Chilled tomato juice-vegetable cocktail
Fritatta with Potatoes & Canadian Bacon (page 37)
Whole Wheat-Flaxseed Rolls (page 63)
Orange & Pomegranate Salad (page 208)
Coffee and tea

This menu provides 2 servings fruits and vegetables, 1 serving whole grain.

Simple Fish Dinner

Sole Florentine (page 164)
Steamed carrots. Steam carrot sticks or mini carrots 4 to 6 minutes.
Brown rice. Cook according to package directions.
Updated Old-Fashioned Date Squares (page 213) with light ice cream or nonfat frozen vanilla yogurt

This menu provides 2 servings fruits and vegetables, 1 serving whole grain.

Dinner with Friends

Beet & Arugula Salad with Walnuts (page 78)
Veal Stew with Mushrooms & Baby Onions (page 145)
Egg noodles. Cook according to package directions.
Green peas. Cook frozen peas according to package directions.
Pear & Dried Cranberry Gratin (page 206)

This menu provides 3 servings fruits and vegetables.

Fish & Greens

Roasted Fish & Potatoes (page 153)
Swiss Chard with Red Peppers & Olives (page 104)
Dried Fruit Compote (page 214)

This menu provides 3 servings fruits and vegetables.

Post-Game Party

Baked Tortilla Chips (page 26)
Black Bean Spread with Cumin & Lime (page 44)
Salsa
Quick Vegetarian Chili (page 172)
Turkey & Bean Chili (page 119)
Rice. Prepare according to package directions.
Spinach Salad with Orange Segments & Olives (page 82)
Wholesome Chocolate Chip Cookies (page 219)
Light vanilla ice cream or nonfat frozen yogurt with sliced strawberries

This menu provides 3 servings fruits and vegetables, 1 serving whole grain.

A Taste of Home

Crispy Ham-&-Cheese-Stuffed Chicken Breasts (page 126)
Garlic Mashed Potatoes with Greens (page 110)
Steamed carrots. Steam carrots sticks or mini carrots 4 to 6 minutes.
Apple-Cranberry Crumble (page 210)

This menu provides 3 servings fruits and vegetables.

Quick & Easy Bistro Dinner

Mustard-Glazed Salmon with Lentils (page 159)
Bulgur. Cook according to package directions.
Spinach. Cook frozen spinach according to package directions.
Broiled Mangoes (page 208)

This menu provides 3 servings fruits and vegetables, 1 serving whole grain.

Pork & Greens

Maple-Mustard Glazed Pork Chops (page 140)
Mushroom-Barley Pilaf (page 94)
Mustard greens, turnips or collards (page 98) or cook frozen greens according to package directions.
Tangerines

This menu provides 2 servings fruits and vegetables, 1 serving whole grain.

Loaf & Ladle

Whole Wheat-Flaxseed Bread (page 63)
Hearty Split Pea Soup (page 56)
Tossed green salad with Herbed Yogurt Dressing (page 73)
Maple-Walnut Roasted Pears (page 212)

This menu provides 3 servings fruits and vegetables, 1 serving whole grain.

Index